REQUIEM FOR A GIANT

For Katia
May truth be your destiny,
Honesty your guide

REQUIEM FOR A GIANT

A.V. Roe Canada and the Avro Arrow

Palmiro Campagna

A HOUNSLOW BOOK
A MEMBER OF THE DUNDURN GROUP
TORONTO · OXFORD

Publisher: Anthony Hawke
Copy-Editor: Andrea Pruss
Design: Jennifer Scott
Printer: University of Toronto Press

National Library of Canada Cataloguing in Publication Data

Campagna, Palmiro
    Requiem for a giant : A.V. Roe Canada and the Avro Arrow / Palmiro Campagna.

Includes bibliographical references and index.
ISBN 1-55002-438-8

1. A.V. Roe Canada — History. 2. Avro Arrow (Turbojet fighter plane) 3. Aircraft industry — Canada — History. 4. Canada — Politics and government — 1957-1963. I. Title.

TL685.3.C338 2003   338.4'76237464'0971   C2003-900356-6

1   2   3   4   5   07   06   05   04   03

Canada

THE CANADA COUNCIL | LE CONSEIL DES ARTS
FOR THE ARTS | DU CANADA
SINCE 1957 | DEPUIS 1957

ONTARIO ARTS COUNCIL
CONSEIL DES ARTS DE L'ONTARIO

We acknowledge the support of the **Canada Council for the Arts** and the **Ontario Arts Council** for our publishing program. We also acknowledge the financial support of the **Government of Canada** through the **Book Publishing Industry Development Program** and **The Association for the Export of Canadian Books**, and the Government of Ontario through the **Ontario Book Publishers Tax Credit** program, and the **Ontario Media Development Corporation's Ontario Book Initiative.**

Printed and bound in Canada.
Printed on recycled paper.
www.dundurn.com

Dundurn Press	Dundurn Press	Dundurn Press
8 Market Street	73 Lime Walk	2250 Military Road
Suite 200	Headington, Oxford,	Tonawanda NY
Toronto, Ontario, Canada	England	U.S.A. 14150
M5E 1M6	OX3 7AD	

The information in this book in no way represents the views, opinions, or thoughts of the Department of National Defence.

All efforts have been made to obtain reprint permissions.

Table of Contents

Preface   9

Chapter 1:   Beginnings   11

Chapter 2:   Jet Jitters   25

Chapter 3:   "Unsellable"   41

Chapter 4:   Criticism   57

Chapter 5:   NORAD   71

Chapter 6:   Who Needs the Bomarc?   89

Chapter 7:   The Arrow: The Pearson Perspective   111

Chapter 8:   How Much is Too Much?   127

Chapter 9:   Termination, Speculation, and the   147
               End of A.V. Roe Canada

Chapter 10:   In the News   159

Chapter 11:   Questions and Answers   173

Appendix: The Secret Files   181

Notes   209

Bibliography   215

Index   221

Preface

It is somewhat ironic, but as I examine the additional documentation I have had declassified, I realize that the quest I began for classified Avro documents in the mid-eighties has been continuing longer than the length of time spent by those who actually designed and flew the aircraft.

My first big break in the search for documents that had allegedly been destroyed occurred in 1987. After reading disparaging information about the program in Canadian history books, I realized that few historians had stated their references and fewer, if any, had searched American sources. I decided to approach the Eisenhower Library. They graciously sent me some key documents but also noted that others remained classified. Not being American, I could not easily gain access. Still, that provided me with clues to Canadian sources wherein I obtained, for example, the documents forming the paper trail answering the question "Who ordered the blowtorching?" To the dismay of some and the delight of others, the answer was *not* Prime Minister John Diefenbaker. This information, plus numerous other documents I uncovered detailing the extent of American involvement in the program, led to the 1992 publication of *Storms of Controversy: The Secret Avro Arrow Files Revealed*, which quickly became a best-seller.

In this book, I reveal the existence of further documents I have had declassified that fill in more of the missing pieces to the story. For example, considerable and surprising detail is provided on the Jetliner, as well as much more on the circumstances surrounding the termination of the Arrow. Since the cost of the Arrow continues to be debated, an entire chapter examines new information on this aspect, with startling conclusions. I am again indebted to the Eisenhower Library for providing some of the new documentation.

I once again wish to thank my wife and children for putting up with my research and writing. I again thank Jim Floyd for his great encouragement and review of the manuscript, the late Owen Maynard and the late Bill Turner for their insights and information, and Roy McCabe for stories and photos. I wish to thank Ian Farrar of the Aerospace Heritage Foundation for assistance with the manuscript and Frank Harvey, also of the AHFC, for provision of photos. I thank Scott McArthur of the Arrow Recovery London group. Both groups host excellent websites on the Arrow. I thank Dave Gartshore for providing me with underwater footage of his discovery of an Arrow model in Lake Ontario, and all the folks who have helped me over the years, such as Glenn Wright from the National Archives and Isabelle Campbell of the Directorate of History, Department of National Defence. I have also had excellent support from various individuals at the Eisenhower Presidential Library as well as from the history group at NORAD Headquarters in Colorado. I thank Christopher Cook for all his support, and a special thanks to Arthur Lee Ray, my computer guru who kept my machine alive. I also wish to thank Les Earnest of Stanford for candid remarks concerning SAGE/Bomarc.

Finally, I thank publisher Jack Stoddart for giving an unknown his first break, and now the people at the Dundurn Group, such as Andrea Pruss, copy editor, Jennifer Scott, design coordinator, and Tony Hawke, editorial director, for assisting in this publication effort.

Palmiro Campagna
Ottawa 2002

Chapter 1

Beginnings

"The future will only belong to Canada if Canada, the people of Canada, have faith in the destiny of Canada and work like blazes to make that destiny come true."
— Sir Roy Dobson at the tenth anniversary dinner of A.V. Roe Canada Limited[1]

Canada emerged from the Second World War with tremendous potential in the field of aviation. A.V. Roe Canada Limited would become one of its largest industrial giants, although few, if any, realized that from its modest early beginnings. By its tenth anniversary, A.V. Roe would demonstrate to the aircraft industries of the world its ability to break new ground and leap ahead in the technology race. Yet, at the height of its prowess, it would be dealt a fatal blow from which it would never recover: the termination of its largest undertaking, the development of the Avro Arrow supersonic interceptor.

In considering the story of the Arrow, it has been said that the management of A.V. Roe was as much to blame for the cancellation as the government of Canada at the time was, if not more so. It has been said that the company had come to depend solely on government money and contracts and that management was not interested in competing in the marketplace because government money would always be available.

It has been argued that company president Crawford Gordon failed to grasp the fact that in the fifties there was an overall shift in emphasis from defence-related spending on military products to spending on consumer items. Consequently, when Arrow development and production was terminated, A.V. Roe had no new non-military consumer products to turn to. In the same era, Boeing successfully transitioned its military business into the commercial jet arena. A.V. Roe on the other hand, in response to the Arrow's demise, fired all of its employees and closed its doors for good. Are the criticisms concerning the company well founded? Did it simply not prepare itself to enter into and compete in the commercial market, or were other factors at play?

In this new millennium, one of the largest corporations in Canada, and perhaps the largest maker of small passenger aircraft in the world, is Montreal-based Bombardier. During the war, the Canadian government contracted L'Auto-Neige Bombardier to build snowmobiles for arctic patrol. Bombardier complied and, in the process, established a lasting relationship with the government. According to a *Globe and Mail* article of January 13, 2001, from this early beginning, Bombardier developed a strategy of determining government needs and then preparing itself to solve them in order to gain acceptance and favour for future work. The article cited Bombardier's acquisition of failing Crown corporation Canadair Limited. A month after Bombardier's rescue acquisition of Canadair in 1986, the latter was awarded a $1.4-billion contract for the maintenance of Canada's F-18 fighters, giving the impression that it had been awarded in response to the takeover.

In an earlier *Financial Post* article dated January 11, Chief Executive Officer John Roth of Nortel noted that nearly half the companies on the Toronto Stock Exchange were in some fashion dependent on government protection. The same article stated that Bombardier was one of those that had received numerous subsidies over the decades. Even

Brian Tobin, the industry minister, was prepared to break international law to help Bombardier win a contract against rival Embraer of Brazil. It had been alleged that the Brazilian government was providing Embraer with unfair subsidies and the Canadian government was simply equalizing the playing field.

Bombardier did win the contract to supply Air Wisconsin Airlines with $2.35 billion worth of aircraft. The Canadian federal government's role, under Tobin, was to provide up to $1.7 billion in loans to Air Wisconsin, under very good rates, to help pay for the deal.[2] In a repeat move in July 2001, the Canadian government once again provided a loan, this time $1.2 billion to Northwest Airlines, to help Bombardier secure another deal.

In yet another instance, the *Ottawa Citizen* of January 27, 2001, quoted Colonel Howard Marsh of the Canadian Department of National Defence. Colonel Marsh spoke of the government's mid-eighties bailout of Bombardier. At that time, the Army was planning to purchase a German-designed vehicle called the Iltis. Cost of the Iltis was in the range of $28,000 if produced in Germany. The government apparently insisted the vehicle be purchased from Bombardier instead. This raised the price to $84,000. From Colonel Marsh's perspective the 250 percent premium, while painful for the Department of National Defence, in fact saved Bombardier and allowed it to move on to bigger and larger projects like the aforementioned aircraft deals.

The point of all this is simply to demonstrate that while the Bombardier deals and alleged bailouts have raised some eyebrows, there does not appear to have been the same degree of criticism as that leveled against A.V. Roe and its alleged government handouts. With sales increasing and Canadian jobs being created, one would hardly wish to attack Bombardier's success.

Also, in a letter to the editor of the *Ottawa Citizen* dated February 7, 2002, Bombardier's Vice-President of Public Affairs Yvon Turcot pointed out how Bombardier had already paid back a number of loans and, through ongoing sales, would continue repayment in accordance with government schedules. He did, however, note that because of the length of time taken to design, develop, market, and sell new aircraft, it could take several years for loans to be repaid. The same would likely have been true if A.V. Roe had enjoyed a similar level of support. What went wrong for A.V. Roe? How did it all begin?

In his writings on the Arrow story, the late Fred Smye, former president and general manager of Avro Aircraft Limited (the airplane-producing arm of A.V. Roe Canada Limited), noted that prior to the start of the Second World War, the Canadian aircraft industry was composed of eight primary companies in the private sector. These were Boeing Aircraft Limited, Canadian Car & Foundry Company, De Havilland Aircraft of Canada, Fairchild Aircraft, Fleet Aircraft Limited, National Steel Car Corporation, Noorduyn Aviation Limited, and Associated Aircraft Limited.

Boeing in Vancouver, a subsidiary of Boeing in Seattle, was producing the Blackburn Shark, a torpedo carrier for the Royal Canadian Air Force (RCAF). Canadian Car & Foundry Company, a producer of railway equipment in Fort William, was producing the airframes for the Hurricane aircraft. De Havilland Aircraft of Canada, a Toronto-based subsidiary of De Havilland United Kingdom, was producing the famous Tiger Moth and was manufacturing and assembling the Anson. Fairchild Aircraft Limited in Montreal, a pioneer in bush planes, was also on contract with Britain for supply of the Bolingbrooke bomber. Fleet Aircraft Limited in Fort Erie was a subsidiary of Fleet Aircraft in Buffalo, New York and was providing the Finch, a trainer, for the RCAF. The parent company later became Consolidated Aircraft when it was moved to San Diego. National Steel Car Corporation had its main plant for railway equipment production in Hamilton, where it still exists today. Then-president Robert Magor saw aircraft production as the way of the future. As a result, he established a plant in Malton, near the airport west of Toronto, for aircraft-related work. Noorduyn Aviation Limited in Montreal was in production of the bush plane the Norseman and was gearing up for Harvard production. Associated Aircraft Limited was established for the production of the Hampden bomber, in cooperation with Canadian Car & Foundry, Fleet, National Steel Car and Ottawa Car, and Vickers. (Ottawa Car and Aircraft Limited was a subcontractor to all the others. Vickers, a shipbuilder, was into the assembly of flying boat aircraft.) Completing the picture was a Crown corporation, Federal Aircraft Limited of Montreal. Federal had been established in June 1940 to oversee the production of the Anson. One of its first tasks was re-engineering British designs to North American standards and specifications, a formidable task. It then had to coordinate the assembly across the various manufacturers in Canada.

According to Smye, at the start of the war this core group of companies, along with several sub-contractors, employed roughly four thousand people and occupied an area of five hundred thousand square feet. By 1944, with aircraft orders from the United States as well as Britain, the area had grown to 6.5 million square feet, with over one hundred thousand people employed in the industry. Aircraft production had also jumped, from a production rate of 40 airplanes in 1940 to an annual rate of 3,600 by 1944.

As Smye points out, the nature of the industry was not based simply on increasing the numbers of aircraft produced. The varied nature of the aircraft necessitated the expansion of facilities, tools, and techniques. Since many of the aircraft were of an almost all-metal construction, the need for precision casting and forging was evident. This in turn required precision engineering and manufacturing skills. The development of these skills benefited Canadian industry in general, and in particular those companies acting as sub-contractors, such as Massey-Harris in Toronto, General Motors in Oshawa, Central Aircraft Limited in London, and the Cockshutt Plow Company in Brantford.

From the original core group, National Steel Car was to evolve into the largest aircraft plant in Canada, and as such, some glimpse into its origins is in order. In 1936, Robert J. Magor, then president of National Steel Car, decided that Canada needed a modern aircraft manufacturing capability. As a starting point, he successfully negotiated a contract to build twenty-one Lysander aircraft for the Royal Canadian Air Force.

In April of 1938, work on a sixty-thousand-square-foot plant was begun, and the first Lysander was delivered eighteen months later. As one of the member companies whose work was being coordinated through Associated Aircraft Company, National Steel Car was given a contract for the construction of centre and outer wing sections for the Hampden bomber. An additional eighty thousand square feet were added to the plant in the fall of 1939 to accommodate this contract.

The outbreak of war in 1939 saw contracts to National Steel Car for more Lysanders, this time Lysander Mark IIIs for the British Air Ministry. This added another 210,000 square feet of floor space to the growing company. Eventually, though, the requirement for Lysander aircraft diminished. This allowed some of the space in the plant to be used for production of Anson aircraft. Still, some considered the capability of the plant and its facilities to be underutilized.

In December of 1940, the Canadian government issued a contract to National for the production of three hundred Martin B26 bombers. The plan was to build thirty per month. To this end, a new 2-storey, 300,000-square-foot building was built for the production of parts and a new engineering and administration building of 63,700 square feet was erected. The expansion continued, as contracts for the war effort were plentiful.

In 1941, however, the government decided to discontinue work on the B26 and elected instead to focus on the Lancaster bomber. In 1942, a new building was added to house the Lancaster engineering team and the associated machinery and equipment. By 1943, the building space would encompass 1,049,465 square feet. When Robert Magor passed away, R.S. Hart became the new chief executive of National Steel Car.

In 1940, as part of the war effort, the Ministry of Munitions and Supply was created within the Canadian federal government, with the aim of procuring and supplying the necessary military equipment for Canada's armed forces and its allies. Its minister was the Right Honourable Clarence Decatur Howe. It wasn't long before his government became concerned that Lancaster production at National Steel Car was being threatened under the new management of Hart. The result was that the federal government expropriated the Malton plant. It was formally turned over on November 5, 1942, and was renamed Victory Aircraft Limited.

John Paris Bickell became the first president of Victory. By the age of thirty, Bickell had already become a millionaire. In 1919, he was president (later chairman) of the gold-producing McIntyre-Porcupine Mines in Timmins, Ontario. During the war, he was appointed to the British Ministry of Aircraft Production, where he served with the aircraft supply board. He returned to Canada to head Victory Aircraft for the continued production of Lancasters.

Originally, C.D. Howe agreed that Bickell could choose his own board of directors to run Victory. Not long after, however, in speaking with his Minister of Labour, C.D. Howe decided a labour representative should be on Bickell's board. He made a selection without consulting Bickell, who objected, feeling that Howe had broken his agreement. In 1944, Bickell tendered his resignation and was replaced as president by V.W. Scully, head of War Supplies, another Crown corporation.

David Boyd, manager of Canadian Car, had originally been brought in as Bickell's plant manager, specifically for the Lancaster bomber production. He eventually became general manager and is largely credited for the success of the Lancaster project. Victory Aircraft eventually went on to produce nine modified Lancasters for passenger service. Called the Lancaster XPP, these aircraft flew the Atlantic carrying nine passengers and mail for Trans-Canada Airlines (TCA), Canada's fledgling national airline company. Other sources have referred to these aircraft as Lancastrians, but this was in fact the name given to the British-modified Lancasters provided to BOAC.

The Lancaster itself was the design of A.V. Roe in Manchester, England, a member of the Hawker-Siddeley Group of companies. Roy H. Dobson, later Sir Roy, was the managing director of A.V. Roe and was also a director with Hawker-Siddeley. Together with Frank Spriggs, managing director of the Hawker-Siddeley Group, he visited Victory Aircraft in 1943. Impressed with what he saw, he decided this was where Hawker-Siddeley should continue post-war aircraft production and design activities.

In the spring of 1945, he returned to Canada hoping to arrange for a takeover of Victory. Dobson secured a lease-purchase agreement with the Canadian government, contingent upon the continued production of Lancaster and now Lincoln aircraft. Fred Smye, who was assistant general manager of Federal Aircraft at that time, was to become the first employee of Dobson's new company once he got the signatures he needed from Hawker-Siddeley. On August 1, 1945, Smye moved into an office at the Victory plant in Malton in anticipation of Dobson's successful takeover. V.W. Scully, Victory Aircraft's president, paid for Smye's salary, since Dobson was not able to arrange for funding from England.

When the war ended the Lancaster and Lincoln contracts were terminated. This effectively cancelled the agreement between Dobson and the Canadian government. Smye was left pondering what was going to happen next. He called Dobson to find out if he was still going to pursue an agreement to purchase Victory and then flew to England to meet with Dobson personally. Back in Canada, the impact of the war's end left only about four hundred of the nine thousand people once on staff at the huge Victory plant. It is somewhat ironic that the release of so many from the same facilities would repeat itself by the end of the fifties with the cancellation of the Arrow.

Undaunted by what seemed to be the collapse of the aircraft industry, Dobson told Smye he was determined to obtain Victory Aircraft even though many believed he was crazy to do so. As Dobson would later say at the tenth anniversary of the founding of Avro Canada, he did not agree with his detractors at the time. He saw Canada as a "great country full of natural resources, all kinds of metals ... and yet lacking in the finer engineering developments and the finer developments in things like aircraft, aircraft engines and so on."[3] He believed an aircraft industry in Canada would be a natural fit if "the people of Canada, have faith in the destiny of Canada and work like blazes to make that destiny come true...."[4] He also knew Hawker-Siddeley could supply some of the much-needed expertise. More importantly, perhaps, he also knew that there was a potentially great market for his products in the United States.

In the Canadian government, there was also considerable discussion as to what to do with respect to an aircraft industry in a post-war Canada. Wilf Curtis, an RCAF officer, had come up short on aircraft during the later stages of the war. In 1942, he was trying to have Hurricane aircraft that had been built under license in Canada allocated to the RCAF. Unfortunately, the original manufacturer had say over where the end product would go, and this forced Curtis to appear before an aircraft allocation committee meeting in London, England to determine who would get the Hurricanes.

In the ensuing discussion, the committee ended up allocating the Hurricanes to Russia. Curtis would later say, "I realized right then, walking out of that room and feeling every inch a failure, that until we didn't have to tip our hats to anyone to get aircraft when we needed them, we'd never have the air force a first-rate nation really deserves."[5] Curtis went on to become chief of the air staff, and he was determined that Canada should have control of its own aircraft supply and therefore its own aircraft industry in order to avoid this reliance on others.

Curtis was not alone in his wish for a Canadian aircraft industry. Under the Department of Munitions and Supply, the Committee on the Postwar Manufacture of Aircraft was formed in April 1943. Chairing the committee was Ralph Bell, director general of Aircraft Production for C.D. Howe. Members of the committee included the RCAF, Trans-Canada Airlines, Canadian Pacific Airlines, the National Research Council, and members from the aircraft manufacturers. Bell encouraged the Minister to continue supporting the design and development of aircraft in Canada. In a July memorandum to Howe he noted that an aircraft industry was of the utmost importance to Canada from the perspective of national defence. As a result the committee recommended a policy to provide contracts for aircraft-related developments over the next ten years.

Members of the RCAF had originally told Dobson back in 1943 that they would support the design and development of a new fighter. Officials at Trans-Canada Airlines told Fred Smye that they were interested in commercial transports. These two requirements combined would give Dobson his impetus for establishing an industry in Canada. After meeting with Smye in England in 1945, Dobson followed him back to Canada to meet with C.D. Howe. He was intent on reaffirming the deal he wanted to make for acquiring Victory Aircraft.

Howe gave Dobson a chance to back out of any deals, but Dobson stood his ground. Initially planning to take only a small part of the Victory plant, Dobson ended up agreeing to take it all. On December 1, 1945, A.V. Roe Canada Limited took over the offices of Victory Aircraft as a wholly owned subsidiary of the Hawker-Siddeley Group.

Fred Smye was appointed assistant general manager. J. P. Bickell, the man who had resigned as Victory's first president, was appointed chairman of the board. Walter P. Deisher, vice-president and general manager of Fleet Aircraft, became vice-president and general manager of A.V. Roe. Edgar H. Atkin from A.V. Roe in Manchester, England was named chief engineer. James C. Floyd, also from A.V. Roe in England, was brought in to lead the civil aircraft engineering section. John Frost from De Havilland in Britain was in charge of military aircraft design. Jim Chamberlin, a native of Kamloops, British Columbia, was hired from Noorduyn Aviation to be the chief aerodynamicist of the new company.

During the war, Fred Smye had spent a great deal of his time at what he termed "begging the British and Americans for engines and other equipment to put in the planes we built here."[6] Much like Wilf Curtis, he vowed this would never happen again. Perhaps as part of this resolve, on May 4, 1946, A.V. Roe took over Turbo Research Limited, a group involved in jet engine research.

Turbo Research began when a group of engineers from the National Research Council in Canada traveled to Britain to study jet engine developments in 1943. They included University of Toronto-trained engineer Paul B. Dilworth. In 1944, Turbo Research Limited was established as a Crown corporation to conduct research and development work on jet engine technology in Canada. By 1946, despite the fact that Turbo had a jet engine design ready, the government was actually looking to let the corporation go.

Offers were made to Pratt & Whitney and Rolls Royce, but both declined, leaving A.V. Roe as the benefactor of this new group of about eighty-six people. The newly acquired group formed the Gas Turbine Division of A.V. Roe and was led by Paul Dilworth. Dilworth's friend Winnett Boyd, another University of Toronto graduate, became the chief designer.

Of the eighty-six people from Turbo Research, the aerodynamicist was not able to come to terms with management at A.V. Roe and did not join the team. The problem was that he was the one with the knowledge to design the necessary compressor blades for the new engine this group was to produce. Boyd was sent to England to seek out a replacement. He found Harry Keast, a twenty-five-year-old, Cambridge-trained aerodynamicist from Power Jets Limited. Keast was hired August 8, 1946, and given five weeks to develop the blades for the new engine.

On March 17, 1948, the experimental engine known as the Chinook was powered up and tested for the first time. What made the test nerve-wracking was that the customer, the RCAF, was on hand. Despite their own confidence, the engineers had no idea what would happen when they pushed the start button. When the big moment arrived, the engine started immediately and became the forerunner of an impressive line of jet engines.

Canada's national airline, Trans-Canada Airlines, had indicated the need for new passenger transports; it was a contract that A.V. Roe was anxious to fulfill with a new development that would be called the Jetliner. But first, some background is in order, given the eventual discord between TCA and A.V. Roe over the Jetliner's development.

TCA had its beginnings on April 10, 1937, when the government of Canada passed the Trans-Canada Airlines Act creating a Crown corporation to establish and coordinate air travel throughout Canada. C.D. Howe was the figure primarily responsible for the formation of the airline. Initially, he had hoped for a combination of private and public funding to help create the new air carrier. Canadian Pacific Railway (CPR) had originally been invited to participate, but in the end, the government forged ahead and made the airline a wholly owned subsidiary of the government-owned Canadian National Railway (CNR).

TCA quickly moved to purchase Canadian Airways Company. The latter had been flying small aircraft on the West Coast. With this acquisition, the first commercial route for TCA was started on September 1, 1937, between Vancouver and Seattle. For this route TCA was using Lockheed 10A Electras carrying ten passengers on twice-daily passenger runs.

While retaining government control of the airline, C.D. Howe hand-picked his managers to run it. In 1941, he made Herb Symington president. In 1948, Gordon McGregor became president, with strict instructions from Howe to keep the airline out of debt.

The first transcontinental routes were established between Vancouver and Winnipeg, where TCA was headquartered and where airports and navigational aids were more advanced than in the east. By February 15, 1940, routes were opened to Montreal and the Maritimes. TCA had established a number of intercity runs, and by 1943, service expanded across the Atlantic. This service was called the Canadian Government Trans-Atlantic Air Service, or CGTAS.

On November 1, 1945, TCA introduced the Douglas DC-3 on the Toronto–New York route and soon replaced the L-10s with thirty twin-engine DC-3s each carrying up to twenty-one passengers. New routes were also opened to Chicago, Cleveland, and Boston.

In 1947, TCA accepted delivery of the first Canadian-built North Star. The North Star was a modified Douglas DC-4 with Rolls Royce Merlin engines. Canadair in Montreal developed it specifically for TCA. Incorporated in 1944, Canadair had taken over the former aircraft division of Canadian Vickers. During the war the company had produced the Canso flying boats. It was to have produced the Lincoln bomber as well save for the intervention of C.D. Howe, who passed the contract to A.V. Roe.

According to Peter Pigott in *The Flying Canucks II*, C.D. Howe persuaded A.V. Roe to take on the Lincoln contract in order to allow Canadair the opportunity to build the North Star. Howe made personal arrangements with Douglas Corp in the United States to allow Canadair the license to build the North Star's DC-4 fuselage, and he made appeals to Britain for the Merlin engines it would need. His wife, Alice, christened the first North Star on July 20, 1946, in Cartierville, Quebec. Howe then sold Canadair in 1947 to the American Electric Boat Company, the forerunner to General Dynamics. This, he claimed, was to help Canada get in on American technology. General Dynamics sold Canadair back to the Canadian government in 1976.

The North Star was a four-engine aircraft that came in both fully pressurized and unpressurized versions. It had a cruising speed of 240 miles per hour. It was described as noisy, loud, and bone jarring. According to TCA maintainers, the poor workmanship of its Merlin engines was a major headache. In addition, the cost of parts was double that of American parts. Still, the North Star was C.D. Howe's baby, as was TCA, and the two were inextricably linked. When TCA requested approval to purchase ten aircraft, C.D. Howe asked the order be increased to twenty. (C.D. Howe also advised the Department of National Defence that they were to receive twenty-four North Stars.) With its new orders of DC-3s and now North Stars, TCA was poorly positioned to accept yet another aircraft, this one from A.V. Roe: the groundbreaking Jetliner.

One must ask as well if C.D. Howe was prepared to accept this new jet aircraft. After all, it had the potential to render obsolete his beloved propeller-driven North Star. When Canadian Pacific Airlines, TCA's only rival, requested permission to fly Pacific routes and routes over the North Pole to Amsterdam, Howe reputedly gave his permission, in the hope that this would bankrupt the rival company. Would he have similar feelings against the jet transport that might threaten the North Star?

When A.V. Roe came calling on TCA, Jim Bain was its superintendent of engineering and maintenance. In late December 1945, Bain had been in the UK and had had talks with Rolls Royce. Officials at Rolls Royce had convinced Bain that the next aircraft for TCA be powered by the new Rolls Royce AJ65 (Avon) jet engine with 6,500 pounds of thrust at sea level. Commercial jet transports were as yet unheard of, and the Avon engine itself was still considered a secret military engine. On his return, Bain insisted the only new acceptable aircraft for TCA would be one powered by the Avon. He rejected an early A.V. Roe proposal for a four-engine turbo-prop, a design similar to the Viscount that TCA would purchase later in 1955.

Jim Floyd was still in the UK when he got the word from Canada to prepare initial designs for the TCA jet transport project. He quickly learned that most of the information he required on the Avon engine remained secret. Nevertheless, Floyd arrived in Canada on February 11, 1946, and on March 27 was sent to Winnipeg to meet with TCA Chief Engineer Jack Dyment to iron out details of the transport design. Meanwhile, TCA was awaiting delivery of the North Star. Would they be serious about a commercial jet transport, especially given that none yet existed?

James C. Floyd was born in England in 1914. He was educated at the Manchester College of Technology, graduating in 1935. While an apprentice at A.V. Roe in Manchester he worked on many projects, including the Anson, Manchester, Lincoln, Tudor, and other aircraft. He was in charge of "stressing" on the York transport after having been engaged in its design. He was also the liaison between A.V. Roe and the Royal Aircraft Establishment test centre at Farnborough. In 1935 and 1936, he had been on loan to the Hawker Aircraft Company for design work on the experimental Hawker "Hotspur," a derivative of the Hurricane. Before he left to come to Canada, he was chief project engineer at the A.V. Roe Yeadon Plant in Yorkshire. Needless to say, he had gained considerable experience that would stand him in good stead to take on development of TCA's jet transport, the Jetliner.

Although eminently qualified for the task,[7] even Floyd could not stem the tide that would rise against the project. After all, jet transport was a new and unproven technology. Perhaps the risks and costs might be too great. Perhaps the jet would undermine the work of the existing non-jet commercial industry, or simply be too much for A.V. Roe to handle.

Chapter 2

Jet Jitters

"The contract with TCA would have to contain clauses to insure that TCA is recompensed for all costs incurred by the operation of this airplane."[8]
> — Jack Dyment, chief engineer at TCA, on the use of
> the Jetliner to explore the potential of passenger jet
> transport, March 19, 1949

Before development of the Jetliner, jet-powered aircraft belonged in the realm of the military. Jet transport for civilians was unheard of. While American aircraft companies remained focused on conventional aircraft engine designs, both Britain and Canada embarked on civil jet-transport work. The British entry was the transoceanic Comet. Canada's entry was the short- to medium-range intercity jet, Jim Floyd's Jetliner.

The Jetliner was approximately eighty-three feet in length. It had a ninety-eight-foot wingspan and weighed about thirty tons. Its carrying capacity was approximately ten thousand pounds, including its thirty passengers. Its cruising speed was not to be less than four hundred miles per hour, with an ability to operate from four-thousand-foot runways and at altitudes in excess of thirty thousand feet. These specifications on the Jetliner represented a quantum leap in passenger air transport at the time. The speed alone was more than double that of some of the turbo-prop transports then in use.

The prototype was designed to carry loads up to 12,700 pounds with 50 passengers. Its range was 1,400 miles with a cruising speed up to 450 miles per hour. Emphasis was on reliability and maintainability with operating costs to be comparable with conventional transports. The Jetliner was to be designed to satisfy TCA requirements using the still-secretive military Avon engines that Jim Bain had seen during his visit with Rolls Royce in the UK. The A.V. Roe sales team under Joe Morley, assisted by Murray Willer, developed and copyrighted the name Jetliner. The copyright to the name did not hold over time because no Jetliners were ever produced in quantity, a stipulation of copyright rules then.

In the negotiations with TCA, A.V. Roe was issued with a letter of intent dated April 9, 1946. This was three months prior to the rollout of TCA's first North Star. The letter was signed by TCA President Herb Symington. It required delivery of the first Jetliner by October 1948 and demanded a fixed price, but did not specify the quantities to be ordered. A draft contract on file in the National Archives of Canada shows that a quantity of thirty would be ordered. This draft never saw the light of day.

The letter of intent further stipulated a maximum price of $350,000 per airplane, an estimate A.V. Roe had derived based on a large production order. According to the letter, if sales were made to other airlines for a lower price, TCA expected reimbursement. Also, if the required specifications were not fully achieved, TCA expected a refund of all advance payments. Finally, the letter noted that neither A.V. Roe nor parent Hawker-Siddeley could sell the Jetliner, or a modification of it, to anyone else for a period of three years. The letter set ridiculous conditions, perhaps spurred on by C.D. Howe's dictum that TCA not lose money and perhaps in hopes that the Jetliner would not be produced in time to compete with Howe's vaunted North Star. Hungry for a deal, A.V. Roe foolishly accepted the terms.

26

The Jetliner was a state-of-the-art development representing a tremendous single advance in aircraft design. It was going to require innovative engineering because nothing like it yet existed. Work with jet-powered aircraft was still in its infancy, even for military users. This meant the cost of the Jetliner project was likely to increase, as any estimates were based on too many unknowns. Typically, cost-plus contracts were used for this type of new development, not fixed-price contracts, as TCA was demanding.

According to A *Dictionary of Accounting* from Oxford University Press, a cost-plus contract is invoked when the cost of the product is unknown or in the case of research work. The contractor is paid costs that are reasonably incurred together with an agreed fixed fee or percentage of cost, by way of profit. The Jetliner design and development fit both categories.

The problem with cost-plus, however, is that the contractor can take advantage by artificially increasing costs, thereby increasing profit. This is supposed to be mitigated through the use of proper and detailed audits. In the case of A.V Roe, some have argued that Avro was seeking cost-plus contracts with a percentage simply to take advantage, when in fact cost-plus was the norm in this type of situation.

For example, TCA wanted cost-plus contracts in work they were providing for the government. In a terse memorandum, Jim Bain of TCA had noted that whenever TCA took on a maintenance contract for the Department of Transport, costs invariably exceeded the fixed prices being quoted. TCA was left having to pay the extra. Bain felt all future such contracts for maintenance should be cost-plus.

Jack Dyment was also a supporter of cost-plus contracting for TCA. On March 19, 1949, he wrote to W.F. English, vice-president operations for TCA. He stated that with the upcoming first flight of the Jetliner, TCA might be asked what the future program with the Jetliner was going to be. He recommended that the government should give TCA a cost-plus contract to operate the Jetliner for a one-year period as a non-scheduled cargo and passenger aircraft.

He further stipulated, "The contract with TCA would have to contain clauses to insure that TCA is recompensed for all costs incurred by the operation of this airplane."[9] He also stated that if the government could not award a cost-plus contract, then cost estimates could be worked out with A.V. Roe and any costs in excess of the estimates would be paid for by the latter. A.V. Roe, though, would have the "privilege" of withdrawing from such an arrangement. Dyment explained that this was to "permit us to learn how to successfully operate a jet aircraft without having to pay for such experience the hard way."[10] And so, while cost-plus was good for TCA, it was not good for A.V. Roe, even though the latter had a potentially world-class product on hand.

While later A.V. Roe contracts would become cost-plus, the letter of intent from TCA for the Jetliner did not leave this as an option. When Fred Smye advised Symington in 1947 that TCA's fixed price could not be met, Symington suggested the project be abandoned. He was just in receipt of his new North Stars. Perhaps he felt that adding yet another new aircraft to the fold, especially one using advanced technology, could be too much to handle and would result in losses.

With the Jetliner project in jeopardy as a result of TCA's unmoving attitude, A.V. Roe asked TCA to release it from its commitment to the letter of intent, and a stop-work order was issued. C.D. Howe attempted to pick up some of the pieces. He provided A.V. Roe with $1.5 million and advised the company to continue work, but at a slower pace. For his part, Dobson expected Hawker-Siddeley would also inject some money to keep the work on this revolutionary aircraft progressing.

Hot on the heels of the TCA pullout was the discovery that the military Avon engines would not be available for the Jetliner. The Avon was still considered secret and was not being certified for civilian use. This would mean an extensive redesign of the Jetliner would be in order to accommodate different engines. Rolls Royce had determined that four civil derivatives of the military Derwent V engines with 3,600 pounds thrust would be similar to using the two Avons but with a penalty in extra weight and fuel consumption.

Back at the drawing board, Jim Floyd was not pleased with the development but soon realized several advantages to using four engines rather than two. Despite the extra weight, he had greater reliability with four engines, and these Derwents were also well proven. They had over 150,000 hours of flying time in military aircraft. There were also advantages in overall design while still meeting and exceeding the original TCA specifications.

The revised design was presented to TCA for approval in October 1947. In February 1948, TCA issued their response. They had effectively changed the requirement. They were now calling for a cruising speed of five hundred miles per hour and greater fuel reserves to make up for the lack of instrument landing systems at some airports. Floyd noted the extra fuel would have amounted to over thirty thousand pounds and was completely unwarranted. Although the Jetliner eventually flew at five hundred miles per hour, Floyd could not understand why TCA had put these revisions in the specification other than to ensure, perhaps, that A.V. Roe could not produce and would give up trying.

Gordon McGregor had now become the president of TCA. In a meeting with Fred Smye and others from A.V. Roe, on April 19, 1948, he made it clear he did not want TCA to be the first airline in North America to fly a jet transport. Did he have a case of jet jitters? The short-sightedness of his statement is astounding but in some ways perhaps typically Canadian: let someone else do it first and if it worked then Canada could copy it. With TCA out of the running, A.V. Roe management reasoned that they should market the Jetliner south of the border.

In 1948, prior to any flights, the November 1 issue of *Aviation Week* magazine carried an extensive description of the Jetliner. Quoting a noted American transport technician, it stated that everything an airline would want for maximum efficiency, safety, and ease of maintenance was incorporated into the Jetliner design. For example, the article noted that given the temperature extremes in Canada, A.V. Roe had paid particular attention to air conditioning. Also, the single-cylinder cross-section of the fuselage was not only practical but would simplify some of the problems associated with pressurization.

With respect to pressurization, the article noted that all such equipment, including refrigeration and smoke clearance equipment, was located in a compartment behind the cockpit. This made inspection simple and fast. This was in contrast to other aircraft designs that placed ancillary units under the cabin floor, thereby complicating maintenance.

Also, while the Jetliner wing was based on the well-developed two-spar principle, it was different in that the stringers were closely spaced, with tapered skin for torsional rigidity. As well, the wing was straight and thick, not swept back. This was due to the fact that the Jetliner was to operate from shorter runways and hence needed higher lift capacity more quickly. It also had a shorter cruising period than the Comet. The straight, thick wing represented the best compromise for all the factors considered. This is important in that some have criticized Floyd's use of the straight wing. After all, the Comet, they point out, had a swept wing. The difference of course lay in the fact that the two aircraft were being designed for different conditions, and the straight wing proved best for those under which the Jetliner would operate.

Already mentioned was the fact that the Jetliner now had four-engine reliability, but in addition, bleed valves and automatic shut-off cocks had been installed to prevent internal vapour explosions. The article also commented on the passenger accommodations, explaining that the front four seats could be removed for a thirty-six-passenger versus forty-passenger aircraft. It described the location of the stewardess panel for controlling lighting, pressure, and temperature and explained that "warm wall" heating was being implemented via a special air distribution technique.

Perhaps the most significant comment was made with respect to the windows. The article noted that the Jetliner was fitted with small-diameter, double thickness, porthole (circular) windows. It stated quite clearly that larger, square windows would complicate pressurization and design factors. Large, square windows would indeed become the Achilles heel of Britain's Comet. Crash investigators would learn that the Comet was breaking apart in flight due to propagating stress fractures originating at the corners of the square windows. Two major accidents with the Comet, in which many were killed, would ground the fleet for years until a solution was found. While the Comet would be taken out of service, the lone Jetliner would continue flying. Jim Floyd explained that he had anticipated the structural problems and that safety of the passengers with a new technology was paramount in his mind.

Today, sophisticated computer programs are used to assist in the design of new, state-of-the-art projects. Writing in *Jet Age*, Scott Young discusses a less sophisticated but no less accurate approach in the Jetliner days. A.V. Roe had built a mock-up of the Jetliner's cockpit section complete with controls. On seeing it one day Jim Floyd remarked that the "nose" would never do. It was sawn off and rebuilt to his calibrated eye. Floyd himself speaks of an incident during vibration testing when the ailerons were shaking violently. After careful deliberation, someone suggested using a type of children's silly putty in the booster jacks. It worked and was eventually replaced with a proper hydraulic damper.

As the Jetliner approached its maiden flight, it was already at such an advanced stage in design that any modifications required by an interested airline company could not be easily incorporated. Instead, the Jetliner could be used to showcase the product, with airline-specific modifications incorporated in subsequent aircraft. In this regard, airline companies, flight certification agencies, airports, and others would all learn from the experience of seeing a commercial jet in action.

Would special landing facilities be required? Would it be as economical to run as the conventional transports? Would it be as safe and easy to maintain? Answers to these questions would influence the design of future jets, and they were questions that could now be answered. In this regard, A.V. Roe decided it had to balance any demonstration flights of the Jetliner against the accumulation of engineering data that would assist in obtaining flight certification and answering the questions.

As the Jetliner was being prepared for its first flight, it was learned that the British-designed Comet had taken to the air — beating the Jetliner by two weeks to become the first jet transport to fly in the world. It captured the headlines with its first flight, which was actually a short hop a few feet off the runway. This was subsequently followed by a proper flight. Still, the early success would not undermine the Jetliner's first flight. The two aircraft were not in direct competition, having been designed for different routes.

News of the Comet was met with the following comments from American Civil Aeronautics Administrator Delos W. Rentzel. He conceded that while the Comet was "a threat to U.S. superiority ... the Avro Jetliner is further advanced than the Comet in terms of U.S. requirements. The American market is wide open for it."[11] In fact, no American manufacturer had a commercial jet in the works, and many had dismissed the idea as being at least ten years away — not a bad estimate considering Boeing finally got the 707 passenger service in operation in October 1958.

Back at TCA, Jim Bain registered his comments in a letter to Jack Dyment dated 1949. He saw the Jetliner and exclaimed that the workmanship was superb and actually better than that to be found on production North Stars, a comment that might have made C.D. Howe cringe. It should also have been a comment that would change TCA's attitude about the Jetliner, but it did not. With TCA out of the picture and demonstration flights looming, the Jetliner was finally readied for its first flight.

It was Wednesday morning, August 10, 1949. At the controls was pilot Jimmy Orrell, A.V. Roe Manchester's chief test pilot, on hand to handle the first flights of the Jetliner. Don Rogers, A.V Roe's chief test pilot, was co-pilot on the flight. Orrell decided to forego the idea of simply taxiing around the runway. This had done nothing but blow the aircraft's tires on earlier trials. Instead, he took the aircraft designated CF-EJD-X or C-102 up to altitudes of thirteen thousand feet.

As Orrell started her up, the engines began climbing in pitch to a high whine followed by a tremendous blast of hot gasses from the outlets. Onlookers heard a whistling roar as the jet climbed into the sky. A formerly confidential memorandum in the Department of National Defence files recorded the following about the first flight:

> The Avro Jetliner took off from Malton Airport on August 10th to be the first pure jet airliner to fly in North America. The flight lasted for one hour and five minutes.
>
> Prior to takeoff the crew had planned to go immediately to the safe altitude of twelve thousand feet before carrying out a study of the Jetliner's characteristics. However, immediately after takeoff the feel of the aircraft inspired such confidence that the flight crew requested and received permission to buzz the field and do very low altitude turns in the process. Throughout the flight, the aircraft performed faultlessly. Its manoeu-

vrability and lack of noise were, in the words of the chief test pilot, "absolutely amazing." From the pilot's point of view, the aircraft handled "like a fighter." As soon as the nose wheels doors closed, the absence of noise on the flight deck was so noticeable that it was thought momentarily that the engines had died. [Compare this to the noisy, bone-jarring North Star.]

Acceleration of the aircraft at takeoff weight (just under fifty thousand pounds) also came as a surprise to the flight crew, which had not expected such a "push" since water injection was not used and the ground temperature was very near 100 degrees Fahrenheit.[12]

The second flight took place August 16 with, according the DND memo, a weight of just under fifty thousand pounds. The takeoff run was approximately two thousand feet. The aircraft climbed initially at about 4,500 feet per minute and then at 2,400 feet per minute. The noise of the Jetliner was significantly lower than that of the two- and four-engine transports that were also over the airfield at the time. The aircraft was taken to thirteen thousand feet to check its stalling speed, but even though excellent stall warnings were given, the aircraft refused to stall even at one hundred miles per hour. It was decided to try again but the main wheels would not come down. Attempts to manually lower the undercarriage were unsuccessful.

The engines did not surge, and when the aircraft refused to stall, the pilot was able to bring it around again and apply full power without any difficulty. The memo noted, "The stability of the aircraft under all conditions has brought forth the highest praise from the flight crew."[13] Finally, unable to lower the landing gear, the aircraft did a belly landing on the grass, sliding to rest with the nose wheel down. The structural damage was slight and easily repaired.

The DND memo stated that although the incident was unfortunate, it showed that the crew and any passengers would be in no danger from this type of landing. The fuselage skin was not broken and there were no propellers to dig into the ground or cause damage. There were no pieces to break and fly off to do further damage. This is just the kind of information passengers would love to hear for any aircraft. In fact, this belly landing, or more appropriately, impromptu drop, shock, and vibration test, proved the integrity of the design.

The problem with the undercarriage lock-up was discovered. It seems the shaking the aircraft received from all of the stall testing had caused the up-locks on the main gear not to release. It was easily solved. For such an outstanding achievement, the Jetliner would eventually receive nothing but continued praise from the United States and nothing but criticism in Canada.

October 4, 1949, marked the first official flight of the Jetliner with all the dignitaries present. C.D. Howe described it as an epic-making event. Perhaps *The Journal of the Engineering Institute of Canada* of November 1949 summed it up best. Under the title "Inferiority Complex" it said, "The thinking that leads Canadian governing bodies, business and industrial concerns, and individuals to turn to the United States for the best in everything — received a rude jolt in the minds of at least a few Canadians...."[14] It went on to explain the success of the Jetliner flights and the ensuing tremendous enthusiasm from the American guests present.

In *Storms of Controversy*, this author postulated that the feelings experienced through the sixties that things Canadian were not as good as those from elsewhere might have been due in part to the demise of the Arrow and the resonant shockwave the termination of that project sent through the Canadian psyche. It seems the inferiority complex was in fact prevalent as far back as the Jetliner days. Perhaps each subsequent termination of major projects simply built upon the first. As for the Jetliner's achievement, American aircraft men of the day told *Maclean's* magazine it would cost them between $20 million and $30 million to design and develop a similar aircraft. A.V. Roe had done it for under $10 million in a typically Canadian approach — seemingly high by Canadian standards, but in reality a shoestring budget.

On subsequent flights other aspects of the Jetliner's flight envelope were checked and it was flown at over 500 mph with cruising speeds of 460 mph, compared with the maximum speed of the North Star of 330 mph with a cruising speed of 240 mph. Despite this, there was still no firm buyer, and because A.V. Roe did not yet have full flight certification, prospective buyers could not even be carried on board to sample the product first hand. This meant that it was not clear what modifications would be needed by interested airline companies in future prototypes and production aircraft.

On the one hand, tests were continuing, in hopes of obtaining flight certification, but on the other, the Jetliner was being booked for demonstration flights in the United States. A.V. Roe soon made a conscious decision to pursue the demonstration flights in hopes of obtaining sales interest in the United States. Under the circumstances of the decision, the Canadian Department of Transport (DOT) was then asked for a limited authority to carry potential customers for such purposes.

This request did not sit well with the DOT. Internal correspondence dated December 17, 1949, shows that Chief Aeronautical Engineer H.S. Rees was opposed. He was of the opinion that unless A.V. Roe saw potential sales looming, they would have no incentive to complete the engineering and design work needed for flight certification. He saw the aircraft as belonging to the government, given the monies that had been advanced, and therefore preferred the engineering test program be completed before any sales-related flights. He relented somewhat, though, and allowed the demonstration flights to move forward, but under severe restrictions.

According to Rees, the aircraft would require several more hours of flight time, to be specified by DOT. Flights with passengers would require flying the aircraft as they would on a normal scheduled flight. Safety belts would be required for all passengers. In the cabin, a conspicuous placard was to be placed in full view with the following inscription: "This is an experimental aircraft and is flying as such without a Certificate of Airworthiness."[15] Each passenger was to state in writing that they understood that the Department of Transport took no responsibility for these flights and that all flights were at the passengers' risk. It is almost surprising that blood samples and last will and testaments were not also required.

Was all this stipulation necessary given the successes of the Jetliner flights, including the crash landing that clearly demonstrated the integrity of the aircraft structure and safety for the passengers? The memo went on to say that in the United States and Britain, the indication was that the Civil Aeronautics Authority (United States) and the Air Registration Board (Britain) permitted such flights without "Type Approval" or certification. In Canada though, "We do not allow passengers to be carried unless the aeroplane has a Certificate of Airworthiness."[16]

In fact, judging from the tone of this letter, the Certificate of Airworthiness was simply designed to absolve DOT of any responsibility should there be a severe accident. Any passengers would know they would be flying in an experimental vehicle. Despite all the stipulations, DOT was inundated with requests from journalists and common folk who wanted to ride in the Jetliner. Perhaps that irked DOT officials even more.

The Jetliner logged about thirty-five hours without incident, save for the belly landing. Rees, though, was concerned that the only hard data he had seen were the pilots' opinions on the handling qualities of the aircraft. He wanted quantifiable data and he wanted DOT pilots to perform spot checks and provide an objective, independent assessment. Des Murphy was selected as the DOT pilot to do just that. He flew the airplane from March to mid-April 1950.

Calling it a docile airplane, he noted that most pilots would be impressed with its performance and handling, and he recommended A.V. Roe be given permission to carry passengers on demonstration flights. Still, given that structural tests had not been completed and that early tests had supposedly indicated certain areas might be under strength, Rees required 2,325 pounds of ballast to be carried in each outer wing tank before granting permission. This is likely what led to C.D. Howe's later famous but poorly informed criticism that the Jetliner needed sandbags in the tail to fly.

C.D. Howe entered the fray on April 12, 1950, when he wrote to Air Vice Marshal A.T.N. Cowley, then director of air services for the Department of Transport. In his letter Howe noted the DOT's decision to allow the Jetliner to be flown to New York for demonstrations, but without passengers. Howe wrote, "This effectively prevents demonstration of the aircraft to prospective buyers, and strikes a serious blow to the Canadian aircraft industry, in that our best opportunity to find a market for those planes in the U.S. is now, rather than six months from now, when U.S. manufacturers will probably have jet planes on the drafting board."[17]

Nevertheless, Howe's only request was for DOT to allow only experienced operators of other aircraft to be taken as passengers. Further, for the trip to New York, only Gordon McGregor was to be allowed to fly, in order to demonstrate TCA's alleged interest in the Jetliner. After all, it would be difficult to sell an aircraft that your own carrier didn't want. Howe agreed with Rees that the Jetliner should not be sent to Europe for demonstration flights until it received its Certificate of Airworthiness. A.V. Roe had been hoping to provide a demonstration flight at the Farnborough Air Show. One can only guess at the level of interest and sales that would have been generated at this international venue had the flights been allowed.

On April 14, 1950, A.V. Roe received permission to fly to New York with McGregor, subject to the conditions described by Rees in his memo. The aircraft flew to New York on April 18, 1950, to an astounding reception, carrying the first airmail by jet transport. Headlines heralded the arrival of the Jetliner across the United States, stating that travel time had been cut in half. Typical of these headlines were, "Jet Airliner Knifes Time To New York" and "Canadian Jet Liner Makes Air History." Years later on the American television show *You Bet Your Life*, the Jetliner was the answer to a question to contestants concerning the first jet transport and air mail to fly in North America.

With respect to this flight and his own experience as a passenger, Gordon McGregor offered two very different opinions. At the time, he noted the lack of noise in the cabin and the smooth ride. Years later, while being accused of killing the Jetliner by non-purchases, he stated that he did not wish to be too discouraging but that the aircraft was unsuitable for TCA. Of course it was unsuitable: it did not have propellers.

On April 24, 1950, Rees wrote to A.V. Roe giving permission to fly bona fide potential customers, subject to all the same restrictions as before. Also, flying with customers would be restricted to the Malton area only. It was also made clear that DOT would not be responsible should a mishap occur.

While all this was going on, the Department of External Affairs in Ottawa received a letter from their man at the Canadian Embassy in

Washington. The letter, dated June 1, 1950, from Gordon E. Cox, stated that the Civil Aeronautics Administration had completed its paper assessment of the Jetliner. Subject to successful completion of the operational tests, the CAA would almost certainly grant "a Certificate of Airworthiness ... the De Havilland Comet would probably not be given a Certificate of Airworthiness."[18] This information appears not to have been passed on to A.V. Roe. Had the latter known, it might have made a difference in their approach to the testing versus demonstration flying.

On September 5, 1950, TCA was brought back into the picture, as Howe wanted route assessments to be made. TCA again asked for a number of modifications before they would take the aircraft for any kind of flight trials. The modifications from TCA have been cited by many as indicators that the Jetliner was a poorly designed and poorly built aircraft. Nothing could be further from the truth.

The Jetliner was first and foremost a prototype only at an advanced stage in design. Modifications to satisfy TCA were simply not possible. For example, TCA complained that the Jetliner wings had not been built to accept the special de-icing pads that would be used on the second prototype and production aircraft. These pads were being developed by Goodyear and represented a new kind of technology for this purpose. Of course they were not ready, so the de-icing on the Jetliner was carried out using interim pads, but this was not good enough for TCA.

By November 1, 1950, Smye wrote to McGregor informing him that A.V. Roe would not turn over the aircraft to TCA but rather would continue with its own testing. This seemed to set TCA off on a course of negative comments about A.V Roe and the aircraft. All the negativism added to DOT's concerns about awarding flight certification. Needless to say, the future of the Jetliner was in grave doubt.

By January 1951, work on the Jetliner had slowed due to priorities being given to the military fighter the CF-100. About 150 flights of the Jetliner had been completed. In the demonstration flights many American officials had taken a ride and been impressed, so much so that some of the American airlines finally began serious talks with the company. One of these was National Airlines. James T. Baker, its president, had been discussing the possibility of acquiring the Jetliner with Dixon Speas, A.V. Roe's marketing and sales specialist.

Speas had been the assistant to the president of American Airlines. So taken was he with the Jetliner that he quit his job at American in order to sell the Jetliner for A.V. Roe. He knew most of the top American officials in the business and carried on numerous discussions with all of them, as well as with the American military about potential military uses for the Jetliner. In Baker's case, although he was interested he asked Speas to determine if the 15 percent duty the Canadian government was planning to impose on any sales could be waived. (This is in marked contrast to Bombardier's situation today, wherein the Canadian government provided American airline companies with generous loans and minimum interest rates to buy Bombardier aircraft.) Would the Jetliner finally have a buyer?

Chapter 3

"Unsellable"

"It never was our intention that if this aircraft [the Jetliner] was required that it would be built by A.V. Roe."[19]
Air Vice Marshal D.M. Smith, July 3, 1951.

R ather than potential sales, what Dixon Speas found on February 5, 1951, was a stop-work order issued by Fred Smye. It seems C.D. Howe wanted all work on the Jetliner to cease immediately, in order to concentrate efforts on the CF-100, whose schedule had been lagging. Speas had to inform Baker that the deal for National to acquire ten Jetliners was, for the time being, off. Baker wrote the following back to Speas on February 26, 1951:

> It will be most appreciated if you will keep in commu-
> nication ... regarding the developments of the Jetliner
> ... It was a real pleasure to ride and fly the Jetliner
> when it was in Miami ... It will undoubtedly have

tremendous passenger appeal … I think its performance at the time I flew it was excellent. It handled well
with one or two engines out and didn't seem to be in
the least bit tricky. I think you have a grand airplane
and it can do a fine job on the airlines if your
Company can build and sell them on a basis acceptable to the airlines.[20]

On March 6, 1951, there was renewed hope for the Jetliner. The
American military was interested and so the plane was flown to Wright
Patterson Air Force Base in Dayton, Ohio. The American military
pilots put it through rigorous test flights, as they would a military fighter. The Jetliner performed flawlessly. The report from the Wright Air
Development Center and Training Command suggested that with a
few modifications, the Jetliner design could be transformed into a pilot
trainer, bombardier trainer, or tanker aircraft.

Word immediately spread that the USAF was ready to purchase
twenty Jetliners and had set aside some $20 million for the acquisition.
Still, A.V. Roe was being told not to pursue the Jetliner and to continue work on the CF-100 military jet. To make matters worse, in July
1951, Jim Floyd was taken off the Jetliner project for six months to act
as a temporary troubleshooter on the CF-100. Even C.D. Howe told
Floyd directly to forget the Jetliner and get the CF-100 on track when
the two met one day at the Avro plant.

In *Shutting Down the National Dream*, author Greig Stewart referred
to the Jetliner as "unsellable." Canadian historian Michael Bliss echoed
a similar refrain in some of his writings on the subject. In addition, one
could argue the USAF interest was only rumour spread by A.V. Roe
people. But what really happened? Was the Jetliner truly "unsellable"?

There is a newly declassified memo from the Department of
National Defence. Dated July 3, 1951, and written by Air Vice Marshal
D.M. Smith, it reads:

> … I do not believe that A.V. Roe would be in any posi-
> tion to build the C102 even if they received an order for
> it. **It never was our intention that if this aircraft was**

> required that it would be built by A.V. Roe [bolding
> mine]. They are fully committed now with their CF-100
> and Orenda engine programmes and anything more
> which we gave to them at this time could only detract
> from these most essential projects. There are other facil-
> ities however in Canada which are still not fully com-
> mitted and a limited programme of C102 construction
> could be undertaken ... During the last few days there
> has been an examination into the C102 by the National
> Research Council, Department of Transport and our-
> selves, and it is the finding of this Board that the pres-
> ent state of the C102 is nothing like as far advanced as
> is advertised by the company ... Perhaps we would be
> unwise at this time to try and sell it at all ..."[21]

The memo speaks volumes. Although some people have accused
A.V. Roe of not getting into the civilian market after the Arrow deba-
cle, it is obvious from this memo that A.V. Roe was only ever supposed
to be a military aircraft development company. Not only C.D. Howe
but also the RCAF saw A.V. Roe as their personal aircraft developer.
The pretentiousness of the above statements is extraordinary. Yes, A.V.
Roe had to dedicate itself to the military requirement, but to say that
it was never the intent to let A.V. Roe build the C-102 is amazing. Did
the board of which the memo speaks consider the hard interests from
the American companies and from the USAF, or did they consider
such interests to be nothing but rumour?

The illustrious board reached its conclusions without anyone from
A.V. Roe present to explain the issues at hand. In *Storms of
Controversy*, this author revealed for the first time how a similar board
consisting mainly of National Aeronautical Establishment (NAE) personnel did a similar hatchet job on the Avro Arrow. The board was
subsequently embarrassed when Avro proved it wrong on all salient
counts before an American arbiter, the National Advisory Committee
for Aeronautics (NACA), forerunner to NASA.

The Jetliner Board convened June 28, 1951, under the title
National Aeronautical Establishment Working Committee on Jet

Transports. The chairman was J.H. Parkin of the NAE. Present were Group Captain R.C. Davis, RCAF; Director of Engineering J.T. Dyment, TCA; Chief Superintendent of Engineering I.A Gray, CPA; Assistant Director Dr. D.C. MacPhail, NAE; Aeronautical Engineer L.M. Nesbitt, DOT; Head Aerodynamics Section T.E. Stephenson, NAE; and Group Captain G.G. Truscott, RCAF. There is no record that any of these individuals had examined the Jetliner first-hand, yet they were ready to pass judgment.

An example of the nature of the discussion is exemplified in an early exchange between Parkin and Nesbitt. Nesbitt wanted operating cost comparisons between the Jetliner and the best aircraft of the day to see if the Jetliner would be competitive. Parkin rather astutely observed "that such a cost analysis was difficult at the moment due to the lack of existing competitive jet aircraft."[22] For his part, Dyment simply argued that TCA would not use the Jetliner unless it was economical. He added that TCA was not going to pay for the development nor was TCA prepared to fly it for the prestige alone.

He also noted that the last paperwork on the prototype of the C-102 was checked and found unsuitable for operation on TCA routes. He rhymed off problems like the lack of de-icing pads and the need for greater fuel reserves because of the lack of instrument landing equipment at airports. He even went so far as to say that though the move from the Avons to the Derwent engines resulted in greater fuel consumption, even if the Avons were now to be used, the aircraft would still not meet the TCA requirements. It seems the man simply did not want the Jetliner and was using every available excuse to keep it away.

At one point in the discussion he suggested the Jetliner should have been designed with a fair margin to be able to meet new and emerging requirements and that it was now limited in space, with no chance of further development possible. Yet the Jetliner had been designed for expansion. The TCA requirement had been for thirty-six passengers. The Jetliner could be reconfigured to carry up to fifty, and its speed was also in excess of original requirements.

A small digression is now in order to address the question of economics and comparisons to other aircraft. Dyment said the Jetliner would have high fuel consumption and hence a high operating cost, and TCA would not consider it unless it was economical. Recall that this meeting was taking place in 1951.

On March 26, 1950, J.R. Baldwin, chairman of the Air Transport Board, sent a copy of a confidential report to Cowley at DOT. The report had been specifically requested by C.D. Howe. Dated May 29, 1950, its title was *Comparative Cost Analysis of the Triangular Route Toronto–New York–Montreal–Toronto When Using Either The AVRO Jetliner, or The Canadair North Star*. Contrary to Dyment's and Nesbitt's assertions a year later, the Jetliner, both then and now, should be compared to the cost of TCA still operating the North Star, and not against some fictitious non-existent competitor.

And what were the results of the comparison? In the report's introduction, the authors set forth the parameters and conditions of their study. The analysis was to provide total operating costs for forty passengers and three round trips each day with allowances for mail, express, and cargo. This was soon expanded to account for fifty passengers. It was noted that Jetliner costs would be based on estimates and that it was assumed the Jetliner would meet the manufacturer's stated performance as well as obtain a Certificate of Airworthiness.

Every attempt was made to minimize any inaccuracies in the estimates. The authors analyzed actual performance and fuel consumption data from Rolls Royce Limited on the Derwent engines and fuel consumption rates from the flight tests that had been performed on the Jetliner to that point in time. The authors stated that calculated numbers were indeed in close agreement with actual numbers.

With respect to the North Star, the calculation should have been more straightforward given that TCA had been operating the aircraft for some time. TCA provided the data but included a lengthy discussion of reservations. Their letter said in part, "the greatest care should be exercised in basing conclusions on them [the data], as in the first place, nearly all such information requires a great deal of interpretive data to be properly used."[23]

Among the list of reasons given that could make the TCA data suspect was the changing price of fuel and the fact that the maintenance facility at TCA was handling more than the North Star engines so it was difficult to isolate North Star maintenance costs. It is rather ironic that on the one hand, TCA was pressing A.V. Roe for hard numbers and accurate information, on the basis of an experimental prototype, but could not itself be confident of numbers it was providing on an in-service aircraft. Perhaps TCA was afraid of the results such a study might produce and needed a way out.

A.V. Roe or Avro had stated in promotional literature that even if the Jetliner consumed more fuel, it would more than make up for it in speed. That is, because it could get to its destination faster than a propeller aircraft, it could make more flights per day and therefore carry more passengers and cargo per day. The authors of the DOT study quickly proved Avro correct. Under the conditions set out above, it would take four North Stars to complete the circuit versus three Jetliners.

The authors then looked at payload capacity, reserve fuel requirements for the Jetliner, wind allowances for the Jetliner flying at greater altitudes, direct operating costs including cockpit crew costs, fuel costs and projected increases in fuel costs, aircraft maintenance costs, flying equipment insurance, aircraft depreciation costs, and various indirect costs. They also examined what they called introduction costs associated with the Jetliner. These included ground handling and servicing equipment costs, modifications, training of aircrew, higher maintenance costs due to lack of experienced ground crew, spare engines, and other factors that might come in to play when using the Jetliner. In all, the assessment was thorough and rigorous.

Several conclusions were reached on the various points considered. The following is a summary from the report:

> It is shown that within the range of conditions chosen for the study the operation can be conducted at a lower total cost with AVRO Jetliner aircraft than with Canadair North Star equipment, at kerosene prices up to $0.267/Imp. Gal. At a fuel price of $0.18/Imp. Gal. the total direct cost of operating the route with Jetliners is approximately 80% of the total direct cost associated with use of North Star aircraft. The conclusions outlined above are only valid if the Jetliner, in daily operation, achieves the manufacturer's flight performance.[24]

The detailed conclusions also noted, "due to the improved standards of comfort and speed the Jetliner can offer, as well as the novelty of such a radically new type of transport, it is very probable that it will generate more revenue traffic than the North Star, so that the difference in net revenue will be appreciably greater than that indicated by the total cost figures given."[25] It is inconceivable that Dyment and company were unaware of this report. Then again, their negative attitude towards the Jetliner and C.D. Howe's fondness for the North Star might have been spurred on by this report.

That the details of this report were not mentioned in either Jim Floyd's or Fred Smye's writings on the Jetliner indicates that Avro was never apprised of the results. In fact, Jim Floyd advised this author he was unaware of this report's existence and it was not available when he wrote his book on the Jetliner. Avro had produced similar numbers, but bias on their part could have been argued. This report, however, was a rigorous, independent assessment requested by Howe that came out in favour of the Jetliner. It is enough to make one believe there was a hidden agenda to scuttle the Jetliner project.

Getting back to the NAE Working Committee, Dyment saw fit to add one more ludicrous comment to his earlier list. He was asked by the chair whether, if someone fixed all the faults he had outlined, he would then consider the C-102 suitable for any kind of large-scale production. Dyment's words summed up TCA's position on the matter thusly: "Mr. Dyment stated that he felt that time had run out on the aircraft now. The original lead gained by the prototype has been cut due to time spent on flights for advertising purposes and because competitive aircraft are now on the way."[26]

What is sadder than Dyment's comments is the fact that no one at the table challenged him and that the RCAF representatives took this nonsense to Air Vice Marshal Smith. The meeting had opened by noting there were no such competitive aircraft. Surely this group was aware that the closest aircraft was the Comet and that it was designed for an entirely different set of circumstances; it was not and never would be in direct competition with the Jetliner.

On July 24, 1951, a group of RCAF members dropped in on Avro to witness some demonstration flights prior to the C-102 going back to

Washington for demonstrations. Nesbitt and Dyment also showed up. Air Vice Marshal John Plant and others flew the Jetliner and the CF-100. All were most enthusiastic about the Jetliner.

The following day, MacPhail and Stephenson joined Dyment and Nesbitt for a meeting with Avro, but this time they also had a pilot, Captain R.J. Baker, with them. Those from Avro included Atkin and Deisher. Noticeably absent was Jim Floyd, who had been seconded to the CF-100. The purpose of the meeting was to address the issues that had been raised by the Working Committee. But the damage had already been done, as witnessed in the Smith memo of July 3.

According to Deisher, the Jetliner had about twenty-five to thirty hours of test-flying left to cover off most of the tests required by the certification agencies. Icing trials had not been completed and all work had stopped on the second prototype as well. Also, the first prototype would not be brought to Certificate of Airworthiness standards. The USAF interest was then noted.

After an in-depth technical discussion from Atkin, Captain Baker "stated that in his view there was no defect serious enough to prevent operation of the aircraft by T.C.A. for experimental purposes."[27] This was hardly the disastrous picture Dyment and Smith were painting. As if to mollify the effect of his comments on Dyment and the others, Baker added that his statements were, of course, "subject to revision following a thorough investigation of all design features by T.C.A. staff."[28]

The group estimated that it would cost about $600 per flying hour to operate the aircraft and the total for one year would be about $600,000. All agreed the money would be well spent and that testing by a joint group from TCA and the NAE would provide an accurate assessment of the potential of pure jet transports. Dyment noted he required TCA management approval for such a proposal.

More meetings were held, and in December of 1951 TCA put forward a proposal for Avro to hand over the Jetliner to the NAE as part of the deal to have an independent party assess the aircraft. TCA would also be reimbursed for the full operating expenses that were expected to be between $500,000 and $600,000 over the anticipated one-year test period. TCA was again looking for a freebie. Needless to say, Avro did not accept the offer.

In fact, R.C. Smith, Avro's resident aircraft inspector from DOT, noted in his almost daily reports that back in July, Jim Floyd had been nonplussed by TCA's seeming belated interest in the Jetliner. He also noted that on July 27, the Jetliner arrived back from Washington. It had been well received, and talks about possible production were at high political levels. The dignitaries who flew in the Jetliner included the Secretary of the Navy and Army, several admirals and top-ranking personnel from the Air Corp and Marines, and several members of the Civil Aeronautics Administration and Civil Aeronautics Board.

This brings the discussion back to those who believe the Jetliner to have been "unsellable." While the NAE Working Committee was dilly-dallying with the fabricated problems of a prototype aircraft, the American military continued with its assessment. Group Captain H.G. Richards at the Canadian Joint Staff in Washington penned the following letter to the Chief of the Air Staff at DND.

It is a letter that has not seen the light of day since it was sent on August 14, 1951. It spoke of the recent flights of the Jetliner to Washington and the reaction from the Americans.

> … The USAF and the USN are both interested in this aircraft but the only **concrete proposal for purchase had come through the U.S. AMC at Wright Field.** It is now **confirmed that the USAF wish to purchase 12 Jetliners.** A recommendation was made to this effect by a specially appointed committee representing all USAF Commands, to the Aircraft Weapons Board. **This Board approved the purchase of 12 aircraft …** the Flight Refueling experimental section at USAF HQ are anxious to get 4 C102s for test in this type of work [bolding mine].[29]

And so it turns out the Jetliner *was* saleable! The rumours of USAF interest had been true all along. They were not fabrications from Avro supporters, and Avro never knew the extent to which they were true. So, what happened? Negotiations had been conducted at high political levels, as noted by R.C. Smith, the DOT in-plant representative.

Those levels would have involved external affairs, DND liaison staff, and C.D. Howe. The axe on the deal likely came from Howe, who, at the time, was the minister directly responsible for the Jetliner and all things Avro, although this is only speculative.

Did Howe kill the American USAF plan to purchase the Jetliner as he did when National was interested? We will likely never know for sure. When this author made inquiries concerning the C.D. Howe papers back in the early nineties, he was told by the archivists that some time after Howe's passing, many of the papers concerning this saga disappeared and have not been seen since.

According to Jim Floyd, Avro would easily have had the capacity to build the Jetliners while carrying on with the military aircraft. This would have kept the Jetliner alive and propelled Avro to the forefront of the civil aviation market. It would have satisfied those who now feel Avro management did not have the foresight to break into the commercial market as Boeing did, and sales would have more than paid for the modest development cost of just under $10 million.

The French Carravelle, a small intercity jet, was certified for passenger service in 1959, after seven and a half years in development. The first flight of the intercity Douglas DC-9 was February 25, 1965. Since then, the Bombardier Regional Jet of the CRJ series that began in 1987 under Canadair has become the most serious contender to the Jetliner; yet in 1951, Dyment was of the opinion that the Jetliner had lost its lead.

By September 1951, rumours were running rampant of senior management changes at Avro. C.D. Howe was most upset at the lack of progress on the CF-100. After all, as suggested in the memo cited earlier, Avro was not to be allowed to produce commercial products like the Jetliner but rather to concentrate on military aircraft. With the Korean War progressing no one knew if a new world war would result, and so military aircraft were desperately needed. On the other hand, perhaps Howe was more upset at the successes enjoyed by the Jetliner.

Unable to cope with the mounting pressures at Avro, Walter Deisher confided to R.C. Smith, the resident inspector, that he had resigned, effective September 6, 1951. He was continuing as director but taking no active part until the new appointee could be announced. This was Crawford Gordon, who took over as president on October 15, 1951.

An Avro press release described Gordon as one of C.D. Howe's key men. In fact the latter reportedly said that Avro's good fortune at gaining Gordon was his bad fortune. Gordon was born in Winnipeg on December 26, 1912. He received his Bachelor of Commerce degree from McGill University in Montreal. During the war, from 1941 to 1945, he was on loan to C.D. Howe's Department of Munitions and Supply as the director-general of organization and assistant coordinator of production.

He then became director-general of industrial conversion in the Department of Reconstruction and Supply. In February 1947 he joined the John Inglis Company, and from February to October of 1951 he was on loan to the government as coordinator of defence production. He was also president and director of English Electric and executive vice-president of John Inglis by this time. On joining Avro, he resigned from these positions as well as those he had held as president and director of Canadian Crocker Wheeler Company Limited and Production Castings Limited. He remained as director of The Canada Assurance Company and as a member of the Dollar Sterling Trade Advisory Council. He arrived on the scene at Avro two days before the first pre-production CF-100 with Mark II Orenda engines was officially handed over to the RCAF at a gala ceremony.

Work on the Jetliner continued despite the changes in upper management. Some test flights continued, but overall, work at Avro had slowed down; on November 2, the plant was shut down over the weekend owing to a water shortage. R.C. Smith noted that since Gordon's appointment, there had been much less interference within the plant itself between shops and engineering. Changes were coming swiftly.

A strike had been averted by discarding a job evaluation plan that had been in the works, and a new appointment was made for a director of industrial relations. As well, rumours began to circulate that Rolls Royce was poised to take over the Turbine division and produce British Avon and Nene engines, with Fred Smye heading up the aircraft division and Gordon the Turbine division. By November 29, Smith was reporting ongoing friction in the Inspection Department. It seems the RCAF was forcing the issue that shop conditions had to be improved and better inspection procedures invoked. The Department of Transport had made similar observations three years earlier. In other words, Avro had to get its act together in terms of production and manufacturing to quality standards.

By December, more flight tests had been conducted on the Jetliner, but on December 5, Gordon announced all efforts had to be concentrated on the CF-100. Another project, the C-103, was also being dropped as a result. By December 7, Smith reported the C-102 was hanging in the balance. Morale was reaching new lows due to all the uncertainty.

Amidst the turmoil there was a positive note. On December 27, Atkin was made technical director and Jim Floyd was made chief engineer. In his daily record Smith noted, "Jim Floyd's appointment as Chief Engineer has everyone's approval, as **Jim is popular, has become a Canadian citizen and is looked upon by all as a real Canadian** [bolding mine]."[30]

There are those who claim that Avro projects were designed by Brits and not by Canadians. They were designed by Canadians, whether those Canadians had been born in Canada or whether they had simply chosen to become citizens (although there remained others who did not choose to become Canadians). The criticism is vacuous at best.

On January 8, 1952, Fred Smye wrote to Rees at DOT and informed him that all work on the Jetliner was now stopped except for minimum maintenance work and the odd flight from time to time. At Avro, though, there was some discussion of the possibility of using the Jetliner as a test bed for the Hughes MG2 fire control system that was earmarked for the CF-100. The Jetliner was best suited for this task as it had been flown like a military aircraft before and had the room required for all the test gear. It was decided to test the fire control system at the Hughes plant in California.

On March 29, 1952, Jim Floyd received a response from Director of Air Services Cowley with respect to permission to fly the Jetliner to Culver City in California for the testing of the Hughes equipment. In the letter, Cowley referred to the restrictions set out in his letter of April 24, 1950, and stated all the same restrictions applied. He added that only Hughes personnel directly related to the equipment being tested would be allowed to be carried as passengers.

There were to be no demonstration flights even though Howard Hughes might be a potential customer for the Jetliner itself, through his airline company TWA.

Demonstration flights could not be allowed, according to Cowley, because Smye's letter of January 8 said all work on the Jetliner had ceased and since "this particular aircraft is not airworthy and will not be modified to make it airworthy, there is no point in proceeding any further with demonstrations…"[31] Not airworthy? Perhaps Cowley thought that Avro would truck the Jetliner to California given that it was not deemed airworthy.

The non-airworthy Jetliner was flown at over 30,000 feet over the Rockies and landed at the Hughes field in Culver City on April 8, 1952. Jim Floyd recounts Howard Hughes's intense interest in the Jetliner and how he held on to it and Avro personnel for nearly six months. Suffice it to say that Howard did everything he could to purchase the airplane for TWA. His plan was to have Convair build it in the United States. The plan was squashed by the American government's claim that Convair had to concentrate on military aircraft. (A reflection of C.D. Howe's and the RCAF's views perhaps?)

The second option was to have Avro build thirty and sell directly to TWA. Before Gordon could approach C.D. Howe through Roy Dobson, Howe got wind of the scheme. On November 14 he ordered Avro to stop all work on the Jetliner and to move the aircraft to a part of the plant where it would not be in the way of manufacturing the CF-100. He reminded Avro of the heavy investment the government had made in the plant, and so he was going to dictate what they would build. The CF-100 would be built for the Korean War effort that was about to end, and Howe's North Stars would be safe from any threat of competition the Jetliner might pose.

The lone Jetliner was kept flying until it could no longer be easily maintained. On December 10, 1956, Jim Floyd received a memo from Fred Smye asking that the Jetliner be dismantled, never to fly again. That was when the Jetliner finally did lose its lead among aircraft of the world. Today, only the cockpit sits as a grim reminder of what was and what might have been, and of the stupidity and short-sightedness of Canadian bureaucrats, and their inability to seize the moment. Today, Bombardier has taken Avro's place and seems to have been given the government breaks denied A.V. Roe.

Reference has been made to the Orenda engine and the CF-100. After the successful demonstration of the Chinook, the first Canadian-designed and Canadian-built jet engine, the RCAF asked for a more powerful one capable of over 6,500 pounds of thrust. Designated the Orenda, it was principally the design of Winnett Boyd and first ran on February 10, 1949. On hand were RCAF dignitaries and other government officials.

As with the Chinook, no one knew for sure what would happen once the button was pushed to start it up. On cue the Orenda ignited without hesitation, to the delight of the onlookers. In subsequent tests it ran for nearly a thousand hours before crashing to a halt. A technician who got too close to it had his lab coat sucked in. In his pocket was a package of razor blades that effectively destroyed the engine's compressor blades. Other problems with compressor blade failures on the first production models acted to delay the program, but eventually this engine went on to become one of the most successful ever built, exceeding 7,300 pounds thrust. Canadian Sabre aircraft using the Orenda flew faster than American Sabres. Total production of the Orenda was 3,838 in operation in Canada, West Germany, South Africa, Colombia, and Pakistan.

The jet engines were to power the CF-100. Unlike the Jetliner, though, the CF-100 was plagued with design problems. The project began in late 1946 with Edgar Atkin as chief engineer. In June 1947, John C.M. Frost was added to the design team. Frost had worked on the De Havilland 108, also known as the Swallow. This was the first British aircraft to fly faster than the speed of sound. Now he was project engineer for the CF-100.

The RCAF wanted an all-weather fighter that could fly higher and faster than the best bombers of the day. Since no suitable aircraft were available, the decision was made to build one. Initially an order for two prototypes was placed, followed in May 1949 by an order for ten Mark II pre-production aircraft with Orenda engines. Despite the difficulties, the first of the two prototypes ordered with Avon engines underwent taxi trials on January 17, 1950.

On January 19, 1950, pilot Bill Waterton took the first of the two prototypes up for its first flight, as Defence Minister Brooke Claxton and other government and RCAF officials looked on. One of the dignitaries, Chief of the Air Staff Wilf Curtis, was particularly satisfied at seeing the CF-100 soar for over forty minutes as various controls and stability were checked out. The second prototype flew July 10, shortly after the start of the Korean War in June. The following June 1951, an order for seventy Mark III aircraft powered by an improved Mark II Orenda was placed. Despite this early success, the CF-100 ran into problems and delays. As discussed above, work on the Jetliner was slowed and eventually stopped, and Jim Floyd was brought in to help solve the problems.

The first of the Mark IIs flew in July 1951. But weaknesses had been discovered in the centre structure and on April 5, 1951, the second of these ten prototypes crashed, killing pilot Bruce Warren and observer Bob Ostrander. The structural weaknesses did not prove to be the cause of the crash, but the program was delayed yet again. The first of the Mark IIIs was delivered in the spring of 1952. In the meantime, the RCAF was already asking Avro for a successor to the CF-100, the CF-103, a swept-wing version. This was the aircraft project Crawford Gordon terminated in order to concentrate efforts on the CF-100. When the first pre-production CF-100 with Orenda engines was handed over to the RCAF on October 17, it was already several months late.

Unfortunately, it and other pre-production aircraft developed wrinkles in the skin at the centre section. The spar web was also cracking. Henry Bennett, chief structural stressman at the Avro plant in Manchester, arrived to examine the problems. The fix was eventually developed by Waclaw Czerwinski, a Polish engineer. It was simple but was going to require considerable rework and more delay.

In the meantime, Crawford Gordon was trying to reassure C.D. Howe that all was under control. According to Ray Footit, who at the time was the RCAF officer principally concerned with the CF-100 development, tensions were building, and accusations flew that Avro was not being truthful. There are also other indications in some archival records that Avro was preparing two sets of reports, one for Howe and one describing what was really happening in the program. Unfortunately, this sequence of events raised suspicions that would also carry over in the development of the Arrow.

By December, Smye went to Britain and asked that Stuart Davies, chief designer at Avro, Manchester, come and assess the situation on the CF-100 first hand. Davies arrived with Harold Rogerson, head of the Stress Office. Both arrived, reviewed the fixes and, with some additional but minor modifications, certified the fixes and the aircraft as airworthy.

Top management at Avro had lost some confidence in the engineering department. Davies recommended Jim Floyd be made chief engineer and this became effective in January 1952. Atkin was moved to technical director. John Frost was put in charge of special projects and concentrated his efforts on a flying saucer for the United States Air Force and Army. R.C Smith described this period in his daily record as chaotic and noted the many serious top-level meetings convened over the CF-100 problem.

The first production CF-100 designated Mark IV with the Orenda came off the line on September 30, 1953. Eventually, a Mark V version with Orenda Series II engines (two-stage turbine) was ordered, each Mark aircraft incorporating new features and equipment. In the final analysis, 692 CF-100s were built for Canada and 53 more were sold to the Belgian air force. The United States, however, steadfastly refused to purchase a foreign military aircraft, partly due to lobbying from their aircraft industry.

As for the cost-plus nature of the contracts, Fred Smye has written that Avro offered a target price proposal on the Mark IVs that was accepted. He noted that the government and the RCAF stated that the cost of the CF-100 was less than what they would have paid for a comparable American airplane. In addition, the money remained in the country, as did the talent and skills that were developed in the process.

Despite the many real problems affecting the CF-100, it became a success. The Jetliner, though, with far greater potential and an untapped American market in wait, lay twisting in the wind thanks to bureaucratic short-sightedness. Perhaps the Americans would not purchase military aircraft from Canada, but there would be nothing like the Jetliner for years to come, and the USAF did want to purchase it in quantity. They were prevented from doing so, and Avro was never apprised of the details. Instead of garnering support and encouragement for its products in Canada, Avro was chastised and criticized.

Chapter 4

Criticism

"I think this company has been subjected to a great deal of unwarranted criticism."[32]

— MP Rodney Adamson of York West speaking in the
House of Commons May 30, 1952

Throughout the development period of the Jetliner, Orenda, and CF-100, A.V. Roe had come under heavy criticism. Writing in *Canadian Aviation* of April 1952, Ronald A. Keith, editor, outlined some of these criticisms. He stated that the rumour mill was declaring the CF-100 a flop, the Orenda plagued with bugs, and millions of Canadian taxpayer dollars lost. He then pointed out that nearly $50 million in government funding had been put into the company in 1946 and there was nothing in the way of production to show for it. But, as he stated, only five years had elapsed and the truth was, no one in Canada had the experience to know how to judge how long it should take to design, develop, and put into production a new engine and a jet fighter from scratch, including a passenger jet. As stated earlier, in 2002, Bombardier noted that design and sale of a new aircraft represented a long-term investment that could take several years.

Keith summarized the developments this way. The CF-100 project was launched in October of 1946, with detailed design commencing in May 1947. Prototype tooling began in January 1948, and the government issued a contract for ten pre-production models in May 1949. The first prototype flew in January 1950, and a production order was finally obtained in September 1950. The total time to reach that point was forty months. Comparable British fighters took between thirty-eight and thirty-nine months to first flight. At least one American fighter took thirty-four months. The conclusion reached was that the CF-100 schedule was comparable to aircraft developments in other countries. Keith also acknowledged the problems and fixes encountered in the CF-100 development. Finally he noted that the CF-100 had been designed to satisfy a rigorous military specification that no other aircraft in the world could match at that time, as C.D. Howe had said himself.

On the engine side, the period from design to first test run was twenty-nine months. Two comparable British jet engines also took twenty-nine months, while the U.S. averaged twenty-five months. In February 1952, the Orenda Mark II, or production version, completed its 150-hour type acceptance run. This event occurred thirty-six months after that first run in February 1949. The American average for reaching this stage was forty-six months, while the British average was thirty-seven months. For the eventual production of the Orenda, a new four-hundred-thousand-square-foot plant was being erected to handle the requirement.

Other articles pointed out that while the Avro developments compared favourably with those of the U.S. and Britain, these other countries enjoyed the advantage of well-developed design engineering capabilities, whereas A.V. Roe Canada itself was new and was starting from scratch in assembling design and development teams. While some engineering expertise was brought in, the rest had to be selected and formed into cohesive design and development units. That there were problems and chaos was perhaps to be expected under these conditions. That these accomplishments were completed and compared well with other countries speaks to the high calibre of the abilities of all who pulled together to make it happen. In the case of the Jetliner, there was no other jet aircraft for comparison.

Speaking in the House of Commons on May 30, 1952, then-MP Rodney Adamson of York West saw the situation with Avro this way:

> Coming to defence production, and with particular reference to the A.V. Roe Company, may I say as a member in opposition to the government that I think this company has been subjected to a great deal of unwarranted criticism. The A.V. Roe Company started virtually from scratch. First of all they endeavoured to design and then produce three things, the Orenda engine, the CF-100 and the Jetliner. For a well-established aircraft company to have tackled these three projects at the same time would have been a major operation; but for a company which has in its formative stage to attempt these three things was almost a heroic venture.
>
> Hon. Members may think that the design and the production of a prototype of an aircraft or a new jet engine is a difficult thing, but compared with making that prototype an item on a production line I feel that the design and development of the prototype is comparatively simple. It was in the hiatus period between the testing of the prototype and putting the engine or aircraft on a production basis that the trouble took place. In part I blame the government for the reason that they did not fully appreciate the difficulties. The Minister of Defence Production probably did, but the Minister of National Defence certainly did not, and the Canadian people have become rather disenchanted with this establishment because of the glowing statements which were made when the prototypes of the Orenda engine, the CF-100 and the Jetliner were first tested.
>
> When the first CF-100 was test-flown two years ago, I believe, there was an unfortunate incident. It

was unfortunate in this way, that when a new aircraft is being tested and test-flown for the first time it is generally the most — I will not say "secret" — nerve-racking performance. When the aircraft is not only a new aircraft being test-flown for the first time but has new engines in it, then it becomes a doubly nerve-racking procedure. Not only are millions of dollars of effort riding on the aircraft but the very lives of the flight crew and test pilot are involved. As somebody has explained to me, test-flying a new aircraft with new engines is like a woman having her first child. She does not want an audience. When this new aircraft was being flown for the first time the Minister of National Defence and a large contingent of top brass appeared at Malton for the accouchement, and the flight crew were so annoyed at what had happened that they very nearly refused to test-fly the aircraft.

The aircraft was flown, but that is an example of the interference with this operation. As I have tried to explain to the committee — and I think the minister agrees with me — the design, development and production of a new aircraft with new engines is an extremely difficult thing to do even if you have a background of years and years of production experience, but to do that with a comparatively new plane of new design is very difficult indeed. To have a top brass of the air force and the Minister of National Defence sitting around and saying now, you had better take off because we have got to get back to Ottawa, would be an intolerable burden.

That is the sort of thing that has bedevilled the A.V. Roe Company ever since it has gone into production. They are producing a good aircraft. They have a good engine...[33]

Adamson went on to explain that a prototype does not mean production and that production could be years away with modifications continually being made to the product. He implored the Ministers to simply tell the truth and said that the Canadian public wanted the truth and needed the truth about our military production capabilities. His main thrust was that political interference was hindering the work at A.V. Roe, and at one point in the House, he called for an inquiry into this aspect. It is too bad he did not have all the details of the Jetliner sales that were shelved. Over the last twenty years, projects of the magnitude of the three at Avro have taken more than ten years to come to production, as noted in the May 2001 *Jane's Defence Weekly*, and at a considerably higher price tag.

As for Avro, despite the early criticisms about being locked into defence production, the company continued to grow with an eye towards diversification into the civil market. As part of this expansion effort, the aircraft and engine components were split into separate engine and aircraft divisions under the A.V. Roe umbrella. On December 2, 1954, the Gas Turbine division became Orenda Engines Limited with Walter McLachlan as vice-president and general manager. Fred Smye was named vice-president and general manager of Avro Aircraft Limited. Both men would become presidents of their respective companies in 1956, with Crawford Gordon as president of the parent company A.V. Roe. In fact, these two companies were created by letters patent on July 29 under the Dominion Companies Act. Both would begin conducting business under their new names on January 1, 1955.

Also announced on December 2, 1954, was the straight acquisition of Crown corporation Canadian Steel Improvements Limited, a company established in 1951. With some four hundred employees, this company produced precision forgings, blades, and other components for jet engines. An expansion program for it was being established, to include magnesium and aluminum foundries as well as a close tolerance forging facility that was to become unique in Canada. These additions opened the company up to the commercial as well as defence sectors.

Supporting the new three-company group were a host of others. Light Alloys Limited of Renfrew had set up a casting facility. MacDonald Brothers of Winnipeg, later Bristol Aircraft (Western) Limited, established a large sheet metal shop to handle the larger parts of the Orenda engines. The Cockshutt Plow Company manufactured combustion cans and smaller sheet metal applications. Acme Screw and Gear Limited, later York Gears Limited, developed gearboxes for the Orendas. Lucas-Rotax of England was asked to set up a fuel systems manufacturing capability.

In September of 1955, Canadian Car and Foundry was acquired. This group not only supplied aircraft but was also branching out to produce rail cars and trolley buses, with its own modern steel foundry. Through Canadian Car, A.V. Roe also gained control of Canadian General Transit, a company supplying tank cars to the petroleum and chemical industry. The expansion was not unlike that of Bombardier today, diversifying into a number of different product lines through acquisition of the respective companies.

In 1956, Canadian Car became a separate company called Canadian Steel Foundries Limited but remained a wholly owned subsidiary of A.V. Roe. At this point A.V. Roe issued five hundred thousand shares valued at $8 million to the Canadian public, as it was no longer wholly owned by Hawker-Siddeley, even though the latter retained control. Management was fully Canadian, and Smye eventually became executive vice-president aeronautical of A.V. Roe Canada in 1957.

Also in 1957, PSC Applied Research was acquired and renamed Canadian Applied Research. A.V. Roe was now estimated to be worth $94 million. A.V. Roe purchased an interest in Algoma Steel Corporation and later made a successful bid for Dominion Steel and Coal Corporation. All these acquisitions shifted the balance of A.V. Roe from its initial focus on aircraft to a greater interest in commercial and industrial-related production. In fact, few realize that by the time of cancellation of the Arrow, the ratio had become 40 percent aircraft and 60 percent industrial and commercial.

By the end of 1957, A.V. Roe was employing close to twenty-five thousand people and had operations across Canada. It had diversified into mining, forging, and casting; producing steel materials; building rail, bus, and other vehicles; manufacturing control instruments; research; and of course aircraft engines and its greatest effort, the Arrow. By 1958, A.V. Roe was ranked among the top eighty companies in North America. It had grossed over $450 million in annual sales and had put back about one third of a billion dollars into the Canadian economy, mostly in the form of sub-contracts on the Avro Arrow. It had also paid out $183 million in wages.

While the Jetliner offered a quantum leap in technology in the civil arena, the Arrow did likewise for the military. Perhaps because of the groundbreaking developments being achieved, numerous rumours and misrepresentations circulated about alleged flaws in the aircraft. Otherwise, how could something that good be terminated? This was not unlike the situation with the Jetliner years earlier.

Those who would criticize Avro's efforts should understand that Avro did not set out to build a bad aircraft, and they did not do so. Technical experts in the international community lauded Avro's achievements. Only in Canada were the criticisms rampant.

Did Avro suffer from poor management early on? Perhaps, but it was a start-up company learning the ropes. This not an excuse but a simple fact. As Adamson pointed out to the House of Commons, people's lives depended on the integrity of the designs, and the company took the necessary actions to correct design problems. Those at greatest risk were the test pilots. To criticize Avro is to attack these people, some of whom lost their lives in ensuring Avro's aircraft were technically sound. One must feel some appreciation of these pilots and the dangerous work they did.

Bill Waterton flew the first CF-100 and was in the cockpit when some of the structural problems were discovered. He left Avro in February 1951, handing the testing over to Bruce Warren. Flight Lieutenant Bruce Warren was the Avro test pilot who gave his life in the pursuit of developing safe aircraft. He and his passenger Robert Ostrander died when their CF-100 crashed in a swamp near London, Ontario. Was it bad design? Was Avro taking shortcuts? The crash investigation team said no.

On April 5, 2001, fifty years after the accident, Mark Matthys, owner of a tobacco farm near the site of the crash, placed a wooden cross as a memorial to the two men who died trying to ensure the safety of Canada's future by test-flying the CF-100. In the words of Matthys, "If he was your grandfather — and he was so willing to serve the country — wouldn't you want something done to remember him?"[34] Who was Bruce Warren and what were the circumstances of the crash?

RCAF Flight Lieutenant Bruce Warren was considered an out-standing test pilot. He had attended a top academy in England. Flying for Avro, he was twenty-eight when he died, leaving behind his wife, Lois, his son, Doug, and his twin brother, Doug. A few days before the crash, he was on a radio show explaining that while test-flying was not a glamorous occupation, he felt it was less dangerous than driving to work with other cars speeding past at high velocity. He was probably correct, but fate would not be on his side.

It was a sunny and cloudless day on April 5, 1951, when Warren and Ostrander buckled in to aircraft number 18102, the second CF-100 prototype ever built. Warren's test route took him over his own home in Etobicoke Creek, but it would be for the last time. Warren climbed to thirty thousand feet and, for four hours, conducted a series of tests and manoeuvres on the aircraft. Then suddenly, at over 38,000 feet, the aircraft nose-dived and crashed into an area of swamp and bush near a Komoka farm in London, Ontario. Crash investigators determined that Warren had experienced a failure in his oxygen equipment. This they presumed had caused him to lose consciousness and thereby lose control of the plane. Today, Matthys is still uncovering pieces of the aircraft at the site.

Test pilot Peter Cope joined the Avro team in May, after the Warren crash, and not only piloted the CF-100 but became one of the test pilots to fly the Arrow. Cope was a graduate from the Empire Test Pilot School in Britain, as was the most famous Avro pilot, Janus Zurakowski.

Zurakowski was born in 1914, of Polish parents, in Ryzawka, Russia. He began flying gliders in Poland and eventually graduated to the Lublin LKL-5 single engine trainer. In 1937, he became a fighter pilot for the Polish Air Force, flying P7 aircraft against the Germans. By 1940, he had made his way to Britain to join the Royal Air Force (RAF) in order to continue his fight against the Germans. He ended up as one of the few who fought in the famous Battle of Britain. During his wartime career he was credited with destroying three German air-craft, with a possible fourth, and damaging at least two. For his efforts he was shot down five times and nearly killed.

Soon after his exploits he was sent to the Empire Test Pilot School to become a test pilot for the RAF. After graduating from there in 1945 he was sent to the Aircraft & Armament Experimental Test Establishment, where he tested almost every American and British fighter at the time. It was here that he began performing his famous aerobatic routines like those he had tried during his glider days. In 1947, he joined the Gloster Aircraft Company, where he continued with his "zurabatics," as they were called, flying a Gloster Meteor in a wing-tip over wing-tip cartwheel. In 1952, he asked to be transferred to Avro in Canada, where he joined a stable of excellent test pilots, of which he was the eldest. He went on to become chief development test pilot, taking the Avro Arrow up on its maiden flight on March 25, 1958.

When Zurakowski was asked why he had selected Canada, he replied, "There is obviously a great future ahead for Canadian aviation and this country is now at the beginning of tremendous developments in the field."[35] He explained the great potential of Canada with its raw materials and its burgeoning development and production capabilities. He also saw excellent sales opportunities for it worldwide. Having flown more than sixty aircraft types, he brought with him a wealth of experience, and, knowing aircraft as well as he did, he saw the tremendous potential in Avro's excellent products. Avro took out a fifty-thousand-dollar life insurance policy on him, considering him to be, given his job, a poor insurance risk. He later claimed that he himself could not get any insurance.

Don Rogers was the chief test pilot. He had proven his cool approach years earlier when he assisted Jimmy Orrell to ever so gently belly-land the Jetliner when the landing gear locked up. This landing had proven the integrity of the design. Rogers was also the first to fly the Orenda-powered CF-100.

Another test pilot, Mike Cooper-Slipper, had joined Avro shortly after Rogers. He had joined the RAF when he was seventeen and had been credited with shooting down nine German aircraft in the Battle of Britain. In one dogfight he rammed his aircraft into a German Dornier bomber. When asked years later why he had done this, he answered that he did it because he was out of ammunition. When pressed he said everyone was doing it at the time as it was the "stylish" thing to do.

For his efforts he won the Distinguished Flying Cross. Downed over Singapore he was captured by the Japanese, but he made his escape through two hundred miles of jungle terrain, then by a Chinese river boat to India. He wanted to fly so badly he ended up joining Avro as a semi-skilled worker making three cents an hour more than the floor sweepers, so that he could fly. Other pilots who joined the group were Chris Pike, Stan Haswell, Glen Lynes, and W.O. "Spud" Potocki, the man who would fly the Arrow to Mach 1.98.

The death of test pilot Bruce Warren was not related to the wing spar problem. This wing spar issue was repaired with a simple design, requiring major modification of the fuselage in order to implement the fix. It is precisely through test-flying that such problems could be discovered. How did the CF-100 modifications compare with those in other aircraft developments? It is said that during Zurakowski's time at Gloster Aircraft, the Meteor required over fifteen hundred modifications to the fuselage and over six hundred to the engines, quite a difference from the CF-100. Unfortunately, as Adamson had pointed out in his address to parliament, Canadian politicians and citizens with no experience in aircraft design and production, and therefore with no feel for these types of problems, would expect everything to be done right first time around and in short order.

The integrity of the CF-100 design was demonstrated by Zurakowski during one of his test runs. As always, he had performed his own calculations and computations with respect to the capabilities of the aircraft. He determined that contrary to what the design engineers were saying, it would be possible to take this straight-winged subsonic airplane and fly it supersonically through the sound barrier.

On December 18, 1952, he did just that. From a height of about eight miles, Zurakowski went in to a steep dive and broke the sound barrier. He then repeated the manoeuvre several more times. As Jim Floyd noted, "The information that came from the test-flying of Zura and the rest of the boys helps lead us directly into the next airplane."[36] And so it did, with Zurakowski becoming the chief development test pilot on the Arrow.

If there was any Avro project that one might attempt to criticize, it was the Avrocar, Avro's flying saucer. In a report sent to the Canadian Defence Research Board in 1953, the American Central Intelligence Agency noted that German engineers had filed patents for flying-saucer-like craft they had supposedly developed toward the close of the war. The CIA had interrogated a number of German ex-soldiers who claimed to have worked on saucer-like aircraft, and there was concern that some of these engineers had fallen into Soviet hands. As it turns out, members of the RCAF and National Research Council had also interrogated some of these German engineers about this strange work.

In 1959, a book entitled *German Secret Weapons Of The Second World War* claimed that flying saucers seen by Allied pilots during the war and dubbed "Foo Fighters" were the product of Hitler's war machine. One individual who believed the Nazis had developed such devices was John Frost, now working on special projects at Avro, after being moved from the CF-100. In his eyes, a vertical takeoff and landing aircraft seemed like a natural progression for such an advanced high technology aeronautical firm as Avro, and the circular-wing vehicle or flying saucer seemed to offer the perfect design.

By 1952, not to be left behind in the technological race for vertical takeoff and landing vehicles, he co-authored two technical reports for the design of a circular wing craft. Initially, the vehicle was more of a horseshoe or spade-shaped design called Project Y. It would sit on its tail at an angle, with the pilot looking skyward, as he would if he were in a rocket. He would land in a similar fashion. This made takeoff and landing rather difficult and uncertain for the pilot. Frost abandoned Project Y and eventually settled on the complete circular wing platform. It became known as Project Y2 in 1954 and was to be developed under intense security at the Avro plant in Malton.

The designs caught the interest of Dr. Omond Solandt, then chairman of the Defense Research Board. Dr. Solandt encouraged Frost in his work and provided approximately $300,000 in development funding. He also brought the project to the attention of the British military and British Minister of Supply Duncan Sandys. The ministry had reservations about the project. Eventually, Dr. Solandt put Frost in touch with General D.C. Putt, head of the USAF Air Research and Development Command, the same man who had welcomed the Jetliner when it was tested at Wright Patterson Air Force Base years earlier.

The United States had been investigating the feasibility of a number of vertical takeoff concepts put forward by companies such as

Goodyear, Chrysler, and Hiller. Impressed by Avro's work on their other projects and convinced by Frost's technical proposals, the USAF settled on Project Y2 and awarded Avro a contract worth $758,000. Like Frost, the Americans had a genuine interest in exploiting the capabilities of this type of technology.

With its vertical takeoff and landing capabilities, Y2 obviated the need for conventional runways and could theoretically be deployed almost anywhere. As a completely circular craft, it would also have inherent stealth characteristics against detection by radar. The vehicle was to reach speeds between 1,720 and 2,300 miles per hour. Maximum height attainable was estimated to be between 71,000 and 80,600 feet, with a capability to hover at 18,000 feet. By 1957, Avro had invested nearly $2.5 million of its own money into the project they called Private Venture or PV 704. The United States Air Force had added another $1.8 million. Encouraged by wind tunnel test results on scale models, the United States Army also decided to join the venture. An integrated USAF/Army program was established with funding of $4,432,497 for the development and test of two vehicles.

Back at Avro, there was some skepticism among the executive concerning the feasibility of the project. Vice-President of Engineering James Floyd was concerned at the amount of time, space, and money that was being put toward the project. He did not believe such a device would work as advertised. He had engineering specialists from the UK examine the design, but they too were not convinced.

The U.S. Army was interested in a subsonic version of Y2. They felt that perfecting a subsonic craft would be simpler than attempting the full supersonic model, while still proving out the concept. The USAF and Avro agreed, and the subsonic Avrocar was born. Also known as Weapon System 606A, the VZ-9A, and covertly by the CIA as Project Silver Bug, the first prototype was unveiled in May of 1959, followed by the second vehicle in August of that year.

The Avrocar was approximately eighteen feet in diameter. It had a gross weight at takeoff of about 5,680 pounds. This included 840 pounds of fuel plus the weight of the pilot. It was "equipped with a 5ft diameter fan [developed by Orenda] situated in its centre, exhausting via an internal duct system to a peripheral nozzle. The fan was driven by means of a tip turbine, which used the exhaust from three [Continental] J-69-T-9 engines … The hot exhaust from the turbine was mixed with the cold flow from the fan in a duct immediately below the fan. This duct passes from the bottom of the fan beneath the cockpits, engine bays, and cargo compartments to the peripheral nozzle around the circumference of the vehicle…"[37]

The first free flight test was conducted in November 1959. Avro test pilot "Spud" Potocki was at the controls. He would hover and zoom as the exhaust from beneath the vehicle blew ice and other debris from off the tarmac. Still, it was readily apparent that the design was running into difficulty. The Avrocar rose only three feet off the ground and achieved a forward speed of thirty-five miles per hour in a sort of skittering motion. It was plagued by instability and power problems.

Several years later John Frost noted that in 1953, what Avro had actually discovered was the principle of the hovercraft. Had Avro not been so intent on trying to fly out of the ground cushion effect created by the downward exhausting air, they could have gotten into the hovercraft business. Instead, they chose to try to solve the instabilities in order to fly like an aircraft, first at subsonic and then supersonic speeds.

The U.S. Air Force Flight Test Center at Edwards Air Force Base examined the design and concluded, "Performance, stability and control of the Avrocar in its present configuration prevents accelerating in ground effect to a free air flight speed. Full scale wind tunnel results indicate that sufficient control is available to conduct a transition into high speed flight … provided that 35 to 40 knots can be obtained with the focussing ring control system …"[38] The report went on to list the areas that would require modification in order to fly.

Frost completed several of the modifications by 1961 and stated technical solutions to the instability problems were also at hand, but the United States decided not to renew the contract. One of the prototypes ended up in a warehouse at the Smithsonian while the other is mounted on a pedestal in Fort Eustis, Virginia. Was the Avrocar a failure? The answer is debatable.

When one reads the technical reports on the Avrocar, it is stated quite clearly that this was a research effort intended for the study of vertical takeoff principles. Indeed, the project was watched closely by the British, and it has been alleged in some circles that the information obtained provided some insights in the design of other vertical takeoff aircraft. And so criticism on this project must be guarded. The Avrocar did not achieve the performance Frost had hoped, but it provided considerable data with respect to power and stability of such problems. In fact, the concept was too far ahead of its time for the technology of the day, but it fell within the realm of bona fide scientific research.

In the early days of operation, some of the criticism against A.V. Roe was justified. There was chaos, some disorganization, and hiding of facts (whether intentional or not). Some of these difficulties were undoubtedly a result of an inexperienced new company breaking new ground. There was also the element of fear of failure. But through it all, the engineering teams delivered the products with which they were tasked within budgets that, though they may have exceeded original estimates, were in fact comparable to like projects in other countries with more experienced and seasoned industries. As MP Rodney Adamson said, the criticisms against the company were and remain unwarranted.

In understanding the eventual demise of A.V. Roe resulting from the termination of the Avro Arrow project, an understanding of continental defence is required. Aircraft like the Arrow and the CF-100 were needed to counter the potential threat from Soviet bombers. The concern was not so much that these bombers would attack Canada, but rather that they would fly across Canadian airspace to attack the United States. Canada was therefore enveloped in continental air defence and, as such, needed to participate within the American air defence network. Hence, the North American Aerospace Defense Command (NORAD) was born.

Chapter 5

NORAD

"I think it is wrong to leave the impression with the Minister and the govern-ment that our air defence plan is primarily for the defence of Canadian ter-ritory when in fact, any defence of Canadian territory is but a by-product or extra dividend to the main purpose, which is the defence of SAC bases and Northeastern United States." [39]

> — Chief of the General Staff Lieutenant-General
> H.D. Graham, in a top-secret letter to Chairman
> Chiefs of Staff Charles Foulkes, August 21, 1958

After World War II, there was no active air defence system in place anywhere on the North American continent. To make up for this vulnerability, the United States established the Air Defense Command (ADC) at Mitchel Field, New York and the Alaskan Air Command (AAC) in Alaska. It wasn't long before the Americans realized that continental defence planning needed to be coordinated with Canada, given that a potential enemy could cross the polar regions and pass through Canada en route to the United States. In May of 1946, the two countries formed the Canada/U.S. Military Cooperative Committee (MCC). The function of the MCC was to provide recommendations concerning mutual defence policy and planning. At its first meeting, the MCC signed documents to this effect and also noted that future threats to the continent would come from supersonic aircraft, atomic bombs, and long-range rockets and guided missiles.

The MCC also stipulated the need for interceptor air bases, anti-aircraft defences, and a combined Canadian and American Air Defense Headquarters for coordination and control over the entire air defence network. In the spirit of this philosophy, in 1947, the two countries established agreements, in principle, for the mutual exchange of personnel and cooperation in testing, training, standardization of weapons, and a host of other initiatives. While not binding on either country, this formed the basis for future collaboration and development of the NORAD agreement.

With Czechoslovakia falling under communist control in 1948, and Russia blockading Berlin and then testing an atomic bomb in August 1949, the world situation was highly unstable. Then on June 25, 1950, the Korean War broke out. In this highly charged atmosphere, one can begin to understand why the RCAF was pushing for the immediate design of the CF-100. Aircraft defences were essential.

In anticipation of possible war, the USAF established a temporary radar net across the United States. In March 1949, funds were approved for the establishment of a permanent radar net of seventy-five stations, with ten stations and two control centres in Alaska. The net became fully operational by 1952. In 1951 a second radar network was approved, and in 1954 a third was given the green light. All were designed to eventually provide a continuous web of surveillance across the continent. The United States Navy helped extend this radar coverage with patrol boats on both coasts. The United States Air Force did likewise using patrol aircraft.

In 1948, the USAF combined ADC with its Tactical Air Command to establish the Continental Air Command (ConAC). On July 1, 1950, U.S. ADC was officially abolished as a separate command under this structure. Also on July 1, the U.S. Army established its Antiaircraft

Command at the Pentagon. By September, Army sub-commands had been established on the east and west coasts, and headquarters was moved from the Pentagon to Mitchel Field, with ConAC. In 1957, Antiaircraft Command was renamed Army Air Defense Command.

In January 1951, the Americans re-established ADC and set it up in Colorado Springs, buried within Cheyenne Mountain for protection. To coordinate forces on the East Coast of Canada and Greenland, the American Joint Chiefs of Staff established their own Northeast Command. Its headquarters was set up on October 1, 1950, at Pepperrel Air Force Base in St. Johns, Newfoundland. At the same time, the USAF formed its Northeast Air Command (NEAC) separate from the Joint Chiefs' Northeast Command.

For its part, the U.S. Army's Antiaircraft Command deployed the Nike Ajax, a short-range guided supersonic missile, in December 1953. By late 1955, the Nike had become the Army's weapon of choice for defensive purposes. An improved version, the Nike Hercules, was unveiled. The systems of weapons, like Nike, the radar nets, and the various aircraft and ships, were all linked through a vast communications network with central control at Colorado Springs.

In Canada, No. 1 Air Defence Group was formed at Headquarters in Ottawa on December 1, 1948. On December 28, the Minister of National Defence announced an expanded program for defence spending, to meet the changing world circumstances. The RCAF also received its first military jet — the Vampire — and anxiously awaited production of the CF-100, while RCAF brass began considering a supersonic successor to it. (CF-100 squadrons were formed beginning in 1953.) The RCAF Air Defence Group moved to St. Hubert, Quebec in 1949. On June 1, 1951, they became Air Defence Command.

In August 1951, Canada and the United States agreed to establish thirty radar stations across southern Canada. Construction of what became known as the Pinetree Line began in 1951, in a this jointly funded effort. Twenty stations stretched across Canada, with ten concentrated on the East Coast. Manning of the stations was shared jointly by both countries. By 1955 all Pinetree Stations were fully operational.

In 1953, the MCC created the Canada–United States Military Study Group (MSG), to study the problems of continental air defence and to focus on the early warning system and the North American air defence systems. As it stood, Canada and the U.S. now had coverage on both coasts by the Americans and in the south by Canada's ADC. The North, however, remained a point of vulnerability. Attacking forces could come over the North Polar regions, across Canada, and into the United States. In 1954, to overcome this problem both countries agreed to build two more radar nets.

Canada built and manned the Mid-Canada line across the fifty-fifth parallel. The United States built the Distant Early Warning (DEW) line, to be jointly manned with Canada, along the Arctic Circle. Its purpose was to provide a warning time of about two hours against a six-hundred-mile-per-hour bomber. It was not designed to detect Intercontinental Ballistic Missiles (ICBMs). This duty would fall on the Ballistic Missile Early Warning System (BMEWS) the first station of which did not become operational until October 1, 1960.

The USAF ADC had been coordinating and controlling the massive complex of varied networks and weapons from the three services and was sharing in the Canadian efforts as well. By 1954 the American Joint Chiefs of Staff decided what was needed was one central coordinating and control agency. This became the Continental Air Defence Command (CONAD), established on September 1, 1954, under General Benjamin Chidlaw. CONAD had operational control of U.S. Air Defense Command, Army Antiaircraft Command, and the Navy's Continental Air Defense Command.

In 1956, with General Earle E. Partridge in charge, CONAD became a separate command with all air defence forces, including those in Alaska and the East Coast, under its authority. The NEAC and Northeast Command were eliminated. During the period of CONAD's formation there was tremendous inter-service rivalry between the Army and Air Commands in terms of whose defence system would prevail for continental defence. The Army had its Nike Hercules missiles while the Air Force began promoting the Bomarc surface-to-air missile. Canada's ADC was not affected by the rivalry and retained operational control of American Air Defense Forces stationed in Canada.

The following excerpt, taken from a discussion in the U.S. House of Representatives, highlights the rivalry:

Competing systems supported by enthusiastic industrial and service advocates tend to create confusion and uncertainty. Great promises, often somewhat nebulous but calculated to get support and contract awards, are held out by the advocates of all systems ... In the air defence area, we have a very definite problem of this type in the competing concepts behind the BOMARC and the NIKE HERCULES ground-to-air missiles.[40]

Both systems were competing for funding as well as continental defence supremacy and were therefore making great claims as to their effectiveness. Having another country like Canada interested in obtaining one of the systems could tip the balance in its favour. This would eventually factor in Canada's decision to obtain the Bomarc.

As per the 1946 MCC recommendations, the United States and Canada decided that one command should in fact oversee all the forces concerned with continental air defence. In 1956, a committee of Canadian and American officers, working under the auspices of the MSG, an MCC subgroup, developed a study designed to determine how to make a joint command politically acceptable to Canada.

Writing in *Dilemmas in Defense Decision-Making*, author Ann Denholm Crosby notes that Canadian Chief of Staff General Charles Foulkes had asked that this study be conducted in secrecy. A study was produced in December 1956 and approved in February 1957 by the militaries of both countries and the U.S. Secretary of Defense. The Canadian government, in the throes of preparing for an election, had not yet had any input to any of the report's recommendations.

The election on June 10, 1957, saw the Conservative government of John George Diefenbaker win a minority election. General Foulkes approached the newly elected Minister of National Defense, former Major-General George R. Pearkes, in the hopes of gaining early acceptance for the MSG report. Minister Pearkes approached Diefenbaker on July 24, and the latter accepted the report without consulting the Cabinet or External Affairs. Since this report dealt with the formation of a joint command, NORAD was effectively born. The report was later accepted by the Canadian Cabinet on July 31.

As a result of the report, on September 12, 1957, an agreement was reached to establish the North American Air Defense Command. Its mandate was to develop defence plans in peacetime, to maintain and operate the vast networks that had been established, and, if necessary, to engage the enemy in the event of attack. The NORAD agreement caused quite a stir in Canada. It was felt that it had been made without the proper parliamentary debate and that there were sovereignty concerns about having the Canadian Forces under the command of an American. Questions were asked: Did this also imply that if the Americans went to war, Canada would have to follow? What did it mean in terms of overall defence planning?

In terms of the latter, it meant that "U.S. pressure for compliance with its strategic perceptions and plans, therefore, became an indigenous pressure operating through the Canadian military, leaving very little room"[41] for Ottawa to influence the planning process. For Canadians, this meant accepting policies that the Canadian government was not necessarily comfortable with, such as the role of and need for nuclear weapons.

According to Ann Crosby, when Diefenbaker accepted the MSG report on the formation of a joint command in July 1957, he committed Canada "to accept nuclear weapons for Canadian air defence forces," since this was a requirement by the United States.[42] Perhaps Diefenbaker didn't even realize the full ramifications of what he had done. Those nuclear weapons, namely the Bomarc, and the anti-intercontinental ballistic missile requirements of NORAD played a pivotal role in the demise of the Arrow.

The NORAD agreement was made official between the two countries on May 12, 1958. NORAD now had operational control of both Canadian and American air defence forces. General Partridge became commander in chief (CINCNORAD) while Canadian Air Force Marshal C. Roy Slemon became deputy commander in chief. On August 1, 1959, U.S. Air Force General Laurence S. Kuter became CINCNORAD after General Partridge's retirement. According to Jon B. McLin in *Canada's Changing Defense Policy*, Partridge had actually resigned because of the continuing inter-service rivalry between the USAF and the Army.

NORAD divided the continent into identification zones or regions. Each zone, also called a division, would have a combat centre with a division commander to oversee the entire battle and allocate resources to the various sub-divisions or sectors. Each sector would have a direction centre and a sector commander to direct any battles over the sector.

Any legitimate aircraft expecting to fly into one of these regions would need to file a flight plan and as such could then be eliminated as a hostile target when picked up on the radar net. If an aircraft were detected that did not correlate with a bona fide plan, communications checks would be made with other commands and civilian organizations to determine if the aircraft was one of theirs. Failing that, it would be necessary to scramble interceptors for a visual identification of the oncoming aircraft. For this reason interceptor aircraft have always been considered essential as being able to positively identify a target as being hostile before destroying it. A missile would not have this capability.

The NORAD defensive arsenal used to repel an attack was and remains formidable. In the 1950s, it consisted of fifty-five squadrons of interceptors. These included the supersonic F-102 Delta Dagger, F-101B Voodoo, the F-106 Delta Dart (the world speed record holder at 1,525 mph), the subsonic F-89, the U.S. Navy's Skyray, and finally the RCAF subsonic CF-100.

The American F-101, F-106, and F-89 were each capable of carrying the MB-1 Genie atomic warhead rocket, which was capable of vaporizing the enemy and the atmosphere for miles around, making accuracy less critical. All of the American aircraft were also capable of carrying the guided Falcon missile. This missile would lock on to its target either by radar or by a heat-seeking device.

The subsonic CF-100, or Canuck, carried relatively ineffective folding fin rockets, which were highly inaccurate. In view of the American equipment, the concept of visual identification, and the increasing ability of potential enemy aircraft, it is readily apparent why the RCAF was anxious to obtain the supersonic Arrow in place of the CF-100. Adding to the arsenal of aircraft were the Nike missiles and the Bomarc.

The American scheme for stopping an attacking weapon was simple but expensive in terms of hardware. An enemy bomber would first be met with manned fighter interceptor aircraft. After this line of defence would come the Bomarc, which could be armed with a conventional or nuclear warhead. Some additional aircraft would also be on hand as short-range fighters if the enemy got past the Bomarc. The Nike Hercules, which could also be fitted with a nuclear warhead, would follow.

Analyzing the data from the various radar stations and coordinating and controlling defensive engagements was a mammoth task. It was initially performed manually by personnel who needed to be in constant touch with one another. In July 1958, an automatic system of control was finally developed for the Air Force. It was called SAGE (Semi-Automatic Ground Environment).

Not surprisingly, the American Army had also developed an automated system. It had become operational in December 1957, before SAGE. It was called Missile Master. Some sources have said that part of the reason for developing SAGE was that the Air Force did not wish to again be outdone by the Army — part of the continuing rivalry between the two services. Eventually, Missile Master and SAGE became fully integrated.

An understanding of what SAGE was is important in terms of understanding its later impact on the Avro Arrow program. The heart of SAGE was a gigantic computer, the AN/FSQ-7. In the 1950s, the Massachusetts Institute of Technology (MIT) was developing the first digital computer, the Whirlwind. What the Air Force needed was a production version.

Mitre Corporation was spun off the Computer Systems Division of MIT's Lincoln Laboratories to design the Whirlwind II. IBM was contracted to build it, and it was designated the AN/FSQ-7. At the time it was the largest real-time computer in the world. Eventually twenty-four SAGE Direction Centers and three SAGE Combat Centers with this computer would be spread across the United States, with one SAGE system in Canada.

The SAGE AN/FSQ-7 was a giant and weighed in at over 250 tons, requiring a 3,000-kilowatt power supply and a massive air conditioning system. It consisted of dozens of cathode ray tube display consoles for multiple users, backed up by over 8,000 vacuum tubes, 600,000 transistors, 170,000 diodes, 7,300 pluggable units, 919 miles of external wiring, 123 miles of internal wiring, and a newly developed memory called magnetic core.

In today's terminology its memory consisted of about 256k — not a lot compared to today's gigabyte hardware desk and laptop computers. Still, it was an impressive twenty years ahead of personal computing. Everything had a duplicate for back-up, and the whole system was housed in huge four-storey concrete buildings. One humorous anecdote has it that when a burnt-out tube was discovered during maintenance, it was found it was not even connected to the circuit due to an earlier modification.

The display consoles of this computer were on the top floor of the building with the computer itself below. The consoles or terminals displayed reference data on a small tube and geographical and aircraft information on a large cathode ray tube or TV-like screen. The operator used a light gun to point at specific targets. Digital data was transmitted from computer to computer and computer to radar via telephone lines. The light guns could be likened to today's mouse, and the interconnecting telephone circuitry to modems.

Interception of an incoming target would occur as follows. Early warning radar would detect an enemy aircraft and feed the information to the SAGE Direction Center. After processing the information, the Center would notify headquarters as well as the interceptors or missile batteries in proximity of the target. The SAGE computer could not only provide direction information to the interceptors but could automatically fly the aircraft to the target. The computer would choose the best attack route and could even compensate for changes in the speed, altitude, and direction of the target. A status update would be provided to headquarters. Likewise, SAGE could not only direct a missile to its target but could actually launch a missile at some distant location. Alternatively, an operator could use SAGE to alert the appropriate defensive systems and then simply monitor the target until it was acquired by one of the defence systems.

The missile designed to work with SAGE was the Bomarc. Between 1945 and 1949, Boeing had been working on the Ground to Air Pilotless Aircraft (GAPA) program to develop surface-to-air missiles. In 1949, the Air Force authorized development of an interceptor missile (IM) to destroy attacking bombers and intercontinental ballistic missiles. What was then called the Michigan Aeronautical Research Center of the University of Michigan took part in the effort and the name BOMARC was born — BOeing Michigan Aeronautical Research Center.

In 1952, the first Bomarc was test-fired. By 1955, forty-one experimental test missiles designated XIM-99 were delivered. Thirty-eight of a newer version, the YIM-99, were delivered by 1957. Finally, the first production model prototype with a guidance system, designated YIM-99A or simply IM-99A, was completed, and on May 16, 1957, Boeing received a production order from the USAF. Bomarc, however, would be effective only against the threat of bombers and not intercontinental ballistic missiles.

All missiles were housed in concrete and stainless steel shelters. The missile itself sat on an erector arm. When the launch signal was given, the roof of its concrete housing would slide open and the arm would raise the Bomarc into firing position.

Because of the highly corrosive fuel used in the Bomarc A, the missile had to be fuelled before launch, as the fuel could not be stored for lengthy periods in the missile itself. This action of raising the missile and fuelling caused a delay in the speed of reaction to an oncoming attacker.

Also, the fuels were of a type that ignited immediately upon mixing. This caused numerous accidental fires, including one on June 7, 1960, wherein a nuclear Bomarc A caught fire. The warhead melted but did not explode. An earlier problem with the Bomarc A had to do with the erecting mechanism acting prematurely. This problem was related to a situation wherein a random signal might look like a launch command and cause the missile to rise. This problem was quickly corrected.

The IM-99A with its rocket fuel booster and ramjet engines had a range of between 200 and 250 miles. The improved Bomarc B used a solid fuel mixture and improved ramjets for a range of 400 miles. The B also had an advanced target seeker and, like the Bomarc A, carried either a nuclear or conventional warhead. There was only one small problem: no conventional warhead was designed for it. Hence when Canada elected to purchase the Bomarc B, nuclear warheads would have to be on board, otherwise the weapon was useless. The nuclear warhead would ensure that the attacking bomber was destroyed.

The first Bomarc B was launched on May 27, 1959, but numerous problems plagued both the As and the Bs, causing a host of failures. The first successful intercept of a drone target by the Bomarc finally occurred on July 8, 1960, much to the relief of the Canadian Minister of National Defence, who had put all his confidence and support behind Bomarc, to the detriment and termination of the Avro Arrow.

The Canadian squadron designated 446th SAM became operational in North Bay, Ontario in November 1963, and 447 squadron became operational the following month in La Macaza, Quebec. Ironically, the USAF began shutting down its Bomarc bases soon after in 1964. Was there a problem with the system?

Les Earnest was a staff member at the MIT Lincoln Laboratories. The group in which he was involved was responsible for the integration of the interceptors and the missiles to SAGE. When Mitre Corporation was formed, he became a sub-section head and later switched to the Intelligence Systems Sub-Department. In 1962 he worked for the CIA, and from 1963–1965 with the Joint Chiefs of Staff, before going to Stanford University. He believed SAGE was a technological marvel with its mammoth computer, radar, long distance data communications, and ground-to-air radio links. But it was not without some major drawbacks.

According to Les, the early SAGE was vulnerable to electronic countermeasures (ECM) and jamming. If an attacking aircraft used active radar jamming or even chaff (tiny aluminum strips ejected from the enemy airplane) SAGE would lose its tracking and be unable to carry out an intercept. He explains that some corrective measures were later used to try to overcome this problem. In reality though, because of this ECM problem, he felt SAGE was in effect only a peacetime tool. Had there been an attack, SAGE could have been overwhelmed.

Les's concerns might be taken with a grain of salt, were it not for some additional corroboration. A similar argument concerning this matter and the ECM vulnerabilities of the radar was raised in the U.S. House of Representatives later in 1960, when the USAF decided to curtail the SAGE/Bomarc program. A USAF General commented, "We attempted various fixes on these radar to improve their electronics countermeasure countering capability, but these are not entirely successful, particularly against the advanced electronics countermeasures we expect in the future."[43]

A technical report by Avro had drawn similar conclusions. Written January 19, 1959, the Avro report noted that in a clear environment in the absence of jamming, SAGE could simultaneously track upwards of two hundred targets in any given sector. Under conditions of barrage jamming from the attackers, though, only a small number of enemy aircraft would need to use the jamming against the ground radar systems to disrupt them. According to the report, these few aircraft jammers would make it almost impossible for SAGE to determine the location, speed, heading, or even the number of attackers.

These jammers would create such a massive target on the display terminal that it would in effect hide other real targets. It could even make it difficult to determine the precise location of the jammers themselves, as they would be indistinguishable behind the large target display on the screen. The effect is similar to trying to look at the stars with a bright street lamp nearby. Remedies to overcome this problem could be met with other, more sophisticated, types of jamming.

The Avro report went one step further in explaining how the Bomarc missile itself could be jammed.

> The present version of BOMARC has no provision for counter-counter-measures and is therefore vulnerable … Later versions will probably be equipped with automatic home-on-jam which comes into action as soon as jamming is started. However, two aircraft which jam alternately would cause the missile to home first on one and then on the other until it finally flew past both without ever being close enough to either for its fuse to function.[44]

A second problem concerned the facilities housing the SAGE computers. According to Les, MIT had recommended placing the SAGE computers and command centres in hardened underground shelters. Hardening means fortifying the buildings to withstand massive explosions. This was deemed to be too expensive, so everything was placed in concrete buildings above ground. This made them perfect targets for enemy bombers. For that matter, it was noted that even the Bomarc bunkers were nothing more than targets for oncoming enemy aircraft.

The U.S. Department of Defense eventually recognized this problem. A recommendation was put forward that modified, more advanced computers would be placed in hardened combat centres called supercentres, guaranteed to withstand a certain blast pressure from incoming missiles or bombs. By early 1960, even this proposal was being rescinded for the following reason:

> ... it was proposed that certain of these advanced type SAGE computers be placed in hardened positions ...you can carry this on ad infinitum and practically put the entire national wealth in this thing because if you harden your centres, to say, a thousand pounds per square inch, then your fighter fields, your subsidiary communications, your BOMARCS, whatever you have, also would have to be hardened because they equally could be destroyed...[45]

Finally, it had been recommended that the SAGE facilities be located away from critical air bases and large populated centres. The Avro report noted that the primary targets in an attack would be the retaliatory strike force on this continent, that is the American Strategic Air Command (SAC) and Naval bases, with civil industrial centres as secondary targets. Despite the MIT recommendations, many sites were placed at SAC bases. Given that SAC bases would also be among the first to be targeted by an enemy, both the bases and the centres could be destroyed at the same time, giving the enemy a nice two for one bonus kill.

There are two at least two schools of thought on the SAGE/Bomarc issue. On the one hand, some great technological strides were made, and it is said that modern computers owe their origins to this system. In addition, the very existence of such a system might deter anyone from attacking.

On the other hand, it is argued that the system should never have been built because it could not and would not work in the event of a real attack, for the reasons stated above. It was also not effective against the ICBM, nor could it be effective against low-flying targets coming in dipping below the radar net. Although it did provide a training ground for programmers and computer designers of the future, it has been alleged that if the money had gone into computer development per se, the world would have had desktops in the sixties, not the late seventies or early eighties. As for Canada, it seems the government was sold a bill of goods when it opted for the system (in particular, the Bomarc), and the Arrow was lost because of it. In reality, though, did Canada have any choice?

This author advised Les Earnest that unlike the American aircraft, the Arrow did not require SAGE. The Americans had pointed this out to the RCAF, as noted in *Storms of Controversy*. Les recalled the Arrow, calling it a sad event, but then made an interesting comment. He claims his group had been asked to determine how the F-108 interceptor would integrate into SAGE. This aircraft was a long-range interceptor with specifications that would best those of the Arrow. Like the Arrow, it too was cancelled. Les makes the point that his group actually showed the F-108 would not require the use of SAGE, and this was the conclusion of a report that was prepared.

He says he was told by the USAF that his group had come to the wrong conclusion. They were supposed to show how the aircraft functioned with SAGE because the illusion of SAGE as a great system had to be maintained. Les believes the F-108 was killed partly because it did not require SAGE. Officially, it was stated the F-108 was cancelled in favour of another aircraft then under consideration, the B-70, a Mach 3 delta-winged behemoth that also never made it to production, but whose design studies began in 1959.

Was the Arrow killed because it did not require SAGE? This is highly unlikely. Rather, it was killed partly because of the introduction of SAGE/Bomarc. The term "unanticipated militarism," when referring to Canadian defence decision-making, has been described as "a gradual acceptance of policies that did not always coincide with the government's own assessment of the exigencies of the international strategic environment."[46] Acceptance of a nuclear air defence role and participation in American missile programs (read Bomarc) are given as examples of this.

The Americans were pushing their defence agenda on Canada for their own interests. Canadian defence and procurement brass, seeing the spectre of fancy missile technology and computers, accepted the American plans and strategies to the detriment of their own programs like the Arrow. SAGE and the nuclear Bomarc were not a Canadian requirement; this certainly seems to be the implication embodied in "unanticipated militarism."

The Canadian Chief of the General Staff seemed also of the opinion that only the American military agenda was being followed. In a top-secret memo he noted that any defence of Canada was simply a by-product of the defence of the SAC bases and Northeastern United States. In his memo, he was rebuking Charles Foulkes for giving the wrong impression to the government that the Canadian air defence plan was for defending Canada.

Specifically, in a document titled *Report on the Development of the CF 105 and Associated Weapon System 1952–1958*, Foulkes had written:

> Canada was primarily responsible for the air defence of
> Canada, and while the United States co-operated with
> Canada, the only arrangement for U.S. support at this
> time dealt with reinforcing after the battle had begun.[47]

It was this paragraph to which the Chief of the General Staff was responding. One can readily understand now why he was upset with what he felt was a misrepresentation to the government by Foulkes.

Typically, one reads that since the Arrow was costing too much, the Canadian government decided to cancel it and introduce the SAGE/Bomarc missile in its stead. In fact, past evidence has suggested that the decision to acquire SAGE/Bomarc was made long before the official announcement in 1959. Ann Crosby has noted in *Dilemmas In Defense Decision-Making*, that in announcing the formation of the NORAD Command in August 1957, Pearkes stated this would require the siting of missiles (Bomarc). The decision on Bomarc can then be traced back to 1957, but it goes back even further.

It was not the cost of the Arrow alone but rather the combined costs of the SAGE/Bomarc and additional gap-filler radar that was going to be too expensive for Canada. George Pearkes's top-secret brief of July 1958 supports this. In that brief, Pearkes stated very clearly that Canada could perhaps make provision for the Arrow in succeeding defence budgets, but that the problem was the cost of all the NORAD defensive requirements (American requirements as discussed above), all coming now at the same time. His top-secret brief reads in part as follows:

> The introduction of SAGE in Canada will cost in the neighborhood of $107 million. Further improvements are required in the radar and other associated communications which will also bring greater expenses ... NORAD has also recommended the introduction of the Bomarc missile ... will be a further commitment of some $164 million ... All these commitments coming at this particular time ... will tend to increase our defence budget by as much as 25 to 30 percent. All these projects also contain a very large element of U.S. content, which may give rise to other fiscal problems.[48]

Recently, this author obtained additional files from the Eisenhower Library concerning this meeting. The Americans quote Pearkes:

> He stated that the problem of developing a defence against missiles **while at the same time** [bolding mine] completing and rounding out defence measures against manned bombers posed a serious problem for Canada from the point of view of expense ... He also stressed that these heavy additional defence burdens were placed on Canada because of its geographic position.[49]

In this brief, Pearkes went on to suggest more in-depth arrangements for production sharing with the U.S., for this extra American required equipment. He also made the rather weak suggestion that perhaps the Americans would share in the costs of the Avro Arrow by purchasing it and equipping the American bases at Harmon Field and Goose Bay with it. Secretary of State John Foster Dulles countered with his own remarks concerning missiles and the need for the Arrow:

> The Secretary concluded his remarks by pointing out that missiles which were now becoming available would be obsolete in a few years and that they were merely a stop-gap until much improved missiles were available. He also thought it might be well for the military people on both sides **to exchange views on Soviet bomber capabilities, as one way of assessing the need for the fighter plane production effort which Mr. Pearkes had discussed** [bolding mine].[50]

It would be the arguments of a diminished manned bomber threat, utilization of missiles, and the alleged high costs of the Arrow that would spell its doom.

Many have argued that the Americans should not be blamed for not having purchased the Arrow. After all, the Americans had never said they would buy it; they had merely strongly encouraged its initial development. One must then ask why Canada should have been expected to purchase SAGE/Bomarc at all, given that it was an American requirement. Was it the soon-to-be-obsolete system the Secretary spoke of? Since Canada was being expected to meet American NORAD requirements for Bomarc, why was not the Arrow considered part of that contribution?

General Putt of the U.S. Air Force Research and Development Command had argued in favour of purchasing Arrows for the NORAD inventory on January 29, 1958, at a meeting between the Canadian ambassador to Washington, Norman Robertson, and Secretary of the Air Force James H. Douglas. Douglas squashed the idea, as did Secretary of State John Foster Dulles, at subsequent meetings with George Pearkes.

Through new documentation, it is now possible to trace more fully the history of the RCAF commitment to purchase the SAGE/Bomarc system and the impact of this decision on the Arrow. The decision was not made in 1959 or in 1957. It goes back much earlier, to the discussions of a combined continental air defence.

Chapter 6

Who Needs the Bomarc?

"If the Bomarc bases are located south of the Great Lakes, the interception of enemy bombers will be done over the area which includes Montreal, Toronto, Hamilton, etc., and higher casualties and property damage would probably result."[51]

> — Memorandum from RCAF Chief of Requirements
> to Chief of Plans, April 25, 1958, discussing the air
> defence concept

Given the vulnerabilities of SAGE/Bomarc, how and why did the Canadian government decide on this as the weapon system of choice? In 1953, the Military Study Group had been set up to study the problems of continental air defence. Early 1954 saw the production in Russia of thermonuclear weapons and a new jet bomber, the Bison. These developments actually acted to accelerate the Arrow development, but also at this time an Air Defense Planning Group (American and Canadian personnel from the air defence forces) was developing plans for the air defence of the continent.

At this early stage, when the Bomarc was not even a developed and proven weapon, the planning group proposed that a line of Bomarc missile bases be set up across the United States and Eastern Canada, at about the forty-eighth parallel. In Eastern Canada this would place them around the area of North Bay, Ontario, a few latitudes north of the nation's capital, Ottawa. These bases were essential for the protection of the American Strategic Air Command force and not necessarily for the protection of the country's capital. That would be merely a by-product.

In September of 1955, the Canadian government decided to reappraise the Avro Arrow program. As a result, the department established an interdepartmental committee, with the Chief of the Air Staff as chair. Members included the Deputy Minister of National Defence; the Chairman, Defence Research Board; the Deputy Minister of Defence Production; representatives from the cabinet Secretariat, the Department of Finance, and the Department of External Affairs; and a representative of the president of the National Research Council.

This group of individuals developed three recommendations that were tabled to the Chiefs of Staff Committee. Each of the three recommendations included installation of Bomarc bases. The recommended option not only promoted continuation of the Arrow but also recommended improvements to the CF-100 and, as mentioned, installation of Bomarcs.

Of special significance was that this group also provided cost estimates for augmenting the radar network as per continental defence requirements. Required were another 26 heavy radar, 123 gap-filler radar, and installation of data processing equipment. The latter was likely SAGE, although Canada was studying the feasibility of developing its own system, called CAGE. The total of these was given as $867 million plus an additional $210 million for Bomarc bases. The group expressed the hope that the U.S. would shoulder a major part of the $867 million.

Given the identified need for these additional defences, the RCAF produced a top-secret memorandum for the Cabinet Defence Committee (CDC) entitled *Authority to Conduct Joint Site Surveys for the Northwest Extension of the Air Defence Combat Zone.* Dated June 11, 1956, it opened with the following:

> A factor of prime importance to the security and lasting peace of the Western World is the deterrent power of the United States Strategic Air Force. This means that the defences of this Continent must be such that this retaliatory force cannot be destroyed or severely reduced by surprise attack … As part of these defences it is proposed to introduce a line of Bomarc guided missile bases from coast to coast …[52]

This document clearly states that protection of SAC was the primary reason for continental defence and that Bomarc would be the chosen weapon. Mentioned later in the document was the fact that protection would also be given to major centres of population and industry in Canada. This further supports the observation of the Chief of the General Staff that Canadian air defence was for protection first and foremost of the American SAC.

The primary thrust of the memo was to obtain cabinet approval for the commencement of site surveys to select the optimum sites for expansion of existing facilities. This meant expansion of ground control radar and computational facilities that would be necessary for the early detection and destruction of enemy aircraft. In fact, this was proposing an extension of SAGE into Canada along with Bomarc.

The memo painted a picture of urgency in order to expedite approval from the CDC. It noted that attacking bombers would soon reach speeds of between 1,500 and 2,000 miles an hour at altitudes of over 60,000 feet (incidentally, the same parameters used in the design of the Arrow). The ground control system then would have to extend beyond the Pinetree Line. Additional gap-filler radar would be required to effectively plug any holes in the network. Finally, improvements were required in automatic data handling. All this was needed for directing the Bomarcs and interceptors to their targets. The memo read as though introduction of Bomarc was a done deal and not simply a proposal. For all intents and purposes, it was a fait accompli.

The MSG had also recommended a further operational evaluation of the effectiveness of the air defence system, under the auspices of yet another subgroup, the Canada-U.S. Scientific Advisory Team (CUS-SAT). Rather than wait for the results of the MSG study the CDC submission said:

> In as much as an evaluation by the Canada-U.S. Scientific Advisory Team is now in progress, there is a natural urge to await its conclusions prior to embarking on any siting program. However, to do so would mean little, if any, progress this summer on site surveys and this in effect would set the whole project back by one year ... Then, as the summer progresses and the results of the Canada-U.S. Scientific Advisory Team's evaluation and the Military Study Group's assessment become available, the balance of the siting program can be confirmed or altered as necessary.[53]

It is clear that the decision on Bomarc was assumed, to the point that even the MSG conclusions didn't matter. It was supposed that they would simply be written in terms of optimizing the existing site choices. It does not appear that there was to be any analysis of the true effectiveness of the system per se. Further, the memo was putting pressure on the CDC, as if to imply that the CDC would be responsible if the site selections were delayed to the point that SAC bases would be in jeopardy. The CDC was not being given much latitude to consider alternatives.

Not surprisingly, in the absence of countering opinion, the CDC accepted and concurred with the memo's recommendations at its meeting of June 13, 1956. Site surveys for additional radar would be allowed. Half a million dollars was allocated for the surveys and American participation was authorized as required. The CDC decision also accepted that the report on effectiveness from the CUSSAT would be forthcoming in the not too distant future.

The CDC also stated that its decision to proceed on all fronts did not mean approval had been given to actually commence construction of bases. Still, despite the few caveats that were imposed, it seems that introduction of SAGE/Bomarc was accepted. Given that this system was linked to protection of the SAC bases and was put forward by the Americans as part of their essential requirement, it became a matter of higher priority than the Arrow. This is critical; while the RCAF clearly wanted both Bomarc and the Arrow, the government would choose only Bomarc.

By September 1, 1956, the RCAF produced its first draft missile requirements report, titled *Operational Characteristic For An Interceptor Missile Weapon System*. (The RCAF could have just copied the Bomarc specifications.) In terms of future implications on the Arrow, the draft made the following observation in its introductory paragraph:

> The RCAF has a supersonic all-weather fighter, the CF105, under development. This aircraft will be capable of countering at least a portion of the enemy threat until approximately 1968 and probably thereafter. It must be augmented, however, by a weapon which is capable of inflicting a high attrition rate on high speed manned bombers as well as upon air-to-surface and surface-to-surface guided missiles. The only defence system which can even approach the attrition rates required against weapons which are capable of such high performance and widespread destruction is a surface-to-air missile system augmented by supersonic interceptors.[54]

Key in this excerpt is the last sentence, which speaks of the missile being augmented by the interceptor rather than the other way around. Surface-to-air missiles had become a higher priority.

When critics speak of the mounting costs of the Arrow, typically the argument centres on the following facts. The Arrow began as an airframe development. Then an engine needed to be developed because none suitable were available. Finally to these developments was added the requirement to develop a fire control system and weapon. One can now add the SAGE/Bomarc and all it entailed in terms of gap-filler radar and the like. Though not officially announced until years later, the SAGE/Bomarc requirement was clearly entrenched as Canada's contribution to

American air defence requirements. There is no denying that the SAC needed protection, but other Canadian options should have been discussed with input from the CDC and parliament. Nevertheless, acceptance of SAGE/Bomarc was a fait accompli, effectively excluding the parliamentary process. It seems that American pressure to have Canada comply with its requirements was behind Canadian military decisions, to the exclusion of outside debate.

Since the missile report was a draft document, it is acknowledged that it did not represent officialdom, yet its conclusions can not be ignored. It provides valued insight into the thinking and priority shifts that were occurring in the RCAF as a result of continental defence planning. It also clearly indicates that the RCAF wanted both systems, not one or the other.

In addition to protection against manned supersonic bombers and air-to-surface launched missiles, the report also mentioned the requirement to defend against intercontinental and submarine-launched ballistic missiles, although Bomarc was not designed to defend against the ICBM. Of greater significance is that the report required the Bomarc missiles to have an atomic warhead as the primary payload, with a conventional warhead as alternate. Was an atomic warhead truly essential? Perhaps, but only because of the technical fact that the Bomarc's accuracy was still questionable. This would not be a problem with a nuclear warhead, as it would incinerate everything for miles around, rendering accuracy inconsequential. Perhaps this is what was meant by the missile providing a higher attrition rate.

An atomic warhead on Bomarc was an American requirement, not a Canadian one. Moreover, an atomic warhead seemed opposed to Canada's unwritten but accepted policy of being nuclear-free. Yet the draft report was establishing the case for nuclear weapons — clearly a case of "unanticipated militarism." Did Canada really not have a choice in the matter?

Jon McLin writes that before the Canadian government's decision to accept Bomarc, discussions between the Canadian Minister of National Defence and the American Secretary of Defense included an appreciation of what would happen should Canada refuse to accept the missiles. According to McLin, "the consequence would be, the Canadians were told, the emplacement of at least one more Bomarc squadron in the U.S., south of the Great Lakes."[55] This meant that any engagement of the targets would mean nuclear devastation directly over the Windsor-Toronto-Montreal corridor, courtesy of the short range of the Bomarc.

The prospect of a nuclear battle over the most populated region of Canada was not lost on the Canadian military planners, as evidenced in the following quote from later correspondence:

> ... the Bomarc in the Canadian Air Defence System would provide greater defence in depth. It would also permit the engagement of enemy bombers before they reach the large centres of population and industrial production in Canada. If the Bomarc bases are located south of the Great Lakes, the interception of enemy bombers will be done over the area which includes Montreal, Toronto, Hamilton, etc., and higher casualties and property damage would probably result.[56]

The situation is no different today. In discussing the American National Missile Defense (NMD) system, Canadian newspapers spoke of dangerous debris falling over Canadian territory and cities. It is hoped the debris from the destruction of incoming missiles would land in Canada's uninhabited northern regions, but there would be no guarantees of this.

In May 2000, the newspapers reported that if Canada did not go along with NMD, the United States would not offer protection to Canadian cities and the NORAD system would break down. Vice-Admiral Herbert Browne, deputy commander of the U.S. Space Command, was quoted as saying that expending missiles for defence of Canadian cities made no sense, as they would all be required for defence of American territory. This prompted the Canadian Minister of National Defence, the Right Honourable Art Eggleton, to pronounce that Canada would not be blackmailed into supporting NMD. In the 1950s, there was no such open discussion of the SAGE/Bomarc issue before it was too late.

By November 1956, the RCAF was actively investigating the various factors for integrating Bomarc squadrons in North Bay and Ottawa. One of the stumbling blocks was that American regulations precluded Canada from having sole custody of nuclear weapons and other sensitive equipment. (This would also become a problem relating to the Arrow carrying nuclear-tipped weapons.) The other was the question of whether Canada would build or purchase the Bomarc from the Americans.

On April 5, 1957, a meeting of RCAF planning and requirements staff was held to further discuss the matter of the introduction of SAGE/Bomarc. The issue was where best to locate the bases in the Ottawa and North Bay sectors. No one seemed to be worried about the effectiveness of the system. The matter of site surveys was again raised as essential in being able to proceed with the timely introduction of a system that was still in premature development. It was even suggested that if a firm decision to conduct site surveys was taken by the Canadian government, it would send a signal of the government's intention to obtain Bomarc missiles. On reading the minutes of this meeting, one can sense the euphoria of the meeting's attendees at being caught up in the exciting possibility of obtaining nuclear-tipped weapons.

One fact should not be lost sight of: John Diefenbaker, the Canadian prime minister seen as responsible for the cancellation of the Arrow, has also been directly linked with the introduction of the Bomarc. The progression of events above removes Diefenbaker, and the Liberal government of Louis St. Laurent before him, from the Bomarc debate; the Canadian decision to adopt Bomarc was made by American and Canadian military planners, independent of whoever was in power.

At the April 1957 meeting of RCAF planning staff, at least one member suggested a slower, more methodical approach to the introduction of Bomarc. In a lengthy reply to the meeting minutes, he suggested that first a series of studies to determine optimal locations would be required, along with a discussion of the pros and cons of producing or assembling Bomarcs in Canada versus obtaining them from the U.S. This would be followed by a complete cost analysis. Still, even his reply did not raise the question of the effectiveness of the missile nor whether it was needed at all by Canada.

The Bomarc discussions continued in a memo dated May 3, 1957, that made reference to earlier correspondence from November 1956

The Jetliner was the first commercial intercity regional jet to fly in North America, almost ten years ahead of similar American aircraft. Avro coined the word Jetliner but, since it never went into production, could not get the name copyrighted.

The Jetliner makes a triumphant flight into New York, carrying the first jet air mail in North America. The design won Jim Floyd the Wright Brothers' medal, the first time it had been awarded to an individual outside the United States.

Over eight years ahead of any North American design, the Jetliner was ordered destroyed in 1956. Note the circular windows. They prevented the catastophic failures plaguing the British-designed Comets in the early fifties.

Concurrent with the Jetliner, Avro was developing the CF-100 Canuck.

The CF-100 is put through its paces.

Despite some early design problems, the CF-100 proved a remarkable work-horse for the RCAF.

CF-100 in flight.

Introduction of the Bomarc missile into Canada was expected as early as 1956 by a joint Canadian and American defence panel, for protection of the American Strategic Air Command.

The heart of the SAGE (used for controlling Bomarc) system was the 250 ton, 256kb AN/FSQ-7 computer, an engineering marvel in its own right.

Controllers for the SAGE computer.

Scale Arrow models were launched over Lake Ontario, from Nike rockets, to test flight characteristics.

The Arrow begins to take shape.

First images of what appears to be an Arrow model in Lake Ontario.

Courtesy David Gartshore

A close-up of the model shows the distinctive double engine exhausts. The wings have been damaged and the tail has been sheared off.

The mighty Iroquois engine is unveiled.

Courtesy Aerospace Heritage Foundation

The Iroquois was tested on a B-47 but not in the Arrow. The B-47 fuselage was damaged from the power of the Iroquois.

The Arrow is taken for a walk.

The old and what should have been the new.

Giants of the industry, the Arrow and below the Avro plant in Malton.

The Arrow comes in for a smooth touchdown, speed brakes extended.

A thing of beauty.

Courtesy Aerospace Heritage Foundation

Just a dream.

The CF-100 and the Arrow part company.

Back on solid ground.

Courtesy Aviation Museum Ottawa Canada

End of the dream. Note that all five Arrows are facing the same direction during destruction. Any photos that show the Arrows in opposing directions were not taken during the destruction but much earlier.

Courtesy Aerospace Heritage Foundation

Avro ventured into aluminum boat building after the Arrow termination, but to no avail. Ironically, David Gartshore used one of these boats when he found the underwater scale Arrow model.

The Avrocar helped in the understanding of the problems associated with vertical takeoff. It never got more than a few feet off the ground.

The Avrocar gets a much needed lift.

The Arrow soars into legend.

Courtesy Aerospace Heritage Foundation

and January 1957. The plan now being discussed was that Canada would supply the base facilities, including shelters, launch equipment, and personnel, while the USAF would supply the missiles and test equipment, while retaining their custody. Of particular note in the May 3 memo was the third paragraph. It stated that the Chief of the Air Staff (CAS) had obtained the approval of the Cabinet Defence Committee for the negotiation and introduction of Bomarc into the RCAF. It further stated that the Americans were in general agreement. Recall, this was in 1957 and not 1959.

On June 3, 1957, CUSSAT finally produced its report, undertaken on behalf of the MSG. The report included the proposal to station two Bomarc bases in Canada, one at North Bay and one at Ottawa, along with the proposed SAGE ground environment for controlling the missiles. (The Canadian environment called CAGE was summarily terminated.) The number one advantage of these installations, according to the report, would be the protection of the American SAC bases in the northeastern U.S. Second to this would be the protection of the region of the Great Lakes. Not mentioned in this report, but not lost on the USAF, was that installation of SAGE/Bomarc in Canada would assure them victory over the competing U.S. Army Nike Hercules system.

A critical but expected assumption made in the CUSSAT report was that the surface-to-air missile in question would be the Bomarc B with an atomic warhead, not a conventional warhead. A second assumption was that USAF interceptors would have the effectiveness of the F-106A, armed with one nuclear-tipped MB-1 and four Falcon air-to-air guided missiles, and that RCAF interceptors were to have the effectiveness of the Arrow, armed with four Sparrow air-to-air guided missiles.

As a result of the report, the American and Canadian Chiefs of Staff agreed that the optimum air defence system, and the one that would provide the greatest flexibility against the manned bomber threat, was a combination of the interceptor and the nuclear surface-to-air missile. The U.S. had long proposed this combined system of defence, and the Canadian military was simply following suit, without the benefit of parliamentary debate.

On January 8, 1958, Chief of the Air Staff Air Marshal Hugh Campbell commented on Bomarc progress to the Chairman Chief of

Staff. He noted that SAGE was currently programmed to intercept non-evasive targets. In other words, if oncoming attackers altered their course, Bomarc would miss its target. He noted the Americans were now rewriting the software intercept program to address this matter. He said the indication was that the new program should be at least 80 percent effective in allowing Bomarc to hit its target. Still, this should have been somewhat disconcerting given that it was nuclear warheads that would be missing, not conventional bombs. He ended with the following:

> The USAF has adopted BOMARC and SAGE as the fundamental missile and missile control system. There is no alternate to this system which would yield an equivalent effectiveness at this time without a greater expenditure of funds and manpower or without further development ...[57]

What effectiveness he was referring to is subject to debate, unless of course it was nuclear incineration of everything in sight. That it was the only system in existence was also not mentioned directly.

The Bomarc was not without some opposition within the Canadian Defence Department. The Canadian Army raised several issues in April of 1958 that garnered responses from the air staff. According to the latter, it was true that the Bomarc could not intercept low-flying targets. This was a limitation of the radar network, but no other system could do so either.

The army had pointed out that the Bomarc was simply filling a gap in American defences in the east where there already existed a heavy concentration of interceptors, while leaving other parts of Canada unprotected. The response was that the statement was only partly true. The placement of Bomarcs had been selected to "thicken" the defences because this eastern sector was considered a critical approach area for oncoming attackers.

As for filling the U.S. gap, "The Bomarcs would partially fill a gap in U.S. defences **and justifiably so as a Canadian contribution to the protection of the deterrent force** [bolding mine]."[58] It added, however, that protection would also be afforded Canadian targets. Protection for the rest of Canada, "under the terms of NORAD, [will] actually be protected by adjacent U.S. interceptors ..."[59] This latter statement is critical in understanding some of the circumstances surrounding the cancellation of the Arrow. Finally, it was noted that the population in the west was lower and that the likelihood of engaging the enemy over western centres was small.

Additional questions were addressed concerning training, but the final one dealt with cost. An estimated cost for Bomarc was given as $104 million over four fiscal years. It was stated that this cost should not prejudice other defence programs. The quoted figure was based on the assumption that the Americans would pay two thirds of the cost, an issue that had not yet been decided and would not be decided until days before the cancellation of the Arrow. It also did not include the costs of SAGE and gap-filler radar. These costs were, however, noted by the Minister of National Defence in his deliberations with the Americans later in July, as seen in his top-secret briefing notes.

The Canadian Department of Defence Production (DDP) also commented on the SAGE/Bomarc matter. In one of their documents the DDP stated:

> The U.S. pressed ahead vigorously with their SAGE concept and by April 1958 it was accepted in Canada that, in the interests both of technical interworking and economy, the only sensible thing to do was to extend the U.S. automation across the border ... In addition the USAF were introducing Bomarc missiles into their automatic network which meant new ground-to-air data communications in addition to voice.[60]

Here again it might be asked why, if we were so ready to acquiesce and take the Bomarcs, would the Americans not purchase Arrows? Why was it always Canada that had to satisfy American requirements? Why couldn't they accept Canadian requirements, as some of their generals, like General Putt of AFRDC, had hoped?

The DDP document went further, commenting on the meeting between the Canadian Prime Minister and the American President that had taken place on July 9 and 10, 1958. It stated that the issue came down to one of defence sharing. Again, it was not in the context of the U.S. purchasing the Arrow, though this point was raised by Minister Pearkes, but in the context of how best to bring in SAGE/Bomarc. As a result, the Canada–United States Committee on Joint Defence was established, and serious discussion on production sharing commenced in August of the same year.

As negotiations continued, the Americans began to sweeten the deal. They proposed, with no firm commitment, their payment of two thirds of the cost of establishing the Bomarcs in Canada. Pearkes, recognizing a possible increase to the defence budget of 25 to 30 percent for all these additional requirements, knuckled under. Presumably much to the amazement of the RCAF, he proposed canceling the Arrow altogether, in favour of installing SAGE/Bomarc. The request for termination is in a memorandum to the Cabinet Defence Committee dated August 8, 1958. It is known that the formal request was tabled August 28, 1958, hence the earlier date may have been a typographical error, or the August 8 memo may have been a draft.

In any event, the memo begins by stating that the manned bomber threat was expected to continue through the 1960–67 period but that ICBMs would replace them as the primary threat. It then states, "Both U.S. and Canadian planning envisage that during this period the Air Defence Weapon System against the manned bomber should be composed of manned fighters and surface-to-air-missiles..."[61]

The rest of the document extols the virtues of Bomarc while talking about the high cost of the Arrow and how this cost could detract from other defence requirements like those for the Army and Navy and those for anti-ICBM research. It then discusses the results of the joint Canadian and American studies that concluded the need for two Bomarc bases in Canada and mentions the USAF willingness to share in the costs of development.

With respect to the Arrow, the memo set out to demonstrate its high cost. There has never been any argument that the cost of the Arrow was significant. But, as this memo and the briefs before it point out, the combined cost with the Bomarc and its associated SAGE and gap-filler radar was going to be too much for the defence budget to absorb. On top of that now was the new and expressed desire to engage in research against the ICBM threat. As the memo notes:

> A study of the financial implications of continuing this programme [the Arrow] and its impact on the overall defence programme, and the necessity of giving consideration to future requirements such as defence against the intercontinental ballistic missiles have necessitated a study of alternative plans.[62]

The reader should understand that defence against the ICBM means an anti-ballistic missile (ABM) program. In 1968 Canada specifically stated it would not participate in an ABM program and had that written into the NORAD renewal that same year. Even the U.S. and Russia began arms control talks that would prevent either country from developing such a system. Now, in the new millennium, the debate is again raging, as the Americans under George Bush hope to once again develop an ABM system, while Canada maintains a wait-and-see attitude, at least at the political if not military level.

What might have been driving the discussion to ICBM defences in Pearkes's memorandum? The answer may lie in a letter sent to Charles Foulkes from the CINCNORAD, General Partridge, dated July 3, 1958. In that letter General Partridge stressed that his views were to be treated as private and not for general consumption by the Canadian government. He explained that the U.S. had under development the Nike Zeus anti-ballistic missile. Unlike Bomarc and the Nike Hercules, Zeus was to counter the ICBM threat. General Partridge had been asked by the U.S. Joint Chiefs of Staff to study the feasibility of siting Nike Zeus batteries in the U.S. and Canada.

In his letter to Foulkes, Partridge stated that as a result of this study and the fact that the Ballistic Missile Early Warning System radar net was to be under NORAD control, the focus for ICBM defence would have to come under NORAD as well. Foulkes would have to have realized that Canada's air defence posture would also have to change to accommodate an ICBM defence. This would explain the remark in Pearkes's memorandum to the CDC that funds would be required for the study of ICBM defences. Likewise, this change in role would have been seen as a further de-emphasis of the manned interceptor, whose role could be replaced by the more economical Bomarc missile. This was the other thrust of the Pearkes memo to CDC.

Was General Partridge pushing NORAD into an ABM focus? Early on in its inception, NORAD had issued a statement linking the DEW line effort with the American Ballistic Missile Early Warning program. Shortly thereafter work began on the development of both short- and long-range NORAD planning documents for continental air defence. These were the North American Defense Objective Plan (NADOP) 1959–1963, a five-year plan, and the North American Defense Objectives (NADO) 1959–1969, a ten-year forecast. Draft documents were prepared in August 1958, and completed documents were presented to Canada in December 1958.

The first priority listed in the ten-year NADO 59–69 was establishment of an anti-ICBM capability. Second on the list was for an improved anti-ICBM. The document projected that the Soviets would have up to two thousand ICBMs by 1966, and this number was repeated when the Canadian Chiefs of Staff were briefed on the subject in January 1959, one month prior to termination of the Arrow. Although the two plans had input from the Canadian Deputy Commander of NORAD, there had been none from the Canadian government, even though the latter had indicated no decisions had been reached in Canada with respect to participation in ballistic missile defence programs. The NADO plan had stated an ICBM capability was required at any cost.

NADO 59-69 made reference to the need for the detection of incoming bombers as only its third priority and interceptors as a fourth. In the latter category, the plan made no mention of specific aircraft types but instead placed emphasis on long-range interceptors and shorter-range surface-to-air missiles. The long-range aircraft required a cruise speed of Mach 3 with a Mach 3.5 to 4 dash capability. They had to operate at all altitudes and have a range of two thousand nautical miles, and there was a stipulation for nuclear armament. Without naming the aircraft, the document was in fact stating the specifications of the American F-108 that was still in its early stages of development. The plan also required all interceptors to carry nuclear weapons.

Specific aircraft types were mentioned in the NADOP 59-63. The document itself remains classified, but this author was able to have the following paragraph de-classified. It reads:

> Existing and programmed interceptors include F4D, F-86, F-89, CF-100, F-101, F-102, F-104, CF-105, and F-106 aircraft ... The CF-100 may be retained in the system after the 1960 time period, but, if so, specific improvements for employment of weapons against a supersonic threat must be incorporated within the Northern NORAD Region. The F-102, F-104, CF-105, and F4D aircraft should be improved by the incorporation of nuclear armament in the normal operational role.[63]

The document further showed nine squadrons of Arrows, with twelve aircraft per squadron, replacing the CF-100 by 1963. Other documents show the Soviets were expected to have ICBMs in quantity (two thousand missiles) by 1966, three years later, but it is not clear how this number was derived.

The NORAD ten-year plan was proposing an anti-ICBM system as its first priority. Given that the air defence of Canada was in fact a defence for the American SAC, one can then understand why it would appear that the utility of the Arrow and continuation of the Arrow program would be considered questionable, especially given its higher cost in relation to Bomarc. The thinking was that since the Arrow would only be in service for three years at best before the bomber threat was expected to switch to ICBMs, it would be better to meet the limited aircraft threat with the less expensive Bomarc. That the anti-ICBM Nike Zeus, Bomarc, and F-108 were not proven or developed systems seems not to have mattered in this equation. That the defence of Canada did not require Bomarc or F-108s seems not to have mattered either.

In an aide memoir for the Minister of National Defence dated August 25, 1958, another factor, as mentioned in the plans, was entered into the equation to abandon the Arrow and get on with the real NORAD priorities:

The abandonment or limitation of manned aircraft in the air defence system, with more reliance being placed on ground-to-air missiles, would bring about a need for arrangements to be made for the use of nuclear warheads for air defence. It is not possible to put a nuclear warhead on the Sparrow missile, and therefore the CF-105 with Sparrow was not the most modern air defence weapon available.[64]

It would appear that some rather technically ignorant bureaucrat, hopefully not the Minister himself, was equating "modern" with "nuclear." There is no connection between the two terms. "Nuclear" equates to mass destruction and overkill, but not to modernity; nevertheless, in the eyes of some bureaucrat the Arrow was not considered modern. Undoubtedly this added to the incorrect notion that the Arrow would be obsolete before it was even put into service. The impact of not having nuclear-tipped missiles for the Arrow's Sparrow missiles was profound. That the Arrow was not considered modern simply because the Sparrow could not carry nuclear warheads is ludicrous.

In January 1959, CINCNORAD arrived in Canada to brief the Canadian Chiefs of Staff on the two NORAD plans. Later revisions of the plan would show that the American planners had called for American air defence expenditures to the tune of $5.5 billion annually in the United States and Canadian air defence expenditures of $300 million annually. Considering the variance between these two expenditures, it is not hard to understand how Canada gradually came to depend upon the American military/industrial complex. These expenses would pay for the full complement of weapons and ground environment envisaged by NORAD.

In commenting on the plans in a memorandum dated February 9, 1959, just weeks before the Arrow cancellation, the Chief of the Air Staff agreed that defence against the ICBM should be given a high priority and that the BMEWS planned by the U.S. would assist to that end. However, he cited the fact that the proposed Nike Zeus anti-ICBM (AICBM) missile was not yet ready and might only come in to force in 1965, at least two years after the NORAD estimate of

1962–63. He further noted that Canada was not able to develop an AICBM system at the present time, and therefore requirements for AICBM were not firm. He proposed limiting Canada's role to providing communications to BMEWS, participating fully in the planning of future AICBM systems but limiting research and development.

Against the manned bomber threat, he agreed that the development of the long-range F-108 should continue. Though it was thought the F-108 would require an extensive ground control environment, he suggested the latter should not yet proceed until the threat was better developed. He also expressed the belief the F-108 would have value even without this extensive ground network.

He further noted that the NORAD five-year plan listed a Canadian requirement for nine squadrons of twelve Arrows. These were to be distributed in Halifax, Bagotville, St. Hubert, Ottawa, North Bay, Gimli, Saskatoon, Namao, and Comox. The RCAF view, however, was for six squadrons located at Chatham, Bagotville, St. Hubert, Uplands, North Bay, and Comox.

The expectation on the part of the RCAF was that American interceptors could be stationed at Saskatoon, Gimli, and Namao, to provide protection to the Prairies. The second reason for reducing the numbers of Canadian aircraft had to do with the perceived diminishing bomber threat, a source of conflict within American intelligence agencies. Simply put, NORAD wanted every type of weapon system to the maximum, but with first priority on ICBM defence.

Canada could not afford the whole package, and Pearkes and Foulkes were questioning why the Arrow was needed at all. The threat from manned bombers was diminishing, and the cheaper Bomarc could take care of these as the ICBM threat grew. Savings from the Arrow cancellation could be set aside for work in this area. Despite this thinking, the bottom line from the Chief of the Air Staff, in his comments to the NORAD plans, was that the Arrow was the best weapon for satisfying Canada's interceptor requirement. Too bad neither Pearkes nor Foulkes was listening, especially since Bomarc itself was in trouble.

In 1959, a House of Representatives Appropriations Committee actually voted to terminate the Bomarc because the system was not yet proven. On the other hand, a Senate Armed Services Committee wished to eliminate Nike Hercules. This led to development of a master air defence plan that allowed both programs to continue but in reduced numbers. On May 26, 1959, the first Bomarc B was test-fired unsuccessfully, an ominous sign of their future effectiveness (or lack thereof). With Bomarc still in jeopardy in Congress, the Air Force was able to demonstrate that Canada was a buyer, and so Bomarc survived.

By March 24, 1960, based on all the shortcomings of Bomarc discussed previously, as well as the fact that the program was slipping and the USAF wished to concentrate on the ICBM threat, the USAF recommended curtailing the Bomarc B program and the advanced SAGE combat supercentres. The plan was to concentrate Bomarc bases only in the northeastern sector while shutting down any earmarked for the west. This shutdown would prove an issue of vulnerability for Canada in the wake of the Arrow cancellation because Pearkes was depending on American Bomarcs to handle protection of the West. Without them, it meant having to acquire American-built interceptor aircraft because the Arrow had been terminated.

While the USAF maintained the Bomarc would be effective, several members of the House expressed great doubt. Typical of some of the American comments are those from the meeting of March 24, 1960:

> Insofar as the moment is concerned, other than General White's statement that he has high hopes and reason for high hopes for the success of BOMARC, there is no proof before this committee that BOMARC has ever proved that it will work to any great degree ... so you scale back but keep enough on order to maintain appearance of defence and bail out Boeing ...[65]

The charge was of course denied, but time would prove it to be true. Canada had unwittingly been part of the Boeing bailout and had cancelled the Arrow, a system that was proving to be working.

Perhaps ironically, it is clear from this meeting that the USAF wished to cancel any further acquisition of the Bomarc B but had to complete those orders that were destined for Canada. That Canada was obtaining the B was mentioned several times in the course of the discussions, but each time the comments were made off the record.

What was CINCNORAD's reaction? It was stated above that NORAD wanted all the weapons. In particular, CINCNORAD wanted the Bomarc program to remain at full strength. He did not want to cancel the super combat centres. He wanted Nike Zeus to its full capacity and wanted to maintain his full complement of fighter-interceptors, including those scheduled for transfer to the National Guard, and he wanted to reinstate the F-108 program, all for $5.5 billion. This, according to USAF generals, was likely impossible.

On March 25, 1961, the U.S. Department of Defense issued a statement concerning air defence projects. It showed that increased emphasis would be placed on ICBM defences such as MIDAS, a satellite detection system, BMEWS, more ATLAS ICBMs, and further development of the Minuteman ICBM. This was consistent with General Partridge's early notions about NORAD and its anti-ICBM role.

Also mentioned high on the list were improvements to American aircraft. If the USAF had purchased the Arrow, they would not have required improvements to their aging fleet of aircraft but would have been getting brand new, state-of-the-art planes. Production of Bomarc B would be curtailed and the SAGE super combat centres eliminated, with the money used to offset the costs of the new plan. As a result of this reprioritization, Canada would have to accept a 75 percent reduction in the missile strength originally calculated for the two Bomarc bases in Canada.

On April 29, the House Appropriations Committee eliminated funds for further Bomarc production. The House of Representatives gave their approval on May 6, though action remained pending in the Senate. According to Jon McLin, there is evidence that this time it was Canada that applied pressure to the U.S. in order to keep Bomarc going so that Canadian orders would be fulfilled. A modest program was continued for this purpose. Bomarcs became operational in Canada in 1962 but were being phased out by the USAF in 1964. On April 1, 1972, Bomarcs in Canada ceased being operational as well. The Bomarc boondoggle had cost the Americans billions and Canada the Arrow.

In addition to the missile debate, yet another variable had entered the "abandon the Arrow" equation, this one dating back to the meeting of July 8, 1958, during which Pearkes made his plea to the Americans to purchase the Arrow. Instead, in the ensuing discussion, rather than purchasing the Arrow, they made agreements for the establishment of the Production/Development Sharing Program and for the official introduction of Bomarc into Canada. The American Deputy Secretary of Defense summarized the matter in a memorandum dated June 1, 1960.

The memorandum, titled *Memorandum on Production Sharing Program — United States and Canada*, stated that Canada decided its defence industry needed business from the U.S. in order to sustain itself. Given this premise, the Arrow was then cancelled and Canada accepted the Bomarc. For their part, the U.S. established a Production/Development Sharing Program in return. It was as though a tit-for-tat deal had been struck. The same memo, because it is reflecting back on events, goes on to explain that the defence sharing arrangements were not working.

A new document obtained from the Eisenhower Library contains some revelations regarding this arrangement and its specific application to SAGE/Bomarc. It states that the Canadian share of about $125 million would pay for construction of the SAGE buildings and that the U.S. would pay for the electronic equipment development. This arrangement, the document noted, was a concern to Canada because the Canadians wanted a share in the high technology work of electronics and missiles, and this relegated them to supplying and effecting construction. The Canadians were concerned and did not want to become a "brick and mortar" economy.

The Department of Defence Production had hoped the arrangements would open the door to American high technology, not realizing that high-tech was already in Canada, in the Arrow project. It naively expected there would be no difficulty in Canadian companies securing contracts in the American sector because the agreement would relax certain restrictions.

The document continues:

> The Air Force has consistently opposed any agreement
> to assure Canada a given share of the production,

108

based on the conviction that technical competence, cost and delivery considerations must be the deciding criteria...A major problem is that the Bomarc, SAGE and radar programs are well along in development as well as in production and extraordinary effort is required to provide opportunity even approaching equality. There are significant roadblocks operating to the disadvantage of a Canadian source; security clearances, release of classified information, licensing agreements, lack of confidence in the knowledge of Canadian capability, qualification problems, inadequate liaison with the United States' laboratories, lack of aggressiveness, and frustration on the part of Canadian industry, and many others.[66]

Did the Canadians know about these factors before jumping into the deal?

The document then delineates the initiatives undertaken to help ameliorate the situation for Canada. It talks of the formation of high-level groups created to study the problems and recommend solutions. It notes that as a result of these efforts some $6.7 million in Bomarc contracts were awarded to Canada and many other requests for bids were being directed to Canadian companies, but only on a competitive basis.

On the Arrow termination, it states:

In the most recent meetings in Ottawa, the Canadians expressed dissatisfaction with progress to date on the basis that the short term objective of filling the gap created by the CF 105 terminations has not and probably will not be fully satisfied. The Canadians have been hoping for a few large items which would satisfy national pride and be significant enough to prove to the public that production sharing will work.[67]

It seems the bright lights in Ottawa got it all wrong. They had just cancelled the Arrow, the largest high-tech program in the country and the pride of Canada, and now were looking for a handout to replace it. This was a truly remarkable demonstration of naïveté at the highest levels in the Canadian establishment.

This revealing American document might also shed some light on the reasons why the Americans did not or perhaps could not purchase the Arrow. This document states that Canadair had just been awarded a contract for production of some Bomarc components. It says, "From a United States point of view, considerable political repercussions can be expected even on this comparatively small item."[68] The implication is that American industry would not allow even this small concession. Imagine then the repercussions in purchasing an entire aircraft. The document concluded that with respect to the aircraft industry, Canada's chances for winning major airframe contracts would be remote without high-level guidance, the 1960s politically correct term for interference.

Regarding the USAF commitment to pay two thirds of the SAGE/Bomarc work in Canada, another American document notes that as of 1960, a formal agreement had not yet been achieved, and it is now clear that Bomarc was in fact being considered a dead duck. No wonder there was hesitation on the part of the Americans to squander more money on it. And what of the Arrow?

Chapter 7

The Arrow:
The Pearson Perspective

"...it was clearly the responsibility of the U.S. government to buy the CF-105 to meet its own requirements and it was the duty of the Canadian government to use all possible ways and means to so convince our American friends."[69]
— Canadian Prime Minister Lester B. Pearson,
notes from 1959

The late Canadian Prime Minister Lester B. Pearson was leader of the opposition at the time of the Arrow termination. The project had begun under the Liberal government of Prime Minister Louis St. Laurent, but in 1957, when crucial decisions would have been made with respect to the program, the Liberals lost the election of June 10 to the Conservative Party of John George Diefenbaker. It was at this time that George Pearkes, Diefenbaker's Minister of National Defence, came to the fore in the Arrow saga.

As opposition leader, Pearson prepared a series of notes that summarized the Arrow situation as he saw it. In the opening paragraphs, he considered whether the decision to initially embark on the Arrow development was indeed a wise one. Some historians who have written about the Arrow have declared that starting the project was the wrong decision and that cancellation was correct. Pearson was of the opposite opinion and provides several reasons why starting the project in the first place was legitimate.

He noted that at the time, the defence concern was that long-range bombers were being developed by the Soviets. Military planners therefore felt this air threat had to be countered and so they set about the task of procuring aircraft for interception purposes. As we now know, from the military perspective it was as early as 1949, while the CF-100 was still in development, that specifications were being written for a new Canadian supersonic interceptor aircraft. Later events gave greater impetus to the Arrow project; for example, in 1953 during the Korean War, the Soviets unveiled a new aircraft, the MiG-17.

The RCAF undertook an extensive series of discussions and studies to determine if there were any other aircraft then in production or development that could satisfy the need for a new supersonic interceptor. For a variety of legitimate technical and strategic reasons, no other aircraft were deemed suitable. The altitude and speed of aircraft of the day were deemed inadequate to counter the new supersonic bombers. Also, most were single-engine craft, whereas Canada required two engines for safety while covering the vast terrain. Other aircraft were of short range and depended on an electronic ground environment, which the Arrow did not, and the RCAF required greater manoeuvrability. Existing aircraft in the U.S. and Great Britain were examined before the decision to build was made.

Among the aircraft considered was the F-101 Voodoo. The Voodoo was in the class of aircraft called the Century Series that included the F-102 and the F-106 Delta Dart. It has been erroneously stated in numerous sources that the Arrow was no better than the Century Series, possibly because an aging number of Voodoos were eventually introduced as the weapon of choice for the RCAF. The fact remains that the Arrow specifications were far superior to these other aircraft. Why then was the Voodoo suddenly suitable for Canada?

One reason not previously discussed is contained in a top-secret memorandum that quotes a December 19, 1961 letter from Minister of National Defence Douglas S. Harkness to the Secretary of State for External Affairs. The letter concerns the provisions for obtaining nuclear warheads for Bomarcs and addresses the arrangement made for obtaining the sixty-six Voodoo aircraft.

> ... Since the time when the original drafts were prepared. Agreement has been reached with the United States whereby Canada acquired F 101 aircraft to replace the CF-100 in the Air Defence force. The F101 is equipped to carry bomber-destroying missiles using atomic warheads ... we are now in the process of replacing 162 CF-100 air defence interceptors with only 66 CF-101 interceptors — which number resulted purely from availability and is short of operational requirements. These reductions are only to a small extent justified by a decrease in the estimated bomber threat. The real justification stems from the equipping of these various weapons with nuclear armament ...[70]

Speed, altitude, and manoeuvrability did not matter as long as one could vaporize the atmosphere with nuclear weapons. That is one of the major reasons the Voodoo became acceptable, not because it equaled the Arrow. Even with that, all of the aircraft in the USAF inventory required major improvements, whereas the Arrow would not have.

If there had been any doubts about the need for a supersonic interceptor, they should have been erased in 1954 when a new Russian bomber, the Bison, was seen making a fly-past during the Mayday Parade in Moscow. The next year an entire squadron was seen, and it was declared that there was a "bomber gap" between the Americans and the Soviets. Believing the Soviets were further advanced in their aircraft technology than was originally thought, the USAF increased its own demands for more bombers and fighters. All the while, the air defence force had been setting up the various radar detection lines such as Pinetree and DEW.

In Canada, the Arrow was discussed at the 574th Chief of Staff Committee meeting on February 11, 1955. At this meeting the Soviet threat from Russian T37 Bison bombers and supersonic aircraft was noted. The Chiefs of Staff subsequently recommended an acceleration of the Arrow program. It was also recommended that the Iroquois engine program be granted approval. No alternate suitable engine was deemed to be available in time for the Arrow, and since the Iroquois development was already underway at Avro, it was selected as the engine of choice.

Aside from the pure military need, Pearson states another reason for embarking on the Arrow program: job creation. The CF-100 was successful, and a supersonic aircraft was a logical follow-up for both the military and for the maintenance of a viable aircraft industry. It also meant increasing numbers of skilled workers who would be providing a foundation for future high technology in Canada. Pearson reasoned then that under these circumstances the government had made the right decision to initiate the Arrow. Pearson did state, however, that the decision to proceed was to be reviewed every six months in light of any changing factors. In fact, this is borne out in the number of Chiefs of Staff Committee meetings that were held.

Pearson also shows in his notes that in 1955, the government had approached the United States about potential sales. While no firm commitments were made, the U.S. did provide encouragement for continuation of the project. Finally, Pearson noted that even John Diefenbaker had stated in the House that he was not condemning the Liberal government for having initiated the program; the Liberal government had no way of knowing of the future potential of nuclear weapons. The argument from Diefenbaker was that perhaps if the ICBM threat had reared its head earlier during the Liberal's term in office, they would not have embarked on the Arrow project but focused their attention on missiles.

Pearson's next point addressed the threat of the ICBM. He first stated that the cost of the Arrow had been increasing but that there was no requirement to alter the program. But, on October 4, 1957, the same day as the official rollout ceremony of the Arrow, Russia successfully launched Sputnik into orbit around the earth. The news overshadowed that of the Arrow and shifted the focus from aircraft to missile defences. Like the "bomber gap" earlier, this was likely the start of the "missile gap." The Soviets had beaten America into space, and this meant the feasibility of ICBMs dropping down on American cities was now very real.

It was also in 1957 that the Central Intelligence Agency declared that the bomber threat from Russia had been exaggerated. The earlier fly-pasts of a multitude of bombers were in fact the same group of aircraft just circling the parade route. The Russian bomber force "consisted of between ninety and one hundred and fifty planes."[71] Further, the CIA added that the Russian industry was not capable of mass production for a number of technical reasons. The threat now was the missile. For its part, the U.S. Air Defence Command believed there still remained a bomber gap and now had the missile gap to deal with as well.

In Canada, the Department of National Defence was quoting Khrushchev, the Russian premier, as saying the manned bomber was obsolete because Russia now had missiles. In a report on the Arrow development dated August 19, 1958, Charles Foulkes stated that the advent of Sputnik had a profound effect on the whole air defence concept. American missile development for Bomarc was accelerated as it became obvious the main threat to North America would come from the ICBM. Unfortunately, the Bomarc would have done nothing against the ICBM. It was an anti-aircraft missile.

Author Jon McLin notes that Canada was highly dependent on American intelligence estimates for bombers and missiles. In 1958–59 these estimates downplayed the manned bomber threat and gave rise to the USAF's revised air defence plan. Writing in the April 1962 edition of *Foreign Affairs*, a U.S. quarterly review, writer Melvin Connant observed that as a result of this change in threat, the USAF urged the Canadian government to accept the Bomarc and to consider the phasing out of the interceptor aircraft force. This was something Canadian Defence Minister Pearkes took seriously.

Documents from the archives show that in fact, Canada and the U.S. intelligence services eventually released a document called simply CANUS 59, in which they mutually agreed the manned threat was diminishing. NORAD continued to doubt this interpretation. While

NORAD acknowledged there might be fewer bombers, it was antici-pated these bombers would have supersonic capability. In this scenario not as many would be required to exact the same degree of damage. On this point, Canada disagreed with NORAD and sided with American intelligence that the manned bomber threat was indeed disappearing.

Pearson was obviously unaware of the ongoing intelligence discus-sions between the RCAF, NORAD, and these other agencies that con-tributed to CANUS 59. In his notes he points out the comments of Deputy Commander Air Marshal Slemon that interceptors would be required. He notes that Slemon was supported by NORAD command-er General Partridge. He also points to the *London Times* of February 21, 1959, which quoted the British Secretary of State for Air as saying the need for fighters would continue. He also noted that Pearkes himself did not contradict Slemon and stated manned interceptors would be need-ed. Pearson was likely unaware of the letter to Foulkes from General Partridge, in which it was expressed that NORAD would focus first on the ICBM threat, and that this meant developing an anti-ICBM system.

In light of the changing nature of the threat from aircraft to mis-siles, Pearson's notes show he agreed that perhaps not as many Arrows would be required as initially envisioned and that this factor alone would increase the cost of the program. (This reduced number was also due to the technical superiority of the aircraft over the CF-100.) He surmised that this cost of the Arrow, when added to the new defence requirements against incoming missiles, might be too much for Canada alone to support.

He states the Conservative government should have begun serious negotiations with the United States for the sale of the Arrow, if in fact the problem was one of finance. This negotiation between governments began in September 1958. In fact it had truly begun in July 1958, but only between Minister Pearkes and American Secretary of State John Foster Dulles. No members of either Air Force or NORAD appear to have been present. There is no indication the matter was discussed between the Prime Minister and the President, except for the subsequent announce-ment concerning the acquisition of Bomarc and initiation of the Defence Production Sharing Arrangements. Pearson believed the government had failed in not trying early enough to solicit sales to the U.S.

One of the reasons put forward for the cancellation was financial. More specifically, the argument from the government was that spending so much money on so few aircraft was not justifiable. A cheaper solution was found in the Bomarc missile and the possible acquisition of inferior American aircraft. This was not an argument based on affordability but rather on cost-effectiveness. The Arrow was not going to bankrupt the country, as some have alleged, but the government should have done more to sell it.

Many believe that the Americans should not be blamed for not purchasing the Arrow, yet it has been shown that members of the RCAF felt it was Canada's duty to purchase the unneeded Bomarc to satisfy NORAD commitments. Why then should it not have been an American commitment to purchase the Arrow? Pearson writes:

> ... If we are to continue to have with the United States a continental system of air defence on a co-operative basis, it was clearly the responsibility of the U.S. government to buy the CF-105 to meet its own requirements and it was the duty of the Canadian government to use all possible ways and means to so convince our American friends.[72]

He goes on to state there was no evidence that any high level negotiations had taken place to convince the Americans of their "obligation" to buy. This could be dismissed as political rhetoric were it not for the perceived Canadian obligation to purchase Bomarc.

Pearson next points to the fact that Canada would be dependent on American interceptors for defence. Pearkes had said that Canada could rely on American aircraft because of the large numbers the Americans had available. Pearson reasoned that if this were true, given their short range, it would mean having American planes based in Canada for the purpose of defending Canada. Pearson said he was not aware that such an arrangement either existed or was even being contemplated.

Such an arrangement had been made, but as far as can be determined, it was never made public. The details were finally revealed by Pearkes himself to Professor Reginald Roy of the University of

Victoria, in a series of taped interviews in 1967. From Pearkes's comments, only Hugh Campbell is mentioned as having had knowledge of the deal. What about Cabinet or the Prime Minister? Following are the salient excerpts:

> *Pearkes:* I took chances. We were defenceless against the high power bomber where we had the old CF-100. It couldn't compete with the modern Russian bombers. We had no supersonic fighter but the Americans emphasized the fact that they had lots of them. Now ... one thing I had to face was, if you scrap the Arrow you've got nothing. What will you do? Will you buy American aircraft to fill this gap? ... Or, say here, you can rely on American aircraft, not having bought them, but putting your pride in your pocket and saying here, we will give facilities [to] American fighter squadrons to come and be stationed in Canada, so that they can get the advantage there or, if not actually stationed in there, when the situation deteriorates they can move forward and operate from Canadian airfields ... I said let us make full arrangements for these American fighter squadrons to come in, to practice from our airfields. Let them store equipment and aircraft if they want to, at places such as Cold Lake and various other points all across Canada, and they came there and then carried out training exercises, moving a squadron up at short notice to one of these airfields. Now, that was how I filled in this defenceless gap during those times. He [name of another author which is not clear on the tapes] doesn't bring that out and I don't know how he would have known ...

Dr. Roy: No, he probably wouldn't. It certainly would-
n't be something that would be advertised
[that the Americans were not just carrying out
exercises but were also to defend us, something that Pearson was unaware of].

Pearkes: It was not anything which was advertised at all
… I had the assurance that the Americans at
this time had lots of fighters. That was when I
was talking to [the] Undersecretary of Defense.
I flew out from Washington to Colorado
Springs the first time I went to see NORAD.
On that aircraft he told me, "We have got lots
of fighters." [Pearkes pounds the table with
each word, for emphasis] We were sitting
together like this talking. He said to me, **and
we can't quote this** [his voice goes soft here],
**"If I was you I wouldn't put all that money
into that aircraft. If you don't want to buy
aircraft from us you may rest assured that we
have got lots of them** [emphasis in voice here]
**which we can use to help in the defence of
the North American continent if a crisis
comes." That's what convinced me more
than anything else** [bolding mine].[73]

Not only does Pearkes reveal the arrangement and the fact that it was
not well advertised, he also reveals the persuasion he received from the
United States. He was prepared to flush Canadian pride down the toilet
for a free American defence. Knowledge of this arrangement would have
been political dynamite for Pearson had he been made aware of it.
Without knowing of the arrangement, Pearson nevertheless provides his
perspective. Pearson writes, "In this respect, at least — that is in the most
important field of manned interceptors — it is not exaggerated to say that
the Canadian air defence system has been assigned to the U.S. air force."[74]

Frank Lowe, associate editor of *Weekend Magazine*, had made a similar observation shortly after the cancellation in 1959. His article,

titled "Is The RCAF Obsolete", featured the famous Herb Nott photos
of the destruction of the Arrows. In the article he said:

> Pearkes told me that the decision was non-political,
> merely something based on U.S. intelligence reports
> ... [and that] the American squadrons will operate out
> of Canadian fields only on "training" missions.[75]

Lowe stated that Canadian airmen believed otherwise and noted
that Canada's North would simply become an American protec-
torate with the RCAF being placed in an inferior role. Yet in 1967,
Pearkes admitted the American interceptors were on more than just
training missions.

Recognizing all the other factors discussed, is it also possible for
Pearkes to have made his decision to scrap the Arrow and have
Americans defend Canada partly on the basis of a conversation on an
airplane? The answer appears to be yes. In a newly released document
from the Eisenhower Library, one sees just how easily Pearkes could be
persuaded. In a formerly Secret Cabinet paper prepared for the
President it says, "...on April 1 [1960] his [Diefenbaker's] Defense
Minister indicated privately to Defense Secretary Gates that Canada
would probably abandon interceptors unless the United States regards
their retention as really important..."[76] This was one hell of a way for
the Minister of National Defence to establish Canadian defence policy. It is unfortunate that Pearson was unaware of any of this at the time.
For their part, the Americans were only too willing to dispense advice.

At the Ministers' meeting in Quebec in July 1960, Secretary of
Defense Thomas S. Gates Jr. stated, quite unequivocally, "that if you
[Canada] want to modernize your forces and contribute to continental
defence, this is the decision [to purchase American Voodoo aircraft] to
be made...."[77] It seems Gates decided to answer Pearkes's private query.
This was a classic example of what Pearson was describing when he
spoke of Canada's dependence on the United States in his notes.

At this same Ministers' meeting of 1960, Howard C. Green,
Canadian Secretary of State for External Affairs, stated in clear terms
the reason the Arrow was cancelled. He said that the Canadians were

"told two years ago that the manned bomber was on its way out and that is why they cancelled the Arrow." Pearkes clarified the statement and said, "We did not cancel the CF105 because there was no bomber threat but because there was a lesser threat and we got the Bomarc in lieu of more airplanes to look after this."[78] He did not, however, add (as he did for Professor Roy) that he initially arranged to have American aircraft defend Canada in the interim period between cancellation of the Arrow and first operation of the Bomarcs.

On the question of the missiles, Pearson made his own observations. Here again he saw that Canada would be dependent on American equipment and technology. He also realized the missiles would protect strategic American sites but do little for Canada. Pearson's notes reflect the fact that he was aware the Bomarc was already being declared obsolete in the U.S. and that production was continuing simply to shore up employment there or for the Boeing bailout and USAF politics. For Canada to contribute to American employment opportunities by purchasing an obsolete weapon was particularly unacceptable to Pearson. He stated, "The conclusion is, therefore, inescapable: the Canadian air defence system has been handed over for all practical purposes to the United States."[79] He noted again that Canada would be dependent on the U.S. for technology, equipment, and policy decisions.

Not to be left out, Charles Foulkes was also party to influencing policy decisions in his discussions with the Americans. His angle was to try to cash in on the Defence Production Sharing Arrangements. At a meeting on November 19, 1958, in Washington, rather than try to sell the Arrow to the Americans, he did the opposite. The previously top-secret minutes of the meeting show that he spoke of the limited numbers of Arrows needed by Canada and how this would drive the unit cost upwards. He believed the cost of producing the Arrow would be higher in Canada than it would be in the United States. (This of course was contrary to the information that had been provided by the RCAF.) His conclusion then to the Americans was that "Canada must, therefore, get into the production of components for joint defence weapons."[80]

Like Pearkes, Foulkes was looking for direction from the United States, and in December of 1958, he stated he would wait for the recommendations of CINCNORAD before deciding on the Arrow. That the Chief of the Air Staff continually stressed the need for the Arrow did not seem to matter. As discussed earlier, CINCNORAD wanted everything: missiles, radar networks, interceptors etc. Since this was not affordable for Canada, and given the conclusion in CANUS 59 that the manned bomber threat was diminishing, Foulkes went along with the decision to go with Bomarc only.

What about the production sharing arrangements? In a memorandum from the United States, it seemed as though the Arrow was cancelled as part of a tit-for-tat deal to secure defence sharing. A secret American Cabinet paper referenced earlier sheds more light on the matter. It states, "The decision to terminate the CF 105 was predicated in part on the agreements to provide Canada with better chances to share in production of defence items of mutual interest."[81] Obviously the Arrow was not of mutual interest.

A second secret document mentioned previously contains the following statement: "In lieu of the CF-105 Canada announced a decision developed by the military establishments of the two countries whereby the USAF would underwrite about two-thirds of the costs of an improved continental air defence system in Canada, which would include 2 Bomarc squadrons, 1 SAGE fire control centre, and improved radar."[82]

The Arrow was terminated because the manned bomber threat, according to the U.S. intelligence, was diminishing. In addition, Pearkes had been told by the American Undersecretary of Defense that Canada did not need the Arrow, since the U.S. could provide all the interceptor requirements. This solved another problem of how to introduce the real American priority, SAGE/Bomarc, into Canada. Foulkes did his part in ignoring the Chief of the Air Staff while accepting the SAGE/Bomarc and pitching for the defence production sharing arrangements in hopes Canada could share in SAGE/Bomarc production.

All of this was not based on whether the Arrow was affordable to Canada but rather on the fact that, in the eyes of Pearkes and Foulkes, its importance had diminished. Spending money on the Arrow was not seen as a cost-effective approach, especially since the American priority was for missile-based defence systems; it was Canada's duty to provide those missile defence systems for the protection of the deterrent force, the American Strategic Air Command.

It has been alleged in other sources that the RCAF had given up on Avro and its cost overruns, and this is why the project was terminated. Nothing could be further from the truth. In the first instance, ex-Air Vice Marshal John Plant had joined Avro to manage the Arrow project. Also, Chief of the Air Staff Hugh Campbell demonstrated in January 1959 that costs were actually decreasing and that the Arrow was required. Further, on February 9, 1959, a few weeks before termination, in responding to the NORAD plans Campbell wrote, "The aircraft best suited to meet the RCAF manned interceptor requirements is the CF105."[83]

Group Captain Ray Footit was the last project manager of the Arrow. On February 18, 1959, two days before the cancellation, he sent out a letter marked "secret" discussing the Arrow flight test program. The letter was sent to the Air Member in Washington, as it involved obtaining American data with respect to flight-testing. In that letter he wrote, "Although there has been no decision, as yet, on the Arrow program continuation the RCAF is proceeding with all the necessary planning as though the project was continuing."[84] This hardly sounds as though the RCAF had given up on Avro, as some have intimated.

Likewise, Minister Pearkes told Professor Roy in their interviews that senior officers in the RCAF wanted the Arrow. They told him it was a wonderful fighter. Specifically, he said that a lot of the air force people, as he called them, wanted it and that this represented a "large percentage."

Immediately after the cancellation, Avro let go of its employees (numbering over fourteen thousand). The Prime Minister blamed Avro for carrying this out, feeling the company was trying to embarrass him in some way. In his attack on the company, Prime Minister Diefenbaker seemed to indicate that the September 23, 1958 announcement to cancel the Astra/Sparrow missile system and introduce SAGE/Bomarc was in fact a cancellation of the entire program.

As noted above, this was not the interpretation of Hugh Campbell or Ray Footit. Pearson also saw the matter differently. As he points out, that September 23 announcement specifically said the Arrow and Iroquois engine programs would continue and be reviewed March 31,

1959. This was a very clear statement. How was Avro supposed to interpret this to mean the program would be cancelled?

Pearson's real point was that Avro had made several proposals for alternative projects to keep its employees gainfully employed. The problem was that the government had ignored these overtures. If the government had truly decided to abandon the Arrow in September 1958, why did it not act on these other proposals? Indeed, over the years others have pointed to the fact that Avro had nothing else to fall back on once the Arrow was terminated. They have tried to pin this on Avro management, but is it justified?

According to Pearson, in addition to proposals for reduced costs in the Arrow program, Avro proposed replacing the Orenda-powered Sabre aircraft in NATO with a Canadian plane. There was also a proposal for a jet transport development for TCA and other airlines, as well as a proposal for a vertical takeoff craft similar to the Avrocar. Orenda engines had been involved with Atomic Energy of Canada with respect to nuclear power, and a proposal was made to extend this effort. There was even mention made of joining with the United States space program. (NASA did end up with some thirty ex-Avro employees, one of whom eventually led the team to develop the Lunar Lander. Imagine if they had remained at Avro. Perhaps the Lander or some other major component would have been developed in Canada.)

The government, as Pearson says, had not responded to or discussed any of these proposals with Avro, even though they had been warned in December 1957 by the Air Industries Technical Association (AITA) that the Canadian aircraft industry was in danger of collapse if new projects were not forthcoming. Even proposals from the AITA were not entertained. Pearson concluded that the government had failed its responsibility to develop alternate plans with respect to Avro and the Canadian aircraft industry. Compare this approach with the actions concerning Bombardier.

Some may argue that Avro's proposals were simply money-grabbing schemes for lucrative contracts from the government, yet projects of the magnitude that Avro was capable of necessitated government funding. Without it, Avro, or its parent Hawker-Siddeley, would not have had the capital to launch a major new development either internally or in conjunction with the United States.

In addition to calling Avro's actions cavalier and unjustifiable, the Prime Minister had stated that there were millions of dollars available until the end of the fiscal year (on March 31) that could have been used to alleviate the unemployment situation. Avro did not have to take the drastic action of letting everyone go. Still, as Pearson points out, the government's decision was announced suddenly on February 20 rather than March 31, as had been stated in the September announcement. This had been done to save approximately $45 to $50 million dollars. This meant that money would not in fact have been available to help alleviate the employment situation at Avro.

More importantly, perhaps, Pearson noted that Avro had not been given prior warning of the announcement to terminate the project. There was no discussion with the company or other departments to arrange for a proper stop-work procedure. Instead, the telegram sent to Avro was quite definitive and clear. It said the company was to cease its work immediately. How would Avro have paid its employees if they had been allowed to continue working? The government, not Avro, was to blame for the massive layoffs and their repercussions.

Finally, others have pointed out that Avro ended up rehiring a number of people. Just after the layoffs, the Minister of Finance had said the government would share the cost of some ongoing technical work by what it called an "essential nucleus" of personnel. As Pearson points out, this was to extend approximately six months but would only involve about a thousand people. What about the rest, and why would the "nucleus" be interested in remaining for just six months with yet more uncertainty ahead? What work would they actually undertake as part of this government salvage operation?

The reality was that the "nucleus" went to NASA and other aircraft manufacturers in the United States and Europe who were more than eager to get them. Employment officials were in the Avro plants within days of the cancellation, snapping up many key individuals.

With a few thousand people, Avro tried developing pleasure boats, but to no avail. (Ironically, nearly fifty years later, it was one of these boats that was involved in the discovery of one of the Arrow scale test models that had been launched into Lake Ontario as part of the early test and development program.) A submission had even been made to develop a hydrofoil boat. This contract was eventually won by De Havilland, but by the late sixties, after the hydrofoil Bras D'Or proved herself in sea trials, that project too was cancelled.

Finally, Pearson's notes conclude with a discussion of the aircraft industry and its demise under the government. He quotes extensively from the AITA document that stated the industry would collapse unless new projects were forthcoming. He also quotes from the Minister of Defence Production, who stated that for production sharing to work, Canadian industry would have to be competitive with American industry. Pearson notes that with a 17 percent tariff imposed on goods, this would mean being 17 percent more efficient than those industries in the United States.

Pearson also pointed to the fact that American industry wielded considerable pressure on Washington for contracts. This would disadvantage Canada even further. The Minister of Defence Production also stated the best results for production sharing would come from subcontracting work. According to Pearson, this would mean Canadian industry would simply become dependent on the "generosity" of American manufacturers. Without drastic measures, he said, "Canada will now move very rapidly to a position of complete dependence on the United States."[85]

Such was the perspective of Lester B. Pearson in 1959.

Chapter 8

How Much is Too Much?

"The greater effectiveness and greater range of the CF105 results in the need for less aircraft and fewer bases. Aircraft for aircraft the F102B is less costly but, dollar for dollar, the CF105 provides significantly more defence ... The burden of cost involved in this course of action [selecting all recommendations], while high, is inherent in an air defence system which is kept abreast of the developing threat."[86]

— Findings of a special government committee on the Arrow, 1955

The issue of the high cost of the Arrow has already been raised. Historians have contended that the Arrow simply cost too much and would have detracted from other government programs. It has been said that as the field was opening for social programs like medicare, money would be needed. Why spend it on an expensive military jet? Others have argued that the Arrow would have taken dollars away from the farm community. Unfortunately these arguments are not supported by the documents, and the Prime Minister himself declared that cost was not the reason for canceling the Arrow.

There is no question that the Arrow was an expensive aircraft. The problem was the issue of cost-effectiveness versus that of affordability. The combined costs of the Arrow and SAGE/Bomarc systems were what would increase the defence budget by upwards of 30 percent, according to Pearkes, not the cost of the Arrow alone.

Both Pearkes and Foulkes had been convinced that the less expensive Bomarc was equal to the task, if not better than the Arrow, for a number of reasons. The Americans had thousands of aircraft that could and would defend Canada, and missile defence like the Bomarc had overtaken the Arrow in terms of the priority defence system for the Americans. Also, the Bomarc and American aircraft were allegedly more advanced than the Arrow because they carried nuclear weapons.

Given that the Bomarc was going to cost less and be subsidized by the Americans, Pearkes and Foulkes reasoned that its acquisition would prove more cost-effective than purchasing the Arrow — even though, according to Pearkes himself, the Arrow was affordable. This less expensive equipment would guard against the diminished bomber threat despite the acknowledgement that the missile, once fired, could not be recalled should the target prove to be a non-hostile aircraft. In this completely flawed concept of defence that ignored Canadian requirements, it was believed the Bomarc purchase would provide the same protection as the Arrow at a quarter the cost while introducing high technology to Canada and affording protection to the American Strategic Air Command bases.

Continual reference has been made to the fact that the Arrow's costs were rising. One must then ask, "Rising in relation to what?" MP Rodney Adamson stated that this country was not in a position to provide accurate cost estimations because the company and the country were breaking new ground in aircraft development and production.

In other words, when Avro first provided its estimates that the Arrow would cost between $1.5 and $2 million, the number had been based on a quantity of about six hundred, without the development cost factored in. Even at that, the figure was likely underestimated for the same reasons as contemporary projects that work on the technological edge. Breaking new ground and attempting to integrate numerous complex systems makes it very difficult to determine costs even by the most experienced corporations, let alone one that was only eight years old when it started the project.

Perhaps too the comparison was being made with the costs of American fighters in mind, but in the case of these, development costs to Canada were not part of the equation. The $2-million figures Canada might pay for American aircraft constituted the fly-away cost, without American development costs factored in.

The only real comparison could perhaps have been made between American fighters and the CF-100. The CF-100 had been produced for significantly less than it would have been in the United States. In terms of supersonic aircraft, there was the comparison with the F-106, established at around $5 million. The cost of an Arrow, without development costs factored in, was $3.75 million — considerably less. In the case of the Arrow there were other significant reasons for increased costs that were entirely unrelated to Avro's work

The 1998 report of the Canadian Office of the Auditor General states that schedule delays and cost increases are typical of defence capital acquisition programs. The case of the Electronic Support and Training project is cited as one wherein schedule delays of 22 months and cost overruns of $22 million occurred. Does this justify the existence of such problems? No, but it does indicate that such occurrences are not unexpected, especially when development and systems integration are essential aspects of a project. Add research to the equation and the project becomes extremely high risk and difficult to estimate. In the case of Electronic Support and Training, the project was cancelled due to insurmountable technical problems resulting in a loss of funds in the $100-million category.

A more recent example concerns the development of new computers for NORAD. Reported in *The Leader-Post* on May 8, 2000, the contract had been awarded to Litton Data Systems in California. The project was to have cost US$40 million and was a joint effort between Canada and the United States. After months of delays and cost overruns, the project was terminated. The two countries had spent a combined $130 million, and Litton estimated that it would cost another US$300 million to complete.

Closer to the Arrow's time, in 1959 the government sought proposals for the development of a hydrofoil vessel. The remnants of Avro actually submitted a bid but lost to De Havilland for the development of the Bras D'Or. This project had all the elements of research, development, and system integration, and sure enough, cost increases occurred. This meant having to return to the Canadian Treasury Board for more funding. This prompted the Treasury Board to observe generally in 1965 that:

> One way in which confidence may be restored in estimates of costs for development projects might be to leave decisions on funding and undertaking hardware development until thorough feasibility and project definition studies have been completed.[87]

In other words, poor estimating has been a feature of large, complex projects. In the cases of the Trainers and the NORAD computers, even though feasibility studies had been conducted, major problems still arose. It should also be pointed out that projects of the Arrow's magnitude have taken between ten and fifteen years to reach first production. The Arrow time scale, on the other hand, would have been about seven years.

What were the cost escalations involved in the Arrow project? Were they related to problems of integration and research? In 1953, the Cabinet Defence Committee of December 2 gave its approval for building two prototype aircraft for a cost of $26.9 million. This was similar to the CF-100 development, in which two prototypes were first requested. Engines and electronic fire control systems were to be purchased either in the United States or United Kingdom. Approximately $4 million had been set aside for this acquisition. It was expected the first Arrow prototype would be available by 1956, with production commencing in 1958.

As has been already mentioned, by 1954 the Soviet Union had detonated a thermonuclear device and produced a jet bomber. This caused a re-evaluation of the Arrow project with the intent of speeding up production. In order for this to occur, more aircraft would be required sooner, to allow simultaneous testing of the aircraft by Avro and the RCAF. An analysis of the numbers of aircraft required, based partly on examination of similar developments in the U.S. and Britain, showed that forty aircraft should be produced immediately. At least twenty from this initial development would be useful for squadron service.

At the same time, the RCAF decided that neither Rolls Royce nor the American engine company Curtiss-Wright would have engines suitable to meet the Arrow's performance specification by the time the RCAF hoped to have the aircraft in service. Pratt and Whitney had the J75 engine, but it too was considered below the requirement. The previous year, Orenda had begun development of the PS-13 engine, putting $9 million of its own money into the project.[88] This engine was a considered a leap in engine technology and was being developed as the most powerful engine in the world. The RCAF noted it was suited to the Arrow's performance specifications and indications were that it was in a more advanced stage in design than the American and British engines examined.

As a result of the above, at the 104th meeting of the Cabinet Defence Committee on March 3, 1955, approximately $261 million was authorized with the intent of producing forty aircraft. Together with $19 million from the previous allocation for the first two aircraft, this brought the total to $280 million. This money consisted of $190 million for the airframe development, $5 million for the acquisition of a fire control system to be purchased outside the country, and $15 million for its adaptation to the airframe. A further $70 million was allocated for the PS-13 engine development, now to be called the Iroquois. Fourteen engines were to be produced.

So, it can be said that costs were rising, yes, but not due to mismanagement or poor work on the part of Avro. The cost increase was justified by the RCAF. As far as Avro was concerned, efforts were being made to keep overall costs down. This is why the Cooke-Craigie development method was used. Under this process, the production tooling would be developed along with everything else so that the first prototype aircraft would not be handmade. They would be produced from the same production tooling as the balance of the production aircraft. This would mean greater flight testing and greater expenses up front but would result in significant cost savings in the long run.

By 1955, much to the chagrin of Avro engineers, the RCAF finally decided the best missile for the Arrow would be the Sparrow 2 being developed by the U.S. Navy. Avro had recommended the Hughes Falcon along with a Hughes fire control system and was developing the airframe for accommodation of this weapon. Selection of the Sparrow 2 meant considerable re-engineering of the airframe. Also, it had been decided to adopt the J75 engines for the first few aircraft so as not to fly an untried airframe with an untried engine. At this time, labour costs had increased, as had the costs of raw materials. Some additional costs were also related to the introduction of the J75 engines into the program and to the Iroquois.

It was determined that some modifications were required to the air conditioning, the electrical and hydraulic systems, and the air intake ducts of the airplane. More importantly and of greater impact was that the program had been further defined by the RCAF. As a result, on-board equipment decided upon by the RCAF required an increase in the number of parts by some 20 to 30 percent. This meant increased tooling and production estimates. In total, Avro estimated an additional $59 million would be required for all the changes, raising the total to about $340 million, from $280 million.

Once again, the increased costs were not the result of mismanagement on the part of Avro, and it was probably recognized that further increases would be in the offing because Avro had not yet been apprised of which electronic fire control system the RCAF wanted. Shortly after the Sparrow missile was selected for the Arrow, the U.S. Navy abandoned its development. Rather than drop it, the RCAF elected to continue its development in Canada. This again added to the cost of the program, but through no fault of Avro.

A re-evaluation of the entire program was authorized at the 106th meeting of the Cabinet Defence Committee of September 27, 1955. A special sub-committee was established consisting of the RCAF, the National Aeronautical Establishment, the Defence Research Board, the Department of Defence Production, and the Department of Finance. Chairman of the committee was the Chief of the Air Staff and in attendance were the Deputy Minister of Defence Production and representatives from the Cabinet Secretariat and the National Research Council.

The conclusions of this group showed the design to be technically sound and superior to other aircraft of the day. It was affirmed that this superiority was required in light of the Soviet threat. The sub-committee recommended continuing the program but also recommended improvements to the CF-100 and the introduction of the Bomarc missile as soon as possible. They showed the total cost of completing the development of the Arrow as approximately $300 million, with production aircraft to cost $2.6 million each. They also called for an additional $308.5 million for improvements to the CF-100 and Sparrow missile, as well as $210 million for Bomarc and $128 million for bases. The sub-committee's findings contained the following observation:

> With manned aircraft and surface-to-air-missiles in the defence system, the system possesses a diversified capability against various threats … The greater effectiveness and greater range of the CF105 results in the need for less aircraft and fewer bases. **Aircraft for aircraft the F102B is less costly but, dollar for dollar, the CF105 provides significantly more defence** [bolding mine] … The burden of cost involved in this course of action [selecting all recommendations, including Bomarc], while high, is inherent in an air defence system which is kept abreast of the developing threat.[89]

The last statement in the quote says such large costs are inherent with respect to large systems. It rests in marked contrast to the comments that many point to from C.D. Howe. He had said the Arrow program gave him the shudders in terms of its magnitude, yet the sub-committee who reviewed the project didn't seem overly bothered and had added in all the additional requirements mentioned.

The costs to implement the full recommendations from the committee were going to be beyond current approved estimates. The results of the study were discussed at the 584th Chiefs of Staff Committee meeting of November 1, 1955. At this meeting, Chairman Chiefs of

Staff Charles Foulkes said it would be desirable if Ministers were apprised of the full air defence picture before tabling the results of the study to them. He suggested providing a briefing on SAGE/Bomarc.

In response to this meeting, the RCAF made several recommendations. They recommended approval to form 9 additional fighter squadrons and approval in principle to include 26 heavy radar and 123 gap-filler radar as well as approval in principle for additional air bases. They further recommended reorganization of the Canadian Air Defence Command for the formation of a new headquarters in Quebec and others in Ontario and the Prairies. There was also a recommendation to open negotiations with the United States for cost sharing. It was further stressed that the Ministers be made aware that the Arrow alone would not solve all defence problems.

As a result, the Cabinet Defence Committee was briefed on November 17, 1955. Given the total costs for air defence under consideration, it was decided to seek assistance from the United States in sharing in the production costs or acquisition of the Arrow. The Americans urged Canada to continue the Arrow development, as they had nothing in their inventory that could take its place, but as far as can be determined, they made no commitments to purchase the aircraft.

The Cabinet Defence Committee was again briefed on December 7, 1955. A modified proposal was put before them. In order to reduce expenditures, the requirement to produce forty aircraft was modified in terms of schedule. It was decided production of the final twelve aircraft could be delayed to January 1958. It was expected the aircraft would have flown by then. In fact, the first flight was March 25, 1958, not that great a delay. Invoking this delay of the twelve aircraft meant $210 million would be required to complete the first twenty-eight aircraft, versus $340 million to complete all of them.

There was some program slippage occurring in terms of production. The RCAF decided that if fewer than twenty-eight aircraft were produced it would cause a one-year delay before entering operational service. This was likely due to the fact that simultaneous testing between Avro and the RCAF would be jeopardized. But, if less than $210 million was to be expended now, then a one-year delay would have to be accepted. The RCAF decided to order eleven aircraft now, with the remainder to be ordered later in March 1958. After that time, if the Arrow proved its worth, the remaining aircraft would be ordered to complete the quantity of forty. All of this creative thinking meant the immediate expense would be reduced to $170 million. If for some reason the Arrow did not succeed, that is all the government would lose.

One can only wonder what havoc these changing numbers wreaked on the company. It has been said the requirement was reduced because the costs were too high. The quantities were not reduced but rather extended over time. In addition, it was the combined requirements for air defence that were problematic. Finally, an artificially invoked one-year schedule slippage in the project would automatically mean increased costs in the long run. The issue of any mismanagement on the part of Avro did not surface in these discussions, because there wasn't any.

The new proposal for eleven aircraft was tabled to the Cabinet Defence Committee of December 7. The committee agreed to accept the revised program and spread the cost of $170 million over three years. In addition, while reducing expenditures for the Arrow, the CDC also agreed that 137 CF-100s be modified for greater altitude and use of the Sparrow, at a cost of $12.4 million spread over three years. They also agreed that $65 million be granted for the procurement of the Sparrow over three years.

Two subsequent meetings of the CDC were held on April 19 and June 13, 1956. Discussion centred on an expansion to the existing numbers of fighter squadrons. The Air Defence planners had called for eighteen squadrons on eighteen bases across Canada. The Chiefs of Staff believed only fifteen bases would be required and some of these could be Bomarc sites. Also, it was decided to reduce the number of auxiliary fighter squadrons of the reserve force. It was felt that having auxiliary squadrons equipped either with the CF-100 or the Arrow would be too much for the reservists to cope with. It was decided to replace the ten auxiliary squadrons with three more squadrons of regular force fighters. Reductions in numbers were also due to the expectation of introducing Bomarc into the air defence plans.

Removal of the auxiliary squadrons meant a reduction in the need for aircraft from between 500 and 600 aircraft down to 100 or 150. The net effect would be that the development costs would be amortized over fewer aircraft, giving the illusion of a much higher cost per aircraft. This is the argument between fly-away cost and full development cost. If an aircraft crashes, the cost of purchasing a new one is the fly-away cost. The total development cost is the cost of dividing the numbers produced into the sum total of production, including research and development. American aircraft were less expensive to Canada because the costs involved were the fly-away costs, since the United States had paid for all the research and development. In all, a total of fifteen fighter squadrons on fifteen bases were finally recommended, along with improvements to existing bases. The plan was to be carried out in two phases.

Further meetings in 1956 addressed the Sparrow missile. The U.S. Navy was not going to go into production of this missile, so its development would be taken over by Canada. This would become another burden on the Canadian defence budget. It would also create delays in the availability of the missile. Then, in 1956, the RCAF finally decided on a fire control system, the Astra. This was to be a new development undertaken by RCA in Montreal, a company that had little experience in the realm of fire control systems. This added yet more costs to the Arrow project, costs that had gone against the recommendations of Avro. The latter were expecting to obtain a developed Hughes fire control system and had begun designing the airframe accordingly.

Selection by the RCAF of the undeveloped Astra fire control system instead of one from Hughes meant more changes required to the airframe. One estimate placed the required changes at between fifty and sixty. With changes come schedule delays, and with both come increased costs; again, not a mismanagement issue but one of reality beyond Avro's control. The selected system was going to require more electrical power and cooling than planned, but since the system did not yet exist, even these were best guesses. Some additional costs that were originally going to be underwritten by the USAF also now fell on the RCAF.

The Iroquois engine had progressed further in design than originally planned, so expenditures that were anticipated for subsequent years could now be moved up earlier. This was good, but it still required more money now, giving the illusion of a cost increase, although savings would result later. In addition, increases had resulted in the need for more flight test instrumentation and ground support. Finally, the union representing many of Avro's employees had succeeded in negotiating higher salaries, so wage rates had gone up along with material costs.

All of these factors increased the planned $170 million by another $46.3 million to $216.7 million (March 31, 1958). The breakout was $19.8 million for the airframe, $20.5 million for engines, and $6 million more for the fire control system. The figures were tabled before the 113th Cabinet Defence Committee meeting of February 6 and 7, 1957. The CDC agreed to the new numbers but also agreed to a reduction from eleven aircraft to eight. It was further agreed to defer the expansion program of fifteen bases along with the additional radar and gap fillers because it did not appear as though the United States was going to provide much assistance in expanding the ground environment into Canada. There was also the notion again that some of the bases would be Bomarc bases instead of aircraft bases.

The proposal agreed to by the CDC would result in a further delay in the schedule. A reanalysis also showed that together with earlier availability of the Iroquois, it meant only thirty-seven aircraft would be required to complete the development and test program, and not the forty originally envisioned. There was also no requirement now to place an order for the remaining twenty-nine aircraft for another year. When this order was placed, however, the total cost could be $500 to $600 million.

By September of 1957, a recommendation was made by the Chiefs of Staff to cancel the CF-100 Mark IV aircraft and the related work on the Sparrow missile. The Minister discussed economies in terms of canceling the introduction of an air-to-air missile for the F-86 Sabre and deferring some construction and Navy-related projects. On October 24–25, the Chief of the Air Staff was asked to prepare a briefing for the Ministers on the expected expenditures for the total air defence package. The Defence Research Board was asked to examine alternate proposals for air defence.

On October 29, 1957, the new Cabinet Defence Committee under John Diefenbaker was briefed. The Committee elected to continue the Arrow program for another twelve months. This included ordering an additional twenty-nine aircraft, for a total of thirty-seven. The Chiefs of Staff submission to Cabinet had shown the costs to March 1958 would not exceed the $216.7 million previously authorized and that the total costs of the program were estimated at $646 million.

According to the documentation, this $646 million was the first time an attempt had been made to capture the costs for the entire program. This was only now possible, since the RCAF had just finalized its decisions on the various required subsystems and equipment. The estimate was still only that and could be subject to change. For example, in 1957 the estimated cost of the Astra was $72 million, but this rose to $208 million by August 1958, a cost that had to be absorbed by the project. Part of this increase was the result of a new RCAF requirement, that of carrying the nuclear-tipped Genie missile in lieu of the Sparrow.

In June of 1958, the Chief of the Air Staff prepared to submit a recommendation to purchase the thirty-seven aircraft as well as an additional order for forty-six, with approval in principle to continue production at a rate of four aircraft per month. But in July, the Army requested that a tri-service group with the Defence Research Board be established to examine the full air defence requirements, with various alternatives to be provided to the Minister. These alternatives included the Bomarc and the F-106 in lieu of the Arrow. In fact, it was the July 8 brief to the Minister prepared by the Chairman Chiefs of Staff that stated all the air defence requirements could add upwards of 25 to 30 percent to the defence budget.

In August 1958, the estimated cost of the thity-seven-aircraft program was set at $789 million. Increases were attributed to better definition of program requirements by the RCAF, which in some instances showed some earlier calculations had been underestimated. Other increasing costs were the result of the usual labour and material cost increases and changes in sub-contractor estimates.

In reflecting on the costs of the Arrow, a document for the Chairman Chiefs of Staff from 1958 stated:

> ... All countries are experiencing difficulties in estimating the cost of new complex systems. The fundamental reasons for this are the compressed time cycle, the rapid rate of technological progress and the complexity: furthermore: The state of the art of designing and devel-

oping a supersonic interceptor has continually been refined. Every advantage had to be taken of new concepts of design. As new information became available, design changes had to be made ... new materials and techniques were introduced ... each selection and subsequent design change in one sub-system invariably affected most of the other sub-systems. For example, the airframe was selected in 1953, the engine in 1954, the electronic system and the missile in 1956 ... The biggest single change in concept was the ordering of 40 development and pre-production aircraft. This came about as a result in the "feasibility" of the programme. It of course considerably increases costs initially, but will save time and money in future, quantity production.[90]

Here again, there was no allegation that the company was at fault for mismanaging the program. The costs were well known, and increases were largely due to the changing requirements of the RCAF. Costs were not spiraling out of control. This was not a case of a company gone mad with greed, as some have alleged.

While researching the material for *Storms of Controversy*, this author discovered a memorandum dated December 4, 1957, from Group Captain R.H. Footit. He was the assistant for the Arrow Weapon System Project; effectively, he was the project manager. In that letter he had accused Avro of mismanagement. Footit wrote to this author explaining the reasons for his concerns; for some reason, he had been unaware of memoranda from Avro that addressed them. Unfortunately, Footit's original memo has resurfaced in other sources and has been used to demonstrate the problems between Avro and the RCAF, without the additional explanation that all concerns were solved.

Here is Footit's letter to this author, written March 8, 1991, which explains his concerns with Avro and their subsequent resolution:

The WSPO [Weapon System Project Officers] spent many long hours setting up committees with the sole purpose of keeping everyone informed, on a regular basis, of the current status of the development. Our unstated motto was, "You have a right to know and we will tell you." It not only stopped may unfounded rumours, but also led to suggested actions to be taken: It was a two way street.

Of course the WSPO depended on getting accurate and timely information from Avro. Some years before the Arrow we had some problem with the Avro Chief Designer at the time [Atkins] on the CF-100 program. I had been personally involved in this, as the company policy at the time was to clam up until a solution was found — of course, all hell broke loose in the RCAF ranks.

I had absolutely no problem previously with Jim Floyd, his key engineering people, or other senior Avro personnel on the Arrow, in keeping us [WSPO] informed. I had the highest regard for Avro's Engineering Department. They were the most professional team I had ever worked with. When the storm broke as outlined in my letter of 4 Dec/57 to Fred Smye, I and the WSPO staff were completely taken aback; was the company reverting to their CF-100 habit of withholding information? Was the previous breakdown of communications referred to on page 2 of the letter just the start of this policy? What about all the miss-information we had spread around with our efforts at keeping everyone informed? Didn't it appear to outsiders that the whole concept of a WSPO had been undermined? And the foundation crumbled?

So the basic idea behind the 4 Dec/57 letter was to get us back on a "Truth with no surprises" basis. The company took it seriously and as I recall, installed Air Vice Marshal (retired) John Plant as president to reinforce their ties with the RCAF. As I also recall, we had no further major problems in communications until the Arrow was canceled.

Footit's letter continues on a discussion of problems encountered:

> When you consider that the aircraft will take a number of years to first flight; then follows the early development stage, production, and continued development through the life of the aircraft in service — you are talking about a specification based on piles and piles of assumptions. So it is common practice in the Western World to try and base the specification ahead of the current state of the art.
>
> Consequently, it would be a miracle if the prototype aircraft met the specification: But you hope that later ones, with modifications, might. But this may be 10 to 15 years hence — or maybe the threat was wrong anyway. Who knows.
>
> But it does follow from this approach that design delays, modifications, schedule changes and cost overruns are a basic part of all developments. The Arrow was no exception.
>
> But the Arrow was probably the most complex piece of machinery ever designed in Canada. And in my opinion its early development was "Normal." If you want to know what might be an "Abnormal" development, plagued by problems, read up on the USAF Bomber, the B-1. From specification to production it has been a development nightmare.[91]

It is clear from Footit's remarks that Avro was not mismanaging anything, but that there had been a breakdown in communications. In fact, proper information had been sent to the RCAF, but Footit never saw the letter from Avro. Still, he saw the development as "normal." This is in line with the earlier quotation from the Chairman Chiefs of Staff. Despite the words of explanation in that memo, given all the factors previously discussed in this book, the Minister of National Defence was going to recommend cancellation of the Arrow program.

On August 21, 1958, the Chief of the Air Staff wrote to the Minister, explaining to him that the Arrow was required. He said he could not go along with any recommendation to cancel it. Pearkes ignored the advice of his air requirement specialist. This is consistent with his interview comments made to Dr. Roy in 1967, when he stated he made his decision after being told by the American Undersecretary of Defense that Canada did not need to spend so much money on the project.

On August 28, after a trip to Washington, Minister Pearkes officially asked the Conservative Cabinet to approve the cancellation of the Arrow as well as approve the installation of two Bomarc bases and the SAGE network, while exploring the use of the F-106. It was noted that the Arrow was going to cost $12.6 million each versus only $5.59 million for the F-106. Here again, the Arrow full development cost was being compared to the F-106 fly-away cost, an unfair comparison.

The cost of the Arrow was later revised down to $8.91 million each when the Sparrow/Astra system was terminated in September 1958. The figure still represented the full development cost based on a quantity of one hundred aircraft with the Hughes fire control system and Falcon missiles installed and on a fly-away cost of $5 million per aircraft. Not mentioned was that a large part of the Arrow cost had gone into setting up the production line, and money would be returned to the economy. In the case of the F-106, the $5.59 million fly-away cost would be lost to the United States. As is known, Pearkes's recommendation to cancel the Arrow was not accepted.

In January 1959, Hugh Campbell summarized the Arrow program and again pointed out that costs could decrease further. In fact, Avro had submitted a proposal to provide the Arrow at a fly-away cost of $3.75 million each, not the previous $5 million. Campbell noted that in this revised program, the figures submitted in 1958 showing projected expenditures for 1959/60 at $385 million, with a peak of $447 million, were now reduced to $162 million in the same time period, to a peak of $245 million. The projection was for one hundred Arrows at $702 million. By February 5, 1959, the number was adjusted to $781 million.

What were the final numbers on the Arrow? Audit reports produced after the cancellation show that the program was for the production of the thirty-seven aircraft discussed plus an additional eighty-three. The thirty-seven were going to cost a total of $576.4 million, a number less than the earlier projected $646 million. This number included all the costs for the production and tooling as well as spare parts support. The remaining eighty-three would be purchased at the fly-away cost of $3.75 million, considerably less than the fly-away cost of the single-engine F-106 and approximately double the originally estimated price of between $1.5 and $2 million. Added to this would be another $181 million for support such as spares and $42.6 million worth of Falcon missiles. The total program, from start to finish with all work complete, would cost $1.1 billion for 120 aircraft.

By contrast, the proposals for SAGE/Bomarc plus the F-106 would cost $967.5 million. This included cancellation charges for the Arrow. Not included, though, was the $236.1 million that had already been spent on the Arrow to that point. If all development charges are to be included in calculating the cost of an Arrow, it would only be fair to add the $236.1 million expended on the Arrow to the $967.5 million, for a total of $1.2 billion, a figure higher than the cost of continuing the Arrow.

Was the Arrow going to bankrupt the country or take money away from social programs or farmers? There are those who would argue in the affirmative and state further that if the Arrow project had gone ahead, it would likely have been considered one of the largest boondoggles ever undertaken. There is absolutely no proof or foundation to the latter statement, and it has no bearing on the situation in 1959, at the time of cancellation. What is of direct interest is the exchange that occurred in the House of Commons Special Committee on Defence Expenditures on May 3, 1960. The Committee was reviewing the expenditure for fiscal year 1958–59.

The exchange took place between Minister of National Defence George Pearkes and Paul Hellyer, defence critic in the opposition cabinet of Lester B. Pearson. Pearkes had just stated that in 1958/59, the Department of National Defence *underspent* its funding to the tune of $262 million. In other words, $262 million was being returned to the government's coffers. Naturally, one might expect this under-expenditure to have resulted from the cancellation of the Avro Arrow. This was not the case. As Pearkes explained, the Arrow cancellation accounted for about $41 million. That left another $221 million. This $262 million was money that parliament had authorized the Department of National defence to spend. It was not "new" money, and the department had not spent it!

Some of the unspent money resulted from savings in salaries. A good percentage was saved in contracts that were not let for one reason or another. For example, slippage in Navy projects created a large under-expense from what was estimated. Likewise Army expenditures were lower than expected. Over and above the Arrow, the RCAF had an additional $24 million in under-expenditures.

> Mr. Hellyer: Mr. Chairman, I have two or three short general questions before we proceed … Mr. Minister, on March 31, 1959, were your army, navy and air force as well equipped as you would like to have seen them? … Mr. Chairman, I think it is a fair question, and one he [the Minister of National Defence], can answer, because when he spent $262 million less than was authorized by parliament, we should know whether this was due to improper estimating or incompetent management. Something obviously is very wrong, and I think the minister should tell us whether he thought at that time he had the equipment necessary for his armed forces, or whether he did not …
>
> Mr. Chambers: I think the member should have listened to the explanations given for the difference between the expenditures and the estimates.
>
> Mr. Hellyer: I did — and I think these were made up by a public relations man, whose orders were to make it as dull and uninteresting as possible, and rationalize everything that has happened.[92]

So, for all the bellyaching that the Arrow was taking money away from much more needed programs, actual monies that had been authorized for spending, to the tune of $262 million, were not in fact spent and were returned. According to the audit records, if the Arrow had not been cancelled on February 20, 1959, a sum of $257.8 million would have been required to complete the thirty-seven aircraft program in its entirety, including the production tooling and support. For $262 million, the Arrow program could have been completed within the parliamentary approved expenditures, with no additional costs with which to bankrupt the nation or deny social program dollars.

It has been said the country was in a recession. What better way was there to support such a recession than to have twenty-five thousand people become unemployed in one fell swoop, while destroying a high technology industry in the process. It was bad enough the Arrow had taken second place to American requirements for the Bomarc missile, but to have it cancelled with funds readily available was criminal. Even if it were not possible to transfer these funds immediately to the Arrow program, they could have been reallocated for social programs then, and the Arrow could have obtained new appropriations in subsequent years. As a result, those twenty-five thousand people would have remained employed. A high technology industry would have survived.

The alternative defence systems being considered were going to cost more, and they were satisfying another country's requirements while $262 million was being returned to the government. In these circumstances, the Arrow program would have been affordable and cost-effective. The arguments that the Arrow would have taken money away from other programs fall short.

Just before Christmas 2001, Canadian Prime Minister Jean Chrétien was interpreted during an interview as saying that spending more money on defence might mean not having those funds available for health care. Retired Major General Lewis MacKenzie wrote in a letter to the *Ottawa Citizen* of December 28, 2001:

> If you were trying to scare the segment of the public that would actually believe such a blatantly untrue and sensationalist statement, you probably achieved your aim. It's unfortunate that the case against increased funding for the military is so weak that facts have to be made up ... There are literally thousands of other sources of revenue within government spending

priorities to source increases in defence spending if deemed necessary.[93]

The same was true in 1959 in the case of the Arrow.

For those who continue believing Avro would have floundered in the long run, then Bombardier should have been shut down years ago, because they too might flounder in the future. Timothy Eaton should never have opened the first Eaton's store in the early twentieth century because he should have known that his stores would eventually collapse, even if it took until the 1990s. Let's shut the country down, because heaven knows what is in store for Canada's future.

Chapter 9

Termination, Speculation, and the End of A.V. Roe Canada

"We are now being stampeded into considering Genie as the weapon merely because it makes a big atomic bang."[94]
— Air Vice Marshal Hendricks, July 29, 1958.

William L. Turner passed away on June 13, 2000, but not before providing some tantalizing information relating to the Arrow termination. In the military, Bill Turner had spent a year in Military Intelligence at Camp Borden and Camp "X." His training had been in the area of weapons systems, and he became the liaison officer on weapons systems between De Havilland in Toronto and Avro. His other affiliation was with the DND Canadian Armament Research Development Establishment. He was involved in telecommunications, cybernetics, rockets, and missiles, and he had become coordinator for the weapons system on the Arrow.

He pioneered the use of Canadian-designed and Canadian-built antennas for use on foreign satellites and spent three years at the Kennedy

Space Center coordinating work on the Canadarm installation. He was given the Kennedy Space Center International Achievement Award for his effort. Upon his retirement, he became a historian and archivist, promoting Canada's aviation and space history. He was a founding member of the Aerospace Heritage Foundation of Canada (AHFC).

Shortly before his passing he spoke to this author about the real reason he believed the Arrow was cancelled. He was preparing an article for the AHFC newsletter, *Pre-Flight*. His article appeared in the March-April 2000 issue. He believed there remains an undisclosed file containing sensitive information about the events surrounding the termination. This author has not been successful in locating such a file.

Turner's story does parallel the previous discussions concerning the Bomarc missile and its impact on the Arrow project. He does, however, make some important distinctions, and he feels it was the inability to obtain an American fire control system, due to American national security regulations, that led to the cancellation of the Arrow. In discussing the issue, he asserts that while Avro had recommended the Hughes fire control system, the United States initially denied the request, as the Hughes MX-1179 was a classified system.

According to Turner, there was great concern on the part of the American authorities that details of this classified system could be leaked to the Soviets. He claims the RCMP, the OSS/CIA, the NSA, the FBI, and others were monitoring Soviet moles in Canada and at Avro, through Operation Keystone. This information was in fact discussed in some detail in *Storms of Controversy* and confirmed yet again by the revelations of a Russian archivist named Mitrokhin in 1998.

He states further that American industries were complaining that their technology kept appearing in Soviet hands immediately after being given to Canada. In *Storms of Controversy* it was demonstrated that a key reason the United States did not wish to sell an American nuclear-powered submarine to Canada in the eighties was fear that the manufacturing secrets would end up in Russia. This was because the Canadian contract bidding process requires all potential contractors be given the same information so they could prepare their offers. Under such circumstances, it would be difficult to monitor all potential contract bidders to ensure they kept the information secret.

A recent example of this involves a Canadian satellite, Radarsat-2. This $305-million satellite required high technology parts from the parent company in the United States. Its success was placed in jeopardy because of a crackdown by the U.S. on "sensitive" information being leaked to other countries. According to an article in the *Globe and Mail*, "the United States is accusing Canada of being lax with sensitive information ... the dispute has put Canada's $5-billion defence industry in jeopardy."[95] (Radarsat-2 is scheduled for launch in 2003.) Perhaps the same was true in the fifties, at the height of the Cold War.

It was because of the inability to obtain a fire control system, according to Turner, that the decision was made to have a system built in Canada. The official USAF position did not want Hughes to bid on the Canadian contract in order to have it concentrate on American projects. Hughes was also not prepared to modify their fire control systems to fire other missiles such as the Sparrow. Members of the RCAF argued that what was needed was a system more sophisticated than the Hughes MX-1179, but perhaps this was simply a way of not having to admit the MX-1179 was unavailable.

The company selected to design the system was RCA in Montreal, a company with little expertise in this area. Because of this, the prime contractor became the RCA parent plant in Camden, New Jersey. Subcontractors included Minneapolis-Honeywell Co., Canadian Westinghouse Co. Ltd. of Hamilton, and Computing Devices of Canada Ltd.

The nature of the Astra system was such that subcontractors would build the sub-components and parts required. Because they too lacked expertise, the component parts would have to be shipped to the RCA plant in Camden for testing, integration, and assembly. This meant having to send component parts and assemblies back and forth across the border as tests and fittings were carried out. This was far from an ideal method of operation. It meant delays in border crossings as well as problems of duty and excise taxes being applied.

At one point on August 1, 1958, the Astra project administrator sent a letter to DND requesting a meeting with the Department of National Revenue to obtain exemptions and establish procedures that would expedite the flow of these parts and components across the border. All shipments, it was hoped, could be stamped "Astra Hustle" to expedite the packages. As mentioned, Astra costs soared from an estimated $72 million to $208 million in less than a year, and it is no wonder, given such arrangements. This massive increase put Avro in a bad light, even though they had nothing directly to do with the Astra development.

Why was RCA chosen, given its lack of expertise in the area of fire control? Bill Turner speculates that Canadian politics helped bring the contract to RCA because of its geographic location. While this can likely never be proven, there have been numerous instances where, rightly or wrongly, it has been believed that location has influenced the awarding of contracts — the alleged Bombardier bailout involving the Iltis vehicle, for example. RCA was also the lowest bidder, and perhaps the only bidder. Still, it lacked the experience, and this should have played a greater role in determining its suitability to carry out this contract.

Many seem to blame Avro for trying to develop a fire control system and adding that development cost to the project. It was not Avro that had wanted this. They had warned against the tremendous cost that would be involved. Perhaps Bill Turner is correct in his conclusion that Astra was initially chosen when the U.S. refused Canada their system on the basis of national security. The facts deviate, though, in September 1958: recognizing that RCA could not produce, the Prime Minister elected to cancel the Astra/Sparrow combination and to attempt once again to obtain a Hughes system.

The United States eventually provided the MX-1179, referred to as MA-1, but perhaps too late. This system was being installed in Arrow RL-202 at the time of cancellation. Still, it was not just the MX-1179 that was being obtained. It was this system and the Falcon missile. Therefore, the MX-1179 would not require much modification. This obviated the need for the U.S. to release detailed sensitive manufacturing and operational data in order for the system to control a Canadian missile. If members of the USAF were no longer nervous about providing a classified system to Canada, one can only speculate what the intelligence agencies in the U.S. were thinking.

There is one other element that may have relevance to this story. As noted earlier, the Arrow was considered obsolete because it did not carry a nuclear weapon. NORAD plans required air defence interceptors to be nuclear equipped. Did this affect the Arrow project? Air Vice Marshal Hendricks, Air Member Technical Services, provides the answer.

On July 29, 1958, Hendricks wrote to the Vice Chief of the Air Staff. He stated that the Sparrow missile had been chosen because it was believed to have a greater kill potential than the other missiles then being considered. It was also more resistant to electronic countermeasures. He then stated rather bluntly,

> We are now being stampeded into considering Genie as the weapon merely because it makes a big atomic bang. I suggest that it still has the same inadequacies as it did when we considered it for the CF 100.[96]

One can only speculate as to who was doing the stampeding if not the U.S. This is consistent with NORAD's expectations. Hendricks then recommended that a choice should be made between Sparrow and Genie as the weapon of choice, but not both. On the same day, the Chief of the Air Staff sent a memo requesting that Avro be instructed to begin the Genie development program.

Avro replied with an estimate that it could take four years from the time the go-ahead was given to proceed with the work to squadron introduction. The RCAF wanted the Genie available at the same time the Arrow would be introduced into service. Air Commander G. Truscott wrote that increases in development would be required to satisfy the RCAF need. The Genie development would have to parallel that of the Sparrow.

Integration of Genie with Astra had been put in the contract with RCA. However, it was stated that this requirement was of a low priority. Consequently, no work had been done on this aspect as concentrated effort had been placed on integrating the Sparrow missile to the system. All of this changed by August 7, 1958. Priority was now placed on the nuclear Genie missile. There was a problem, though, in obtaining necessary data on the missile. For example, Avro required information on flight characteristics, trajectory, range, method of launch, methods of calculating safe time of flight, accuracy requirements, and the like, but this information was classified. Not only could Canada not obtain the Hughes fire control, as Bill Turner suggests, they could not get the weapon of choice.

Faced with these issues and those described in earlier chapters, by August 11, 1958, Pearkes had a report to cabinet prepared, recommending termination of the whole Arrow program in favour of the Bomarc. As mentioned, the Astra development had ballooned to $208 million, up from $70 million the year before. This Genie NORAD requirement would push that figure even higher — if the specifications on Genie could even be obtained.

From RCA's perspective, the Astra could be developed to work with either Sparrow or Genie but not with both, in the time available to squadron service in 1961. A major problem was the development of an electronic counter-countermeasures capability for Genie. RCA was of the opinion that Genie was particularly vulnerable to electronic countermeasures. This opinion had been the view of several RCAF members, including Air Vice Marshal Hendricks. The bottom line was that it was going to be a very difficult development.

The situation was summarized as follows on September 8, 1958, a few weeks prior to termination of the Sparrow/Astra development. Writing to the Chief of the Air Staff, Wing Commander G.B. Waterman, a detachment commander at Avro, stated that under some basic assumptions, Avro could deliver a Genie/Astra weapon system by 1961. First of all, the Genie program required government financial authority to proceed by November 1, 1958. Secondly, if the Genie launch system did not present too many difficulties to Avro engineers, engineering drawings could be ready by May 1959, with an experimental weapons pack ready by the summer. Production weapons packs would be available by March 1961.

All of the above was predicated on the overall assumption that Astra could also be modified in time to work with Genie. Still, according to Waterman and Avro engineers, the capability would probably not satisfy the full RCAF requirement for the Genie system. To satisfy all that the RCAF wanted from this system in the time available would, in the words of Waterman, require "...astronomical amounts of money...[to] the Genie/Arrow Weapon System, which will be delivered early in 1961..."[97] Yet again, it was not Avro that was bleeding the government dry for funds; it was the changing RCAF requirements, following the American requirements, that were creating delays and cost escalations — only now it was in the Astra program.

There was another complication to the Genie development in addition to its classified specifications. Avro had stated that its engineers, like those of RCA, would require security clearances in order to be able to work with the American classified data on the Genie. Even with RCAF help, clearances for their staff could take up to a month, thereby making it very difficult to meet the necessary deadlines. If, for any reason, Avro was not allowed full access to the information required, the deadline could never be met. These were not unlike the comments RCA had made when Genie use was still a lower priority. For all intents and purposes, given the American requirement for nuclear missiles on Canadian aircraft, Avro and RCA could not produce in the time allotted without vast sums of money and fewer security complications.

On September 21, 1958, the Canadian government finally cancelled the ill-fated, ill-conceived Sparrow/Astra system. Approval to obtain and install the Hughes MA-1 electronic fire control system, with Falcon and nuclear Genie missiles, was finally granted by the Minister of National Defence on November 5, 1958. The option was discussed with the USAF and agreed to, and soon work began to acquire and install the system in Arrow RL-202. This had the effect of substantially lowering the cost of the Arrow.

There remained the question of incorporating Genie, although this no longer presented the problem it had with Astra. For one thing, the Hughes fire control was already adapted for the Genie in American aircraft. It also meant not having to disclose classified information to anyone other than Avro engineers. But use and handling of American nuclear weapons by Canadians was still somewhat problematic and needed to be sorted out. Overshadowing this was the higher priority being accorded the Bomarc.

Thus the reasons expressed by Bill Turner were not that far off. Inclusion of the Genie requirement by NORAD created more design difficulties for both RCA and Avro. This had the added effect of causing schedule delays and a tremendous increase in cost, in order to satisfy the imposed RCAF deadlines. There was also no guarantee that Avro and RCA engineers would be provided with sensitive information concerning Genie specifications. In addition, satisfying the new RCAF deadlines would require astronomical sums of money. This was not due to Avro mismanagement but to trying to expedite the project. Any project manager worth his salt today would tell you it was complete insanity to add and change requirements the way the RCAF did. That Avro still kept fly-away costs to $3.75 million per aircraft is amazing.

One item of interest that Turner explains has to do with the RL designation. Avro had been asked to brief some USAF personnel in Washington. A small-scale model of the Arrow was presented with the RL designation on it. When asked what this registration meant, it was said that the markings were arbitrary and simply there to make the model appear more realistic. According to Turner they were in fact the initials of a prominent staff member. Speculation is that the member in question was Robert Lindley, chief engineer for the Arrow. It has also been said that the initials stood for Roe Limited.

One question that has always been difficult to answer is why the Iroquois engine was not allowed to go into production. As reported in many of the Arrow books, contracts were being negotiated to sell the Iroquois to the French government for use in the Mirage jetfighter. The discussions were terminated because of rumours the Arrow was going to be cancelled. There had been additional information that companies such as Curtiss-Wright in the U.S. were interested in producing the engine, perhaps under license.

The Iroquois was produced under the team of Charles A. Grinyer, vice-president of Orenda and chief engineer on the Iroquois. His assistant chief engineer was Harry Keast, and his chief design engineer was Burt Avery. The Iroquois compressor was constructed primarily of titanium, a lightweight, strong material resistant to high temperatures. With a thrust of 26,000 pounds with afterburner, compared with the 18,500 pound thrust of the J75 with afterburner, the Iroquois weighed in at roughly 2 tons versus the J75's 3 tons. Its power could accelerate the Arrow to a world speed record. In laboratory test runs, the Iroquois had sucked the insulation off the walls of the test cell it was in before being shut down.

Chief test pilot Mike Cooper-Slipper was going to test-fly the Iroquois. With him were test pilot Leonard Hobbs and flight engineer John McLachlan. Canadair had mounted the engine to a specially designed pod affixed to the tail end of a B47 bomber on loan from the USAF. It would be flight-tested in this manner before actual installation in an Arrow. The first flight test in the B47 took place November 13, 1957. The crew had trained for this moment by learning to fly the B47 at Strategic Air Command training base McConnell, near Wichita. Learning of their mission a Texan reportedly said, "Do you mean that you little old Canadians have got the biggest engine in the world? And you're going to put it in the tail of a B-47? Man, you're crazier than we are."[98]

They were even crazier. Two days before the flight, a small fuel leak had been discovered. It would take a month to change engines, but the RCAF wanted to see it fly. It was decided to run the test engine anyway, but at idling speed only. Clouds began rolling in over the test flight area in Malton. Parachutes strapped in place, they decided it was time to go. It was noon. Without the aid of a ground starting motor, the B47 would have to fly fast enough to get the Iroquois blades spinning at 25 percent of their potential revolutions per minute.

Cooper-Slipper increased the speed of the aircraft to 328 knots at about 14,000 feet. The blades had reached only 18.8 percent, not the required 25 percent, when, at 12:27 P.M., the Iroquois came to life. After six minutes, the decision was made to land. The Iroquois engine was shut down during the descent. This procedure was carried out for safety, in the event of any leaking oil. The test flight, though brief, was quite literally a roaring success. For the pilots, it was something of a relief that everything went so smoothly (they never did need those parachutes).

At the time of cancellation only seventeen engines had been built. Six were described as serviceable and one, designated X116, had achieved flight standard and was at Avro, presumably in Arrow RL 206. The rest were in various stages of assembly or had been stripped down. The engines had achieved a total running time of 7050 hours and a total flight time on the B47 of 34.5 hours. They had achieved 303 hours of wind tunnel test time at simulated altitudes of 70,000 feet and Mach 2.3 forward speed. Model performance specification had been achieved at 25,550 pounds thrust versus the rated 26,000. The critical fifty-hour Pre-Flight Rating Test (PFRT) had been achieved, clearing the aerodynamic configuration of the engine. A third-stage compressor blade or disc failure had prevented achieving the mechanical configuration, but this was deemed a minor problem. Engine X-106 was in the B47.

After the cancellation on March 19, 1959, Earle K. Brownridge wrote to Minister of Defence Production Raymond O'Hurley. He stated that the government would have to decide how it wanted Orenda to continue its operation. Would it produce other engines on license, or spare parts and other components? Depending on the decision, the company would have to reduce in size. Orenda, with its affiliated companies — Canadian Steel Improvements Limited, Lucas-Rotax Limited, York Gears Limited, Renfrew Aircraft & Engineering Company Limited, Bristol Aircraft (Western) Limited, and Light Alloys Limited — had grown to a total floor space of 1,600,000 square feet but would likely need to reduce down to 780,000 square feet. A final plea was made to salvage the Iroquois program, but it was not to be. Instead, in the summer of 1959, the RCAF chose the Lockheed F-104, and Orenda was selected to build its engine, the GE J-79, under license. What was a vibrant, thriving, independent Canadian company capable of its own development was effectively reduced to being an American branch plant operation.

By December 1960, there were five complete engines in storage at Orenda. Four more were being stored in various stages of completion. Seven more engines no longer existed, and there were many spare parts, enough perhaps to complete twenty engines.

One complete engine, number X116, had been shipped to Bristol/Siddeley in the United Kingdom. It was the rediscovery of this engine, placed in storage by the Royal Air Force Museum, that created news headlines in the late nineties. In fact, members of the Aerospace Heritage Foundation of Canada had been quietly attempting to get the Canadian government to have it returned to Canada when news of its existence hit the media. The attempt by AHFC failed, as none of the original shipping documents were available, having been destroyed after cancellation. It seemed that even though this engine remains property of the Crown, the government will not claim ownership without those documents.

The USAF had expressed some interest, and Orenda had submitted proposals to have the engines installed in a B58C aircraft or for short takeoff and landing (STOL) aircraft. Unfortunately, the USAF indicated that their studies for their B58C aircraft had been terminated and that any application for STOL aircraft would use existing engines. The Iroquois was dead. It is presumed that the remaining engines at Orenda were scrapped. On May 26, 1964, Orenda advised the RCAF they still had all tool drawings and other data on the engine. On June 5, 1964, a reply from the RCAF noted that there was no requirement to continue holding the data, and disposal was recommended.

It has always been asked why American manufacturers did not pick up the Iroquois. At the stage it was at, the Iroquois still had some development and test work left. With the program development shut down, Orenda was unable to continue the work, as the engine was Crown property. Another company like Curtiss-Wright, although prepared to license a completely developed engine, might not have been ready in terms of money or facilities to complete the development of one that was not finished. A great Canadian achievement, the Iroquois, like the Arrow, was reduced to scrap.

At the time of cancellation, A.V. Roe had grown into the third largest company in Canada, behind the Canadian Pacific Railway Company and the Aluminum Company of Canada. Adding to its size was the acquisition of Dosco and its complex of about thirty-three companies.

After cancellation, most of the top executives resigned from the company or were fired. On June 17, 1959, Sir Roy Dobson wrote to John Diefenbaker, advising him that he had asked for and received Crawford Gordon's resignation. Fred Smye submitted his own in July of that year.

In an effort to survive, Avro took over the management of United Marine Incorporated's Richardson Boat Division, with the intention of building large aluminun-hulled executive cruisers. Unfortunately, two other large aircraft manufacturers in the United States had done the same a couple of years earlier. The result was that the venture was not profitable.

Likewise, with cheaper road and aircraft transportation, Avro's rail divisions began running into difficulty. Adding to this were the problems of the coal industry from the Dosco group of companies. On the aircraft side, the American government had terminated its contract on the Avrocar.

In July 1962, De Havilland was instructed by Sir Roy Dobson to take over the Avro facilities at Malton. Hawker-Siddeley in Britain had acquired De Havilland Canada through its acquisition of the parent company in 1961. Jack Ames, former chief of product design, had become general manager of Avro and was the man who handed over the keys of the Malton plant to De Havilland Canada. The name A.V. Roe Canada ceased to exist, and the remaining companies fell under the auspices of Hawker-Siddeley Canada. Dosco was eventually sold off in the mid-1960s. In 1966, 40 percent of Orenda was sold off to United Aircraft in the U.S. The remaining 60 percent became Orenda Limited. In 1973, Orenda Limited bought back the 40 percent. It now forms part of the Magellan Aerospace Corporation as Orenda Aerospace Corporation.

Hawker-Siddeley Canada continued until 1995, when it began selling its assets, including Orenda. Then, in September 2001, with Hawker-Siddeley about to declare bankruptcy, an offer of purchase was made by Vancouver-based publisher Glacier Ventures International Corporation. Glacier Venture's offer of $6.2 million was accepted over a competing bid of $5.8 million from Coastal Investments of Winnipeg. In announcing their bid, Glacier noted they wished to preserve the Hawker-Siddeley name, given its history in Canada. And so the name will go on. After all, the Arrow most certainly has.

Chapter 10

In the News

*"THE ARROW is a work of dramatic fiction inspired by real events.
Certain characters, scenes and dialogue are fictional composites..."*
— Part of the disclaimer at the start of the CBC showing
of *The Arrow*, a production by The Film Works,
Tapestry Films, and John Aaron Productions, 1997

Over the last few years, the Arrow has been in the limelight on a
regular basis. It has been one of our enduring legends, the
Canadian equivalent perhaps to the events surrounding the assassina-
tion of John F. Kennedy. It has also continued to be a matter of heated
controversy because of the fact that many of the files were only recently made public. The movie *The Arrow* aired on the CBC in 1997, and
it was partly responsible for the renewed interest.

The Internet has picked up the cause, with nearly a thousand sites
dedicated to some aspect of the Arrow story. The sites of the Aerospace
Heritage Foundation, at www.ahfc.org, and of Avro Recovery Canada,

at www.avroarrow.org, are excellent. With respect to the movie, many seem to have missed the disclaimer that appeared during the opening credits, stating that the movie was a fictionalized account based on the book *Shutting Down The National Dream.*

As a result, this author has been asked if certain representations in the movie were true. For example, one individual wanted to know whatever happened to the female engineer portrayed in the movie. The female engineering character was fictional. She may have been written with Edith Kay Shaw in mind, an aviation engineering tech-nologist who authored one of the first books on the subject, *There Never Was An Arrow.* While there were many other women working in various capacities, there was no female in the position described in the film, though Barbara Reed, now a retired judge, worked as an under-graduate engineering student testing engine parts for the Arrow.

Another fictionalized portion involved the portrayal of June Callwood. Callwood was a reporter following the Iroquois engine development. She was not, however, the individual who took the now famous photos of the destruction of the Arrows on the tarmac. That honour belongs to Herb Nott, who rented a small airplane and flew around the Avro plant snapping photos of the wanton destruction.

Was there any truth to the scene showing Prime Minister John Diefenbaker with President Eisenhower, out on a fishing boat? In that scene the President urges the Prime Minister to rethink the Arrow. Such a fishing trip between the two was contemplated. According to confidential notes prepared by the embassy in Ottawa, on his upcom-ing visit to Ottawa, the President could go salmon fishing in New Brunswick. He would fly in his personal aircraft, the Columbine, and then be driven to a provincial lodge on the Miramichi River. Involved in the trip would be Bill McDonnell, then considered a leading Canadian fisherman. The venue was subsequently changed to Snow Lake for trout fishing, but it has not been established if the trip occurred. In reality, George Pearkes revealed that he was advised by the Undersecretary of Defense to drop the Arrow in favour of American aircraft, while on a trip to NORAD with him.

Another scene in the film showed the CIA as anxious over the fact that one could purchase a model of the secret Arrow in a toy store. In fact, Air Vice Marshal Jack Easton provided this author with corroboration of a mole operating within Avro. Then in 1998, Vasili Nikitich Mitrokhin entered the world scene with a best-seller.

Mitrokhin had been an archivist working for the KGB in cataloguing and storing hundreds of thousands of files. Over the span of twelve years, he began making notes from these files. He eventually fled to Britain, with a cache of tens of thousands of pages of highly sensitive notes. These pages were used in the preparation of the exposé *The Sword and the Shield: The Mitrokhin Archive and the Secret History of the KGB* by Christopher Andrew, head of the faculty of history at Cambridge University and a foremost historian on foreign intelligence.

Among the information revealed by Mitrokhin was confirmation that a mole was in the Avro plant. He is described as being of Irish descent, with the code name "Lind." This information corroborates the idea that the Soviets had an interest in the Arrow. Ex-RCAF members have stated that of course the Americans would have been concerned about information on the Arrow falling in to the wrong hands. They knew how advanced the Arrow was. So why have we not seen a Soviet Arrow?

The secrets behind the Arrow design were not so much in its outward appearance as they were in its manufacturing. Working with titanium and breaking new ground in hydraulics, engine design, and the like were required to build this type of advanced airplane. It was many of these same engineering and manufacturing secrets that the United States was protecting during the design of the secret SR-71 Blackbird aircraft. These would have been the most crucial secrets to obtain, and if the mole got them, one might not necessarily know it by simply looking at a Soviet plane. Certainly, some of the MiG series of Soviet jets displayed some of the Arrow's characteristics and power, but this does not necessarily mean they benefited from the information the mole provided.

On another note, the film showed a model of the Lunar Lander being tossed into a box in Jim Chamberlin's office. It gives the impression that Chamberlin was working on lunar landing concepts in 1959. In fact, Chamberlin and some twenty-five others did join NASA almost immediately after the cancellation. Chamberlin had a hand in all of NASA's programs, playing a key role in the final design of John Glenn's Mercury capsule and directing the multi-million-dollar Gemini project. The job of overseeing the design of the Lunar Lander, or Lunar Excursion Module (LEM), as it was called, actually went to ex-Avro engineer Owen Maynard.

Another ex-Avro engineer, Brian Erb, had the task of developing the heat shield that would protect the astronauts' capsule on re-entry into the earth's atmosphere. Old photos of the Gemini space capsules show that the doors swing open from the middle outward. The task was to have doors that could be opened and closed immediately. This particular idea had been influenced by the design of the clamshell canopy opening of the Arrow cockpit and incorporated into the Gemini capsule.

From these few examples it can be seen how elements of truth were woven together to produce a drama that made the points with respect to the overall story but was in fact fictional in many of the details. Still, it makes for interesting viewing. The flying sequences and in particular the recreation of the rollout on October 4, 1957, are well worth watching. The full-scale replica used in the sequence was built by Alan Jackson, a sales estimator and hobbyist in Edmonton.

With respect to flying an Arrow, three separate news items spoke of groups trying to build models of the Arrow. In Toronto work has been in progress on the rebuilding of a full-scale mock-up of the Arrow. Some fifty volunteers have donated their time to producing the museum-quality replica. Some of these volunteers, like Peter Allnutt and Bill Kee, had worked on the original, and they bring forth the experience and memories of those days gone by. Work is being done at the Toronto Aerospace Museum in Downsview Park in Toronto. The model is made out of aluminum and steel and will not fly. It may be fitted for taxiing.

The Arrow 2000 Project includes a museum in Calgary, Alberta dedicated to Avro Canada. One of their projects is to build a non-supersonic, flying, two-thirds-scale replica of the Arrow. The craft is being built under Canadian Recreational Aircraft Legislation. The aircraft will be powered by lightweight engines driving ducted fans. It will be considered a high-performance recreational aircraft and will be flown at air shows. First flight of this aircraft is scheduled for March 25, 2008.

Notwithstanding Project 2000, the most ambitious project announced is to rebuild an actual flying, full-scale supersonic model. Peter Zuuring, author of *The Arrow Scrapbook*, is spearheading this effort. First flight is scheduled for February 23, 2009, according to page 233 of his book.

This author has had several queries about what it would take to achieve a flying, supersonic model. The real question regarding rebuilding a flying, supersonic Arrow is whether it is indeed feasible. From an emotional perspective, rebuilding a flying Arrow makes for an excellent news story. Indeed, newspapers and magazines across the country have carried it. But emotion aside, there are specific issues that need to be addressed by anyone considering such an endeavour. These issues, as seen by this author, are presented here to give an idea of the daunting complexities involved and the challenges to be faced.

Over the years many parts and pieces of the Arrow have surfaced. It has been asked whether enough found parts could make the task of rebuilding easier. Certainly, such parts could be incorporated into a static museum display model. For a flying aircraft, though, refurbishing these forty-year-old parts would likely be impossible. Many were uniquely designed and would require the necessary tooling, all of which was destroyed when the project was cancelled. Even if a warehouse full of brand new parts was discovered, each would have to be inspected against the original drawings to satisfy Department of Transport requirements, and most would need to undergo testing to ensure integrity. Aircraft parts have a certain shelf life, which can not be altered.

Could original drawings be used, but with new materials and the aid of modern computer-aided design programs? A number of the original drawings exist, which might be used in the project. But there is a major challenge here. Those drawings were developed based on engineering calculations and computations and thousands of hours of testing for the characteristics of the existing materials of the day. Changing those original materials and replacing them with modern ones would obviate the use of all those original drawings. Everything would have to be recalculated and retested from scratch. Centre of gravity, weight, drag, thermal coefficients, and load and stress factors would all change — to name just a few. The task is a formidable one. If it were not, the major aircraft builders would not be spending hundreds of millions of dollars in aircraft development. The fact is that the design would have to be redone. Computer tools would help, but specialists would be required to manipulate those tools to produce a meaningful design.

Engines represent a major dilemma. Modern engines would need to be used, and this would again nullify the use of any existing drawings. One has only to look back at the real Arrow to understand the cost and engineering impact on design with respect to altering the engine types. The engine inlets and airframe structure would need to be redesigned. With different engines and new materials, the result could be made to look like an Arrow in terms of outward appearance, but it would not be an Arrow.

What would it cost to build an aircraft from scratch for a one-off prototype? According to audit records cited in previous chapters, the original research and development on the airframe was approximately $100 million in the 1950s. One can well imagine what would be required today. Considerable sums would need to be raised. Assuming the money was available, considerable design and testing of parts and sub-assemblies would still be required, a major effort in itself. Some of the original test rigs alone would create their own challenges in design.

The Arrow required a highly skilled workforce. Even for a one-off aircraft, the same would be required today. How many specialists would it take? How many hours would be required? Who would actually do the work of manufacture and assembly? What safety measures would have to be put into effect? These are all questions that require an answer. Project 2000 is working with volunteers, as is the museum in Toronto for their static displays. A supersonic effort would seem to require the use of paid professionals with the necessary resources to get on with the task.

Rebuilding a flyable seventy-seven-foot supersonic aircraft requires a lot of specialized tooling for final and sub-assembly, and a lot of floor workspace. The original Arrow also required specialized wind tunnel testing. Presumably, the logistics of such an undertaking have been or are in the process of being worked out.

The issue of money has been mentioned. Certainly, a project of this magnitude requires considerable funding and a timeline within which to complete the task. Hopefully, any organization contemplating this endeavour would have a cut-off point by which a go/no-go decision would be required. In the case of a no-go, a mechanism would likely be required for dealing with unspent accumulated funds. This would mean having a solid project management organization that would develop the risks in such an undertaking to ensure the project would deliver as advertised.

Finally, the aircraft would require flight certification. Proof would be needed that the aircraft was built to all pertinent standards in order to satisfy Transport Canada requirements. It would not qualify as a military aircraft as it would not be built under a military contract. It would require Department of Transport certification.

Such an undertaking would also need to consider the consequence if the aircraft crashed on initial flight. Plans would be required in terms of shouldering responsibility for such an event. And, would such an event be another blow to national pride? Even though it would be a different aircraft, would the critics use the event to insinuate the original Arrow was also a technical bust? Rebuilding a supersonic aircraft that looks like the Arrow is definitely possible, but the ramifications discussed above would have to be very well thought out, as presumably they have been.

Following cancellation of the Avro Arrow Program, all completed aircraft were destroyed. *Storms of Controversy*'s first edition in 1992 clearly showed the trail of memos and the players involved in the destruction affair and reproduced the key documents from government records specifically declassified by request. Despite this, a former member of the Diefenbaker Cabinet, Pierre Sevigny, then associate defence minister, made some unbelievably ignorant comments about the affair. He said it was Crawford Gordon who ordered the destruction. He even went so far as to state the Diefenbaker government wanted to keep at least one model, even though memoranda exist showing his boss, Defence Minister Pearkes, was arguing that no planes could or would be kept. What these documents showed was that it was neither John Diefenbaker nor Crawford Gordon.

As first reported in *Storms of Controversy*, shortly after the cancellation, the RCAF advised the National Aeronautical Establishment, an arm of NRC, that five aircraft and fourteen engines could be made available for supersonic research. On March 11, 1959, the RCAF received a reply that the NAE was not interested. Had it said yes, we would have Arrows today. Two days later, Chief of the Air Staff Hugh Campbell wrote to Defence Minister George Pearkes and advised him of the NAE decision and added that with the Minister's approval, the RCAF would take steps to dispose of the Arrow and engines.

On March 19, Pearkes wrote back to Campbell concurring with this, but added that he wished to be informed of the method of disposal. On March 26, Campbell wrote to Pearkes recommending the Arrow and engines be reduced to scrap. Pearkes sent the letter to his deputy minister asking for his advice and comments. Why would he require such advice if he already had Diefenbaker's order in hand or if Gordon had already ordered the destruction? On April 8, 1959, Pearkes agreed with Campbell's recommendation to scrap. There is more to the trail, but it will end with the words of George Pearkes, written on June 9, 1959, to a man in Brantford, Ontario who had asked that one Arrow be spared for posterity:

> Although I sympathize with your desire to preserve the Arrow as an item of historical interest, I cannot grant your request for economic reasons. At the present time the completed aircraft are being stripped of equipment and will be scrapped in the near future. We will be able to salvage several hundred thousands of dollars."[99]

The trail led to Chief of the Air Staff Hugh Campbell having made the recommendation and Defence Minister Pearkes having accepted it after conferring with his deputy minister and members of the Department of Defence Production. This paper trail partly exonerated Prime Minister John Diefenbaker. As was expected, some Avro supporters took some exception to this, as it has long been believed that it was Diefenbaker alone who ordered the destruction in order to erase all memory.

The following points should be considered by those who cling to this belief. First of all, the paper trail that exists and was declassified for *Storms of Controversy* would never have existed if the order came from the Prime Minister. More importantly, though, under such an order, a completed aircraft would never have been offered to the National Research Council for test purposes. There would have been no aircraft to offer.

Likewise, the nose section of Arrow RL 206 would not exist if not for the fact that the destruction orders clearly state it was to be kept for research and testing purposes by the Defence and Civil Institute of Environmental Medicine (DCIEM) in Toronto. Finally, the destruction itself did not occur until several months after the cancellation — not within twenty-four hours. A direct order from the Prime Minister would have resulted in immediate destruction and disposal. This latter point is germane to the question of whether one got away.

In *Storms of Controversy*, a sequence of photos of the destruction is shown in which one aircraft, Arrow RL 202, seemingly disappears from the pictures. Did it escape the torch crews? The *Arrow Scrapbook* offers additional photographs taken by a photographer named Russel from Fed News, which purport to show the destruction of RL 202 along with the rest, but is this really the case? The issue is one of sequence. When were the newly published photos by Russel actually taken in relation to the Herb Nott photos, and what do they really show?

The Russel photo sequence of the five Arrows on the so-called death row was taken at various angles and heights. In fact, the coloured photo showing RL 202 allegedly being dismantled in the foreground of the picture was actually published in the book *Arrow*, by the Arrowheads. This photo shows RL 202 with a hose coming from the spine of the aircraft and crossing the wing. Also in the photo is what appears to be a ground power unit on wheels, near the airplane. Several pockmarks are visible across the wing and tail that give the illusion of the airplane being disassembled. These in fact are access or service panels that have been opened. The radome, the black cone at the front of the airplane, has been removed.

Adjacent to RL 202 is RL 205, and it is pointing in the opposite direction. This scene is what appears in the Russel photos. It is clear in these photos that RL 205 is not yet in a state of disassembly. However, RL 205 is in a state of disassembly in the Herb Nott photos.

The first photo of the sequence, reproduced in *Storms of Controversy*, shows five aircraft from an overhead shot in a photo whose source is actually unknown. It is not at all like the Nott photos in terms of clarity and angle. Unlike the Russel photos, all five Arrows are pointing in the same direction, with one in an obvious state of disassembly. This is RL 205, which is in the foreground of the Herb Nott photos. All tail numbers in the Nott photos are clearly visible. Missing in the Nott photo is RL 202. It appears to have been moved between the time the unidentified over-head shot was taken and the time Nott snapped his shots.

This examination of the photos clearly demonstrates that the Russell photos, with RL 205 intact and pointing in a different direction, were taken some time before the torch crews were sent in, since in the overhead shot in *Storms of Controversy*, RL 202 is intact and RL 205 is partially disassembled. This is corroborated by the accompanying note, which indicates the Russel photos were taken on May 8, long before the Nott photos.

The date is significant. Memos reproduced in *Storms of Controversy* clearly show that as of May 12, all five Arrows were being held intact, pending news of possible interest from Great Britain. This is consistent with the Russell photos. On July 7, a letter was sent to the Crown Assets Disposal Corporation confirming that all aircraft were to be reduced to scrap. Was this final order carried out? It is impossible to tell from any of the photos in question.

If anything, the newly published Russell photos just add to the mystery. They do not show RL 202 being taken apart. In fact, one might interpret the photos to show RL 202 was being serviced for flight. It is unlikely that Arrow 202 was saved, and in *Storms of Controversy* it was noted that RL 202 was probably still in the hangar when the Nott photos were taken.

On October 10, 2001, the *Hamilton Spectator* carried a story about Henry Daciuk, who had salvaged some pieces of the Arrow. He had taken them as a boy from the Hamilton scrapyard of Sam Lax, the man who paid about $300,000 for the Arrows and turned them into melted scrap. One of the pieces salvaged is an aluminum plaque that is stamped with the number 2 and C105, Mk 1. Does this prove that 202 was destroyed? Lax claimed that the weights of the aircraft he smelted had to coincide with the weights of delivery to ensure nothing escaped. Clearly this did not happen, given all the pieces that have turned up over the years. Furthermore, in 1995, this author attempted to obtain the records of the Crown Assets Disposal Corporation to verify what was delivered to Lax. It was discovered that the files on this particular transaction were in complete disarray and unintelligible. The mystery of the disappearing Arrow continues. Sam Lax himself passed away February 5, 2002, at age eighty-six.

In 1999, the headlines reported that Arrow models had been found. What had been found was quite possibly one of the one-eighth scale models launched into Lake Ontario to test the aircraft's shape and design for stable flight characteristics. In 1988, this author wrote an article in the engineering magazine for the Professional Engineers of Ontario suggesting that perhaps some day these models might be found. In the early nineties, the search began in earnest.

Gerald Saunders was an ex-Avro employee and founding member of the Aerospace Heritage Foundation of Canada. His son Bob is a certified diver. It became his son's dream to locate one or more of these models, bring them to the surface, restore them, and put them on display, as a matter of national pride.

It was not long after Saunders began his search that aviation buff Bill Scott entered the fray. Hailing from London, Ontario, Bill founded Arrow Recovery Canada with the goal of finding the Arrow models. He assembled a team of volunteers, including divers, but he needed a boat. He teamed up with Trenton marine mechanic David Gartshore, who owned a boat. Bill moved in with Dave's family with the idea of helping Dave restore the boat. This boat was in fact the last of the aluminum craft Avro produced after the cancellation. Dave's father had worked at Orenda and came into possession of this boat, which had never been in the water.

With the boat restored and the help of side-scan sonar, the two set out to look for the models. During the course of the searches, some dives were made with no results, as reported by Gartshore's divers. Eventually Bill and Dave had a falling out. Bill Scott went back to London, but Dave continued searching on his own.

On June 19, 1999, the *National Post* carried the story that Dave had found what he thought was one of the models. Underwater photos of the zebra mussel-encrusted model do show the delta shape outline with two large engine exhausts at the back. By week's end, Bob Saunders's group announced they too had discovered a model. Photos of it clearly showed it was perhaps a rocket but definitely not one of the models. In Gartshore's model, the wings appear to be bent inward, and the tail rudder has either been sheared off from the impact or is embedded in the lake bottom, if the model is upside down.

Unlike Bob Saunders and the AHFC or Bill Scott's Avro Recovery Canada, Dave Gartshore did not have a permit to search for the models on his own. As a result, he could be subject to a $50,000 fine should he ever try to raise the model from its resting home in the water. According to the Ontario Ministry of Citizenship, Culture and Recreation, permits are required for looking for the models and additional licenses are required to bring them up. As of this writing, without revealing the location of what Dave refers to as "his" model find, he has given up his quest to raise it. Neither the AHFC with Bob Saunders nor Avro Recovery Canada has reported any other finds, but the searches continue.

In the September-October 2002 issue of the AHFC newsletter *Pre-Flight*, an interesting announcement was made. According to the letter, the AHFC acquired the salvage rights and gratuitous transfer of all nine models. This means that anyone else locating them will now have to hand them over to the AHFC. This still leaves the models that were launched from Wallops Island in the U.S. available for salvage by others.

Ex-Avro personnel also made the headlines. Test pilot Jan Zurakowski was honoured in March 2000 by the Department of National Defence. The DND named the Aerospace Engineering Test Establishment in CFB Cold Lake in Zura's honour.

For accomplishments in both the American and Canadian space programs, in particular the Canadarm, ex-Avro simulator specialist Bruce Aikenhead was awarded the Order of Canada. One who should also be so honoured is James C. Floyd.

On May 19, 2000, Jim Floyd was awarded an honourary degree as Doctor of Engineering from the Royal Military College of Canada. This was added to his list of achievements, which have included being awarded the Wright Brothers medal in 1950, the J.D. McCurdy Award from the Canadian Aeronautical Institute in 1957, the George Taylor

Gold Medal from the Royal Aeronautical Society in 1962, a Lifetime of Achievement Award from the Air Industries association of Canada in 1988, and a host of others. In 1984, Challenger space shuttle mission 41B carried a plaque in Jim's name, signed by mission commander Vance Brandt.

James Arthur Chamberlin was inducted into Canada's Aviation Hall of Fame on June 16, 2001.[100] Chamberlin passed away in Houston, Texas in 1981 after a distinguished career first at Avro and then with NASA. The latter had awarded him the Exceptional Scientific Achievement Medal and the Exceptional Service Medal. He was described as one of the most brilliant individuals to ever work at NASA.

In keeping with the tradition of work in space, a team in London, Ontario has entered a global race to build the first commercial space shuttle. They have named it the Arrow, after the Avro Arrow.

On a sad note, the Arrow has been in the news in the reports the deaths of its creators. Wladek "Spud" Potocki passed away in 1996. Born in Poland, he escaped the occupation and, like Zurakowski, became a pilot at the British Empire Test Pilot School. When he immigrated to Canada in the early fifties, he joined Avro Aircraft and eventually became test pilot of the Arrow. He flew the Arrow more than any of the other pilots. He was also the last to fly it, and he achieved a speed of Mach 1.98 at *three quarter* throttle from the J75 engines. After the cancellation, he flew as a test pilot for North American Rockwell before losing an eye in an unrelated accident.

Air Vice Marshal John Plant passed away in May 2000. In 1957, he became president of Avro. This was a move that, in part, helped solidify relationships between the RCAF and Avro brass. It was his voice over the public address system that informed the Avro employees that the program had been cancelled.

Charles Grinyer passed away on March 10, 2001. He joined Orenda in April, 1952, becoming chief engineer of the Gas Turbine Division on January 1, 1954. He was appointed vice-president of engineering for Orenda Engines Limited on January 1, 1955, when Orenda became a separate company. He led the design team of the Iroquois engine and was awarded the McCurdy Award in 1959 for his contribution to aviation engineering in Canada. After the Arrow termination he joined Atomic Energy of Canada Limited as vice-president of engineering at the Chalk River Ontario nuclear plant. In 1962 he was appointed to the board of directors and the executive committee of Atomic Energy of Canada Limited.

Owen Maynard was an aeronautical engineering graduate of the University of Toronto in 1951. He had worked on the Jetliner and the CF-100 before becoming a senior structural engineer at Avro. When the cancellation was announced, he joined the group of Avro employees who went down to NASA. Responsible for the development of the Eagle, the LEM that put Neil Armstrong and Buzz Aldrin on the moon, he became chief of the systems engineering division for the Apollo Space Program. For his efforts he was twice awarded NASA's Exceptional Service Award.

The Award, presented in October 1969, reads as follows:

> For superior achievement and contributions to the success of the Apollo program. His leadership, professional skill and personal dedication were essential elements in the fulfillment of this Nation's commitment to achieve the goal, during this decade, of landing a man on the moon and returning him safely to earth. The scientific and technological capability demonstrated by the Apollo 11 has opened for all mankind the new era of interplanetary travel.

Owen Maynard passed away on July 15, 2000. Canada and the world lost a great space pioneer.

With the cancellation of the Arrow and the demise of A.V. Roe, Canada lost many giants.

Chapter 11

Questions and Answers

*"I think it is true that Canada would have gone ahead and had the best fight-
er plane in the world…"*[101]

> — Russel Isinger, a history student at the University of
> Saskatchewan, to *The Beaver*, Canada's history
> magazine.

O ver the years, many questions have been asked about the
demise of the Arrow, including questions about its capabilities,
or lack thereof.

1. **Would Avro still exist if the Jetliner had not been cancelled?**
    Typically the question asked is where would Canada be today if the
    Arrow had not been cancelled, but in fact termination of the
    Jetliner may have been more significant. When one considers that
    the first American commercial jet transport did not fly until the
    late fifties, while the Jetliner flew in 1949, one realizes the com-

manding lead Avro had in this area. This was recognized by both the American airline companies and the American military, who wished to purchase it.

Precisely because there was nothing comparable, it is likely those sales would have been made. This would have established Avro in the passenger transport market, so the impact of canceling the Arrow might not have been as great. In fact, revenue generated by Jetliner sales might have altered the decision to terminate the Arrow. The Jetliner would have been modified with time in much the same way Bombardier has been developing its regional jet, resulting in differing versions. The British and French teamed up to produce the Concorde. One can speculate that Avro and some American firm might have teamed up to produce a North American supersonic transport — after all, Jim Floyd did consult on the Concorde.

2. Was the Arrow an advanced aircraft?

Other sources have said the Arrow was no better than the Century series of American fighters. *Storms of Controversy* showed that the Arrow was far more advanced. The Century fighters included the Voodoo and F-106. Even the analysis performed by the Americans themselves showed the Arrow was far more capable than these in terms of speed, altitude, and manoeuvrability. The fact that the United States had thousands of Century fighters is irrelevant. One does not equate quantity with quality.

On this note, some Canadian historians now agree. Writing in *The Beaver*, Canada's magazine of Canadian history, a young history scholar researching the Arrow was quoted as saying, "Technologically, I think the historians have gone too far in their criticisms ... I think it is true that Canada would have gone ahead and had the best fighter plane in the world."[102]

3. So how advanced was the Arrow?

The Arrow broke ground in what was then called "electronic stability augmentation." If this feature failed, the aircraft would lose control and crash because it was designed as an inherently unstable platform for greater manoeuvrability. This electronic stabilization was the forerunner to what later became known as fly-by-wire in aircraft like the F-18.

The Arrow employed a four-thousand-pound-per-square-inch hydraulic system, which did not show up again until the stealth bomber. Other aircraft of the day were at three thousand pounds. The engine intake was of a unique design. Avro moved the field of telemetry forward with its scale model rocket test program as well as with the aircraft itself. Arrow employed special alloys to combat heat stress build-up. The Iroquois engine was being developed using titanium in the compressor, whereas other manufacturers in the U.S. were trying to use a mix of titanium and other metals. According to American sources, it was one reason the Americans felt the Iroquois would work while their designers were running into troubles. There were a number of these types of leading-edge achievements embodied in the aircraft.

The Arrow was supposed to be capable of a 2-g turn at Mach 1.5 at 50,000 feet without loss of altitude or speed. It was never tested to this specification, but other aircraft of the day were in the 1.3-g category at much lower altitude and speed; this again is from American sources. It is not so much that the Arrow had so many firsts as it was pushing the state of the art in so many different areas of design all at the same time on the same airframe.

4. **Would the Arrow still be advanced by today's standards?**
No. It has been said that the Arrow would still compete with modern fighters. While this may bear some truth, the point is that each class of fighter interceptor has been developed for differing roles. So, while the Arrow might be faster than the FA-18, the fact is the FA-18 was not designed to go any faster than it does. One has only to look at the SR-71 Blackbird for an aircraft that would outperform the Arrow in given circumstances. The Arrow, however, would have evolved over time. Avro had designs for different variants. The Arrow of 1959 would be much different today if Avro had been allowed to continue its evolution.

5. Did Diefenbaker order everything destroyed?

John Diefenbaker is only partly to blame here. *Storms of Controversy* shows the entire paper trail, which was not destroyed, although it was alleged to have been for over thirty years. Chief of the Air Staff Hugh Campbell made recommendations to the Minister of National Defence that the aircraft be destroyed. Destruction began more than two months after this recommendation, during which time the Canadian National Research Council and British Ministry of Defence were offered the aircraft. Neither took the offer. If Diefenbaker was the bad guy here, destruction would have occurred immediately, not two months later, and there would not have been a paper trail. At the time of the cancellation, Paul Hellyer was the opposition defence critic. He firmly believed Diefenbaker was the culprit. Writing on April 6, 1995, after having received documents from this author, he stated, "Mr. Campagna: Thank you very much for your letter of March 19th and the enclosed photocopies of DND documents. I must say that surprise is much too mild a word to describe my reaction! You have destroyed one of my most cherished myths!"[103]

6. Who was responsible for the Arrow's cancellation?

This is a complex question. Chairman Chiefs of Staff Charles Foulkes and Minister of National Defence George R. Pearkes became convinced that the Bomarc missile was every bit as good as the Arrow and could do the same job, but for a lesser price. This is where there is disagreement with the historians concerning the cost aspect.

Pearkes and Foulkes were not saying the Arrow was unaffordable. They were saying the Arrow would not be as cost-effective as the missile. (Put another way, if you need a truck and have $50,000 to buy it, but you become convinced that a $10,000 car will do the job you want, you will probably save the $40,000 and purchase the car. But you could have still bought the truck, since the money was there.)

In addition, they had no real choice in that the missile and the SAGE computer network was a NORAD requirement. It was believed by some that NORAD's requirement was automatically

Canada's obligation. There was also the problem that NORAD's first priority was for an ICBM defence system, with interceptors as the fourth choice. In the case of interceptors, NORAD's emphasis was on the long-range F-108. NORAD also required nuclear-tipped missiles. The Arrow's Sparrow missile could not carry a nuclear warhead. Because of this, Canadian bureaucrats labeled the Arrow as not a modern aircraft.

Finally, Pearkes admitted in an interview that his decision to cancel the Arrow was given impetus by the Americans, who advised him they could take care of air defence because of the numerous fighters they had. Pearkes admits to having set up a deal in this regard that few people were aware of. Had he not said any of this in his interview, we would not know it today, as there was no paper record of his actions. Pearkes went so far as to say that Canada would get rid of her entire interceptor requirement unless the U.S. really thought they were needed. This fact would also not be known today if it had not been recorded in a classified American document.

How many other confidential discussions were held that were never recorded or that had records destroyed? This raises the question of American motives as well. One cannot know for certain what American thinking on the Arrow was without seeking out the documents of the key American players, and even then, discussions might not have been recorded. Either way, there was certainly American influence in the decisions made about the Arrow, and this fact can not be ignored any longer.

7. **Did the RCAF cancel the Arrow because they became disenchanted with the company or the project?**
This is a myth with no basis in fact. The RCAF supported the Arrow to the end. Minister Pearkes admitted this in his interview with Dr. Reginald Roy in 1967. There were frustrations on both sides, but this is true of all major projects of this scale. The documents in this book certainly show the RCAF support for the aircraft. It is clear that the RCAF wanted the Bomarc missile as well, but not to the exclusion of the Arrow.

8. **Where would we be today if the Arrow or Jetliner had not been cancelled?**

Most books speak of the tremendous brain drain that ensued when the Arrow was cancelled. In addition, the aircraft industry was decimated. Edith Kay Shaw, author of *There Never Was an Arrow*, notes that Avro was placing supply orders across the country, obtaining Canadian-made parts, and keeping Canadians employed. The parent companies of American branch plants, however, were not allowing their branches to purchase Canadian components. While Avro was building up Canadian suppliers, the others were not. We became a branch plant economy. Avro was also promoting research and development in Canada and had a multitude of patents for processes and design. All that was lost. One thing is certain: today we do have a world-class aircraft manufacturer in Bombardier, but it has taken us about fifty years to get back to where we were in the Jetliner days, and we still haven't repeated that tremendous leap from turboprop to the Jetliner to the supersonic Arrow.

9. **Are any original blueprints of the Arrow remaining, and if so, are they of any value?**

Yes, there are a number of original blueprints. The value of these has more to do with historical significance than monetary considerations, unless some collector is willing to pay large sums for them. The blueprints can not be used to rebuild a supersonic flying Arrow. They were developed for the existing materials of the day. Use of new materials today would require all new calculation and testing.

10. **How much would the Avro Arrow project have cost if it had been completed?**

Audit records show the project was going to cost about $77.9 million dollars to complete the research and development. The government was expecting to pay out over $100 million in cancellation fees, but this number came closer to $33 million. Without the cancellation charges, the whole program, from start to finish of production, was going to cost $1.1 billion. The alternate system of F-106/SAGE/Bomarc was going to cost about $1.2 billion when you add in the $318 million that had already been spent on the Arrow project at the time of termination. One must remember that this money was being cash phased over several years, as any program of this size is.

The $1.1 billion included all the research and development and setting up the industry. In the case of F-106/SAGE/Bomarc, the $1.2 billion was just to buy the end items and spares from the United States. That makes a major difference. If an Arrow crashed, the replacement or fly-away cost would have been $3.75 million, not much at all for such a sophisticated aircraft. If the Arrow had gone into production, the fly-away price for an additional one hundred aircraft would have been about $2.6 million each. The replacement cost of the less sophisticated F-106 was close to $5 million. The politicians claimed the Arrow would cost about $12.5 million each. This was the full development cost plus the cost of the Sparrow and the Astra fire control system, simply divided by one hundred for the one hundred airplanes.

11. What happened to A.V. Roe Canada Limited?

The company never recovered from the shock of the Arrow termination and closed its doors for good in 1962. Orenda continued on and still exists today. Some of the other divisions in steel products also survived, but parent Hawker-Siddeley eventually succumbed as well.

12. How fast would the Arrow have gone with the Iroquois?

An Iroquois Arrow was rated for Mach 2, but speculation is that it would have achieved Mach 3. The Arrow with the less powerful J75 engines achieved Mach 1.98 at three quarters throttle.

13. How far away was the Arrow from flying with the Iroquois?

Arrow 206 was fitted with Iroquois engines at the time of cancellation. However, there would have followed a series of taxi trials and ground tests before attempting a first flight. It might have been several weeks if not a month away from a full-fledged flight, and several more away from a speed record attempt.

14. Why did the United States not purchase the Arrow?

Even though the Arrow was advanced, the U.S. had its own aircraft industry that lobbied against purchases of foreign-made equipment. The American military claimed the USAF and Army would not be willing to accept "at this advanced stage of development, a plane which they played no part in designing."[104] This statement was not entirely correct, as the U.S. had supplied wind tunnel testing as well as other advice on the design work.

Appendix

The Secret Files

TCA FORM
4-45
DISTRIBUTE
AS CHECKED
BELOW ✓

VICE-PRESIDENT

ASST. TO VICE-
PRESIDENT

PERSONNEL
ASSISTANT

RESEARCH
ASSISTANT

OPERATIONS
MANAGER

ASST. OPERA-
TIONS MANAGER

OFFICE
MANAGER

SUPT. OF FLIGHT
OPERATIONS

SUPT. OF COM-
MUNICATIONS

SUPT. OF PASS-
ENGER SERVICE

SUPT. OF CARGO
SERVICE

SUPT. OF
TRAINING

SUPT. OF ENG'RG.
AND MTNCE.

ENGINEERING
SUPT.

OVERHAUL &
MTNCE. SUPT.

AUDITOR

STORES

FU_____

Montreal, May 2, 1949

Avro C-102   1400-10 ✓

Mr. W. F. English,
Vice-President, Operations,
TC. - Winnipeg.

Further to my memo of this date in regard to the experimental
operation of the C-102, I can bring you up-to-date on my last
talk to the Avro Company during a recent visit on my return
from the Ethyl Corporation in Detroit.

It appears to me that we still have some time to get lined up
with both an agreement to operate and the operational method.
Within the Avro Company the earliest estimate of the first
flight is late June. My own estimate is the middle of August
and possibly September. The main cause of delay in production
has been with the bought out assemblies, principally the Dowty
undercarriage and some of the supercharger equipment. Although
some representative sections of the fuselage have been pressurized
beyond normal operating pressure, it yet remains to proof pressure
test the assembled aircraft. Past experience would indicate
that this will cause some delays in first flight date.

Should my approximate estimate of first flight date turn out to
be accurate, and if we allow a minimum of three months for
manufacturer's flight trials and preliminary certification, it
would appear that there is little likelihood of us being asked
to service test the C-102 much before the end of the year.

In reviewing some of the operational reductions now being
prepared as sales literature, the curves produced by the Avro
Company (if they mean anything at all) indicate that the C-102
is more than competitive with any existing aircraft used on
similar range operations. I did not take time to attempt a
thorough check of their economic reduction but from what I did
see, it appears that they are not taking all of the advantage
which they might. I was left with the general impression that
Avros are handling the whole affair in a very conservative
fashion. It was interesting to see the evidence of interest
shown by most of the major airlines on this continent. In
particular, Eastern Air Lines are serious enough in their discussions that the second prototype will be built with the

In this independent assessment of the Jetliner, Jas. T. Bain, director of
engineering and maintenance for TCA, notes that Avro has produced
conservative estimates that show the Jetliner to be more than competitive with other aircraft, and that Eastern Air Lines is quite interested.

DISTRIBUTE
AS CHECKED
BELOW ✓

VICE-PRESIDENT

ASST. TO VICE-
PRESIDENT

PERSONNEL
ASSISTANT

RESEARCH
ASSISTANT

OPERATIONS
MANAGER

ASST. OPERA-
TIONS MANAGER

OFFICE
MANAGER

SUPT. OF FLIGHT
OPERATIONS

SUPT. OF COM-
MUNICATIONS

SUPT. OF PASS-
ENGER SERVICE

SUPT. OF CARGO
SERVICE

SUPT. OF
TRAINING

SUPT. OF ENG'RG.
AND MTNCE.

ENGINEERING
SUPT.

OVERHAUL &
MTNCE. SUPT.

AUDITOR

STORES

FU_____

− 2 −

double slotted flap which will meet Eastern's low landing
speed requirement.

A physical examination of the aircraft showed a quality of
workmanship which I have never seen surpassed on a prototype
aircraft nor indeed by many production aircraft. Taken by
and large, the skinning and metal work is beautiful and far
surpasses the quality achieved by Canadair in production
North Stars. They appear also to have left very few ends
untied and even in the prototype the general equipment installation design shows enough care and foresight to make the C-102
a really modern aircraft incorporating the best of present
installation knowledge.

Jas. T. Bain,
Director Engineering & Mtce.

cc − J. T. Dyment

ACKNOWLEDGE BY INITIAL AND DATE − THIS COPY MUST BE RETURNED TO THE FILE

He then remarks on the superb workmanship that has gone into the
development of the Jetliner prototype. (National Archives)

/56

WASHINGTON, June 1, 1950

Dear Mr. Plumptre:

      Larry Vass, the officer dealing with economic affairs in the Dominion Affairs Office of the State Department, told me yesterday that the Civil Aeronautics Administration had completed its examination "on paper" of the Avro jet liner, C-102 and, subject to the successful completion of the operational tests now in progress, the aircraft will "almost certainly" be given a Certificate of Airworthiness by the C.A.A. He also remarked that the de Havilland Comet would probably <u>not</u> be given a Certificate of Airworthiness.

      All concerned with the production of the C-102 are, of course, aware that the aircraft was designed and engineered to meet C.A.A. specifications but this is the first remark I have heard from any official indicating that a Certificate of Airworthiness will probably be forthcoming.

      Yours sincerely,

      GORDON E. COX

F.W. Plumptre, Esquire,
  Economic Division,
    Department of External Affairs,
    OTTAWA, Ontario.

This letter from the Canadian liaison staff in Washington indicates the American Civil Aeronautics Administration is prepared to give the Jetliner a certificate of airworthiness subject to completion of tests. It is noteworthy that the CAA probably will not give such a certificate to the Comet. It does not appear this information was ever passed on to Avro management.

47

CHAIRMAN
A. FERRIER
J.P.R. VACHON

AIR TRANSPORT BOARD
OTTAWA

22-7-7

Confidential   June 26th 1950.

A/V/M A. T. Cowley,
Director of Air Services,
Department of Transport,
OTTAWA, Ont.

Dear A/V/M Cowley:-

　　　　　　　　I have pleasure in enclosing, for your information,
one copy of the report "Comparative Cost Analysis of the Triangular
Route Toronto-New York-Montreal When Using AVRO Jetliner, or
Canadair North Star Aircraft". This report was prepared by the
Board's Research Aeronautical Engineering Branch following a
request made by Mr. Howe, and is to be treated as confidential
material.

　　　　　　　　　　　　　　　　　Yours very truly,

　　　　　　　　　　　　　　　　　J. R. Baldwin,
　　　　　　　　　　　　　　　　　Chairman.

ENTERED
ON CARDS

Given Avro's conservative estimates of competitiveness, C.D. Howe
requested the Air Transport Board to perform an independent analysis.
(National Archives)

Certain advantages will accrue to the airline which first employs a jet transport in domestic scheduled transport operations and these are believed to be sufficiently important to warrant a brief examination. Firstly there should be an increase in traffic due to the superiority of turbine-engined aircraft over conventional types, with respect to passenger comfort. Increased speed will also be an attraction. Both these factors assume greater importance as the stage length is increased. The very novelty of such a radical advance in type of equipment will also be of benefit. A temporary advantage in low fuel prices may also go to the first airline to introduce turbine-powered aircraft, though this advantage is expected to disappear as the demand for kerosene increases.

This study suggests that the Jetliner can be operated at a lower direct cost than the North Star for the route and schedule frequencies chosen even though the stage lengths are well below the optimum for the Jetliner. It is quite possible, however, that a comparable analysis of direct cost under the same conditions for a modern twin-engine transport powered by reciprocating engines (such as the Convair 240 or the Martin 404) would show lower direct costs than those estimated for the Jetliner. In comparison with such aircraft the Jetliner might still be more attractive, however if all factors are taken into consideration, since increased revenues are expected to result from the improved standards of comfort and speed which the Jetliner offers.

Conclusions.

Provided that the Jetliner in normal scheduled operations demonstrates the performance submitted by the manufacturer the comparative operating cost analysis of a 40 passenger version of the Jetliner and of the North Star when operated on the triangular route Toronto-Montreal-New York-Toronto with three daily flights in each direction indicates that:

1. The service requires three Jetliners (including one as reserve) as against four North Stars (including one as reserve).

2. The direct operating cost of the Jetliner, with the present price of kerosene in tank cars at Malton, varies between 79% and 81% of the North Star direct operating cost. Assuming the price of kerosene to rise to a level of $0.05 less per Imp. gal. than the price of high octane aviation fuel, direct operating cost of the Jetliner will still be lower than that of the North Star.

3. An equal indirect cost (as calculated from TCA data) was applied to the Jetliner and the North Star alike. On this basis, which is rather unfavourable to the Jetliner, the total operating cost of the Jetliner varies between 88% and 90% of the total North Star operating cost.

4. The introduction cost of the Jetliner in the proposed service will probably be of the order of $860,000.

5. Before any jet-engined transport is introduced on a particular route special studies with respect to traffic control and winds at cruising altitudes will have to be made. The calculated maximum wind at 30,000 ft. is indicated by the Meteorological Division, Department of Transport to be of the order of 250 mph. Such a wind will seriously affect operation of the Jetliner.

6. Increased frequency of service, or an increase in stage length up to 900 miles, either of which will result in a larger number of aircraft than specified in para. 1, will have the effect of lowering the direct operating cost of the Jetliner from the levels indicated in para. 2.

7. Due to the improved standards of comfort and speed which the Jetliner can offer, as well as the novelty of such a radically new type of transport, it is very probable that it will generate more revenue traffic than the North Star, so that the difference in net revenue will be appreciably greater than that indicated by the total cost figures given in para. 4.

8. It is very probable that under the basic route and schedule conditions assumed in this study, direct operating costs lower than those for the Jetliner would be achieved through use of a modern twin-engine transport such as the Martin 404 or the Convair 240, since the stage lengths involved are so far below the optimum for the Jetliner. The greater attraction of the Jetliner might, however, even out-weigh the higher cost level, particularly during the initial period during which no other North American operator would have jet transports in operation.

The overall conclusions of the Air Transport Board say it all. The Jetliner would be more cost-effective and would likely attract more business. Until now, this report has never been publicly released. (National Archives)

APPENDIX A

Extract From A Letter From The President Of Trans Canada Airlines

Dated April 13, 1950; Which Accompanied A detailed

Breakdown Of T.C.A.'s North Star Operating Costs

"the greatest care should be exercised in basing conclusions on them, as in the first place, nearly all such information requires a great deal of interpretive data to be properly used, and secondly the answers to many of the questions are altering quite rapidly due to such changing conditions as the bases of warranty claims, fuel prices, corrective effects of modified design, replacement of major units of aircraft equipment, reduction in number of maintenance bases, schedules, etc.

Furthermore, apart from interpretation and continuous change, the figures themselves are in many cases of very questionable accuracy, for very good reasons. To cite one example, the cost of engine repair on a per-mile basis has been requested with respect to the North Stars. Our engine repair base at Winnipeg, as you know, handles both the Pratt & Whitney twin row, and the Merlins; both these types of engine come into a common disassembly room, after which all components go through a common parts-cleaning and initial inspection process. The acid cleaning baths and the "black light" inspection for flaws will have parts of both types of engine in process at the same time. This is just a minor example of the impossibility of segregating costs accurately when two different types of equipment are being dealt with in an efficient and logical pooling of equipment and manpower."

The detailed breakdown of North Star Operating Costs is on file in the Research Aeronautical Engineering Branch.

In preparing the report, the Air Transport Board requested information from Avro and TCA. While Avro freely provided theirs, TCA had a host of excuses and caveats. (National Archives)

NATIONAL AIRLINES
3240 N.W. 27th Ave.
Miami 42, Florida.

February 26th, 1951.

Mr. R. Dixon Speas,
U.S. Representative,
A. V. Roe Canada Limited,
P. O. Box 111 - La Guardia Field,
New York Airport Station, New York.

Dear Dix:

It will be most appreciated if you will keep in communication with
J.D., regarding the developments of the Jetliner. As you know, we
are interested and ready to do business if a reasonable basis for so
doing can be reached.

It was a real pleasure to ride and fly the Jetliner when it was in
Miami a few weeks ago. It will undoubtedly have tremendous passenger
appeal after the average passenger's first fears have been reduced
or eliminated by knowing it is in scheduled operation. A great many
people are anxious to fly in it but are naturally a little shy of
such a new development, as they were 30 years ago in flying the old
Jenny's.

I haven't been in the plane when it was fully loaded, but I think its
performance at the time I flew it was excellent. It handled well
with one or two engines out and didn't seem to be in the least bit
tricky.

Ramp handling was no more difficult than a conventional type aircraft.
The heat from the jets was not noticeable.

While the noise level in the rear of the plane was a little higher than
it was in the front, it certainly was less than in a plane powered with
reciprocating engines.

I think you have a grand airplane and it can do a fine job on the
airlines if your Company can build and sell them on a basis acceptable
to the airlines.

Best regards,

"B. T. Baker" - President.

GTB:mst:A:M

More kudos for the Jetliner. (National Archives)

NATIONAL AERONAUTICAL ESTABLISHMENT

WORKING COMMITTEE

ON

JET TRANSPORTS

Minutes of Meeting held in Ottawa

at 10:00 a.m., 28 June, 1951

Chairman:

| Mr. J.H. Parkin | N.A.E. | Director |

Committee Members:

Davis, Group Captain R.C.	R.C.A.F.	Director of Operational Requirements
Dyment, J.T.	T.C.A.	Director of Engineering
Gray, I.A. (represented by Siers, T.A.)	C.P.A.	Chief Superintendent of Engineering
MacPhail, Dr. D.C.	N.A.E.	Assistant Director
Nesbitt, L.M.	D.O.T.	Aeronautical Engineer
Stephenson, T.E.	N.A.E.	Head, Aerodynamics Section
Truscott, Group Captain G.G.	R.C.A.F.	Deputy A.M.T.S. (Development)

In June 1951, the National Aeronautical Establishment convened a working committee on jet transport. A.V. Roe personnel are noticeably absent. At that June meeting, it was said the Jetliner should be competitive with the best aircraft foreseen. It was quickly pointed out that there were no other competitive jet aircraft. (In fact, there would not be for years to come.)

Dr. MacPhail and Mr. Nesbitt replied that the small engines would not have sufficient time on them to be of use in the transport field when they were needed.

The comparison of the C-102 with the requirements listed for the express domestic transport was next considered.

Mr. Nesbitt pointed out that when considering the C-102 there should be the added requirement that it should be competitive with the best aircraft foreseen on the basis of operating costs. Mr. Parkin observed that such a cost analysis was difficult at the moment due to the lack of existing competitive jet aircraft.

Mr. Dyment reiterated Mr. Nesbitt's point on the cost requirement and stated that T.C.A. would only consider the aircraft if it were economical. They couldn't afford to fly it for prestige alone. T.C.A. were not prepared to pay for the development of the type. An Air Force order or a subsidy from some outside agency was required to develop such an aircraft since the manufacturers couldn't afford to develop one on airline orders alone unless these orders were for quantities in excess of 200 aircraft.

Mr. Parkin asked for the cost figures to be used when comparing the 102 to other aircraft and Mr. Dyment countered with the statement that there was no such aircraft as the C-102. There have been too many changes in design. The last paper prototype was checked for operation on T.C.A. routes and found unsuitable. T.C.A. want actual operating data before committing themselves but will not be satisfied with operating data from the first prototype since it is too different from any of the proposed production models - no slotted flaps, low tankage, incomplete de-icing equipment, cabin pressurization not checked, etc. The second prototype may represent a salable aircraft but as proposed now, it would not be capable of flying the Toronto-Winnipeg leg non-stop.

Dr. MacPhail asked Mr. Dyment if he felt that the second prototype would be salable in the absence of experience with the first.

Mr. Dyment replied that the second prototype may represent a salable aircraft and that T.C.A. would fly it on service trials if someone paid for the flights as a source of general operating data but would not wish to test number one.

The TCA representative stated that the airline would only consider the Jetliner if it were economical. Absolutely no mention is made of the Air Transport Board report the previous year, which showed the Jetliner to be more economical than the North Star that TCA was still flying. (National Archives)

M I N U T E (3)

1   Reference your Minute (2) I do not believe that
A. V. Roe would be in any position to build the C102 even
if they received an order for it. It never was our intention
that if this aircraft was required that it would be built by
A. V. Roe. They are fully committed now with their CF100
and Orenda engine programmes and anything more which we gave
to them at this time could only detract from these most
essential projects. There are other facilities however in
Canada which are still not fully committed and our limited
programme of C102 construction could be undertaken, I believe,
without too great difficulty.

2   During the last few days there has been an examination
into the C102 by the National Research Council, Defence Research
Board, Department of Transport and ourselves, and it is the
finding of this Board that the present state of the C102 is
nothing like as far advanced as is advertised by the company,
and that in fact, the aircraft lacks many desirable features
before it could be put into production. Perhaps we would be
unwise at this time to try to sell it at all. The Board is
however going to continue their investigations by an "on the
spot" visit to A. V. Roe and when their complete report is
available, I will forward it to you.

(DM Smith) A/V/M
AMTS

3 July, 1951.

This secret report of July 1951 shows that A.V. Roe really didn't have
a chance of breaking in to the civilian market. "It never was our intention that if this aircraft was required that it would be built by A.V.
Roe." The assumption was made that A.V. Roe was committed to other
projects, but did anyone ask A.V. Roe? Jim Floyd has indicated that
they could have handled this production. (National Archives)

IN REPLY PLEASE QUOTE

No. ....S.1038-C.102(C Staff O)

Department of National Defence
CANADIAN JOINT STAFF
1700 MASSACHUSETTS AVE., N.W.
WASHINGTON 6, D.C.

14 August, 1951.

Referred to.. /1. I.I.I.S.

AUG 17 1951

File No. S. 60 3. 71

Noted in ....

Chief of the Air Staff,
Department of National Defence,
Ottawa, Ontario, Canada.

Avro Jetliner C.102

1.   Recently the Avro Jetliner was flown
from Toronto to Washington for demonstration. The USAF
and the USN are both interested in this aircraft but
the only concrete proposal for purchase had come through
the US AMC at Wright Field.

2.   It is now confirmed that the USAF wish
to purchase 12 Jetliners. A recommendation was made to
this effect by a specially appointed committee representing
all USAF Commands, to the Aircraft and Weapons Board. This
Board approved the purchase of 12 aircraft.

3.   The USAF intend to use the C.102 as a
high-speed bombing trainer.

4.   There is another application for the
C.102 which is of exciting interest, this being high-speed
jet fighter refuelling. It is not known, at present,
whether an order has been placed but the Flight Refuelling
experimental section at USAF HQ are anxious to get 4 C102s
for test in this type of work.

NOTED
C.A.S.

SEP

(H.G. Richards)
Group Captain
for Air Member
Canadian Joint Staff

This confidential memo is written proof the USAF wished to purchase twelve Jetliners. It was not passed on to Avro. (National Archives)

Montreal, November 1, 1951
1410-1

Mr. A. M. Sutherland,
Director Mtce. & Overhaul,
TCA - Dorval.

I have read with interest your letter to Mr. C. T. Travers,
Supt. of Air Regulations, on the subject of the Department's
DC-3 and the work done on it at Winnipeg.

It is not the first time that the DOT have lead us up the garden
on the work required on an airplane; in fact it is almost the rule
that the programme has greatly exceeded the work on which quota-
tions were given. The resulting bellyache from the Department
habitually puts us in the wrong, and I think that on any future
occasion when we are requested to do work, we should advise the
Department that our past experience indicates a cost-plus basis
would be the only realistic arrangement, or that we will give
a quotation on the work they demand but not proceed with any
other work without separate individual approval of the extra
costs involved.

Jas. T. Bain,
Director Engineering & Mtce.

jtb'djp

The pot calling the kettle black. While TCA forced Avro into a fixed-
price contract rather than a cost-plus contract, despite the unknowns
in the Jetliner development, they too were of the opinion that cost-
plus contracts were more realistic given all the unknowns. In this
memo Jas. Bain of TCA expounds on the issue. (National Archives)

TOP SECRET

THE DEVELOPMENT OF THE INTRODUCTION OF THE BOMARC
GROUND TO AIR GUIDED MISSILE AND THE MB-1 AIR TO AIR
GUIDED MISSILE ON CANADIAN MANNED INTERCEPTORS FOR THE
RCAF FOR THE DEFENCE OF CANADA
- -

    In 1953 the Chiefs of Staff of the U.S. and

Canada set up a Joint Study Group of Military and

Scientific Experts to keep in constant study the problems

of air defence on this continent, and in particular, to

study those aspects of the North American air defence

system in general, and the Early Warning System which are

of mutual concern to Canada and the U.S.

    With the emergence of the soviet thermonuclear

weapons and long range jet bombers an Air Defence Planning

Group of the U.S. Continental Air Defence and RCAF Air

Defence Command were actively participating in plans for

the air defence of this continent. This Air Defence Planning

Group proposed to introduce a line of Bomarc guided missile

bases from coast to coast crossing the U.S. and Eastern

Canada at roughly the 48th parallel of latitude. To the

north of this and entirely within Canada the proposal was

for a line of all weather interceptor squadrons, nine of

which were already in existence. Further, in order to

control these weapons the adoption of the necessary ground

radars and computing systems. To do this an extension was

proposed of the ground environment in Canada northward to

increase the depth of the combat zone for tracking and inter-

cepting hostile raids.

    As a result of this, the Cabinet Defence Committee

agreed at its 110th meeting on 13 June 1956 to recommend

that site surveys be authorized in 1956 for additional heavy

radars and gap fillers for this purpose. At that meeting

it was also stated that further operation and evaluation of

../2

This top-secret brief notes that the joint Air Defense Planning Group
proposed the introduction of Bomarcs in Canada long before 1956.
(Directorate of History National Defence Canada)

S1920-105-4 (AMTS)

3 May Ontario,
29 Apr 57

Air Member,
Canadian Joint Staff,
2450 Massachusetts Ave. N.W.,
Washington 8, D.C. USA

BOMARC - Liaison Activities

1   Please refer to the following:

    (a) Our S1920-105-4 (AMTS), dated 12 Nov 56;

    (b) Your 825-14-2 (AFCS), dated 3 Jan 57;

    (c) Your 25-14-2 (O Staff O), dated 25 Jan 57.

2   As indicated in reference 1(a) above, consideration of the many factors associated with activating BOMARC squadrons in the North Bay and Ottawa areas is continuing. Because these bases are essentially to accommodate the requirements of the integrated defence system of North America and because present US regulations preclude Canada from having sole custody of atomic and other sensitive equipment, a mutual USAF-RCAF effort is now favoured over the original concept of Canadian manufacture. In this latest proposal, the RCAF would supply all base facilities including shelters, launching equipment, and personnel while the USAF would supply missiles and special test equipment. In this way the bases would be assigned a priority suitable to CONAD and the USAF would be able to maintain direct custody of the sensitive equipment. It would be necessary for the RCAF to procure in the US and/or have manufactured in Canada the necessary installed and ground support equipment. Also, the USAF would be required to absorb the training of RCAF personnel.

3   The CAS has obtained the approval of the Cabinet Defence Committee to negotiate the introduction of BOMARC into the RCAF and the USAF are generally aware of and agree with the above concept. However, until our operational and planning staffs have completed the detailed requirements, decided upon the best weapons deployment, and formulated the associated programme, little detail can be discussed with the USAF. Similarly, pending the foregoing, technical effort beyond maintaining current data on the system is also being held in abeyance.

4   Because the demand for current technical information is now at a peak for planning purposes, the course of action proposed in references 1 (b) and 1 (c), above, is concurred in and should be completed as soon as possible. In the absence of a firm programme, your suggestion of a single Canadian authority or project office for handling BOMARC information and liaison is considered premature, except as now practiced unofficially within AFHQ.

5   The presently conceived limited RCAF provided equipment will decrease the number of agencies and personnel who will require direct liaison with the USAF and BOMARC contractors. Initially, this can be restricted to a very few CJS (W) and AFHQ staff members; a list of those involved at AFHQ can be provided as you have suggested at any time the present clearance procedure appears inadequate or cumbersome.

....../2

196

SECRET

- 2 -

6   Until this matter is further pursued by various AFHQ staffs, it is considered your endeavours should be directed towards:

    (a) Re-establishment of the curtailed flow of current technical information, not only as a facility to planning but also to obviate much of the visiting which might otherwise become necessary;

    (b) Keeping the USAF informed of the evolution of our intent towards BOMARC so that they will be better disposed to providing information and assisting in the fulfilment of our ultimate programme.

DWG/hs
AEng 6
2-4943

(H.N. Hendrick) A/V/M
for CAS

cc: VCAS (3)

    CAE
    AMTS
    Orig
    Circ
    File

(D.W. Goss) W/C
AEng 6
(2-4943)

(H.R. Foottit) G/C
DAEng
(2-5485)

(G.G. Truscott) A/C
CAE
(6-6273)

This secret 1957 memo shows the Cabinet Defence Committee had given its approval for the Chief of the Air Staff to negotiate introduction of Bomarc. (National Archives)

S E C R E T
~~S1038CN-183~~(AMTS)

L/038CN-183-5

M E M O R A N D U M

29 Jul 58

VCAS

Arrow Weapon System - Genie

1   The attached memorandum at working level is brought to
your particular attention on the task involved in fitting Genie
to the Arrow.

2   You will recall when we analysed Genie versus Sparrow
in the CF100 we came to the conclusion that both were of the same
kill probability, and that the Sparrow was probably to be preferred
because it had no side effects on aircrew, no escape problem and
was far better against countermeasures.

3   We are now being stampeded into considering Genie as the
weapon merely because it makes a big atomic bang. I suggest that
it still has the same inadequacies as it did when we considered it
for the CF100, and that an analysis of the kill probabilities of
the Sparrow versus the Genie on the Arrow may well show that the
Sparrow is to be preferred again. Therefore, I urge that we be
practical in our decision to use Sparrow or Genie, and base it on
our estimate of the kill probability of the Weapon System.

4   If the kill probability of Genie is adequate, then we
should make a decision to have one weapon only on the Arrow as
an interim weapon until a suitable guided atomic headed airborne
weapon is available, that the interim weapon should be either
Genie or Sparrow II, and the decision as to which it should be,
should be made now.

(MM Hendrick) A/V/M
AMTS
2-2743

Air Vice Marshal Hendrick complains of being stampeded into accepting nuclear missiles for use on the Arrow. In fact, this became the
requirement, thereby placing the development of Astra, and eventually the Arrow program itself, in jeopardy. (National Archives)

Secret

S1038CN-183 (AAAS)

Ottawa Ont
18 Feb 59

Ref (1) CAE Report No. 21, Issue 2, dated 12 Jan 59 - "General
Policy and Programme for the Development, Demonstration
and Evaluation of the Arrow Weapon System" (sent to
CJS(W) on G-11 dated 6 Feb 59.

Air Member,
Canadian Joint Staff,
2450 Massachusetts Ave. NW,
Washington 8, D.C., USA.

Arrow Flight Test Programme
Data Required from Convair

1   Stage 1 of the Arrow Flight Test Programme, as detailed
in reference (1), is intended to clear the Arrow Weapon System to
a minimum standard in a predominant portion of its combat envelope
by an early date. The basic assumption underlying this "minimum"
approach to flight testing is that use can be made of the extensive
data and analysis which have resulted from the USAF F-106 programme.

2   The matter of obtaining F-106 data from Convair was discussed with the F-106 WSPO at WADC on 5 Dec 58 by representatives
of this Headquarters. The F-106 WSPO stated that they required
authority from USAFHQ to release Convair F106 flight test data and
analysis to the Canadian government and contractors. Further, the
F106 WSPO stated that, upon obtaining USAFHQ authority, they would
hold a meeting, with representation from HAC, Convair, AVRO and the
RCAF to define Canadian data and analysis requirements.

3   Although there has been no decision, as yet, on the
Arrow program continuation the RCAF is proceeding with all necessary
planning as though the project was continuing. You are therefore
requested to arrange for the necessary authority from USAFHQ which
will permit the RCAF and AVRO to obtain relevant flight test data,
analysis and results immediately the Arrow program goes ahead.

4   An interim report on the progress of negotiations is
requested.

(H. R. FOOTTIT) G/C

(H.R. Foottit) G/C
for CAS

F/L-K Thomassen/JM
2-0548

AMTS
Orig
Circ
Local (1)
Local (2)
File

This memo dated two days prior to termination proves the RCAF was
still expecting the Arrow program to proceed. (National Archives)

CANCELLED

10336N-80 (CAS)

APR 2 1959

MEMORANDUM

26 Mar 59

The Minister (Through Deputy Minister)

Arrow Cancellation - Disposal of Material

1   In your approval to my recommendation of
13 March 1959 on courses of action to be taken in respect
to disposal of materiel arising out of the cancellation of
the Arrow, you desired to be informed before final action
was taken on the method of disposal being considered for
the disposition of the airframes and the Iroquois engines.

2   Two methods may be followed:

(a) Declaring as surplus materiel to Crown Assets
Disposal agency. This course is not recommended for the reason that this agency has
the prerogative of selling this materiel in
its original state. This course could lead
to subsequent embarrassment, that is, airframe and engine could conceivably be placed
on public view or even, in fact, used as a
roadside stand. This, I am sure, you will
agree is most undesirable.

(b) Relinquishing any DND interest in the airframes and engines to DDP for ultimate
disposal by that agency. In this case DDP
can reduce it to scrap. This course is
recommended.

3   I would appreciate being advised whether you
concur in the method recommended.

(Hugh Campbell)
Air Marshal
Chief of the Air Staff.

cc: Deputy Minister.

D.M. May I have your comments
please Send/Leaders

This memo was first revealed publicly in *Storms of Controversy: The
Secret Avro Arrow Files Revealed* in 1992. In 1959, it was this memo
that began the chain of events leading to the physical destruction of
the Arrows. Note the written script by Pearkes. He is asking his deputy
minister for comment. Pearkes would not have required comments
from anyone if the order to destroy had in fact originated with Prime
Minister John Diefenbaker.

- 3 -   TOP SECRET

concerned lest we spend too much on rounding out the defence against

the manned bomber and not have the funds available to participate in the

development and production of defence against the ballistic missile.

Our second problem, which is much closer to us, is the rounding

out of the defence against the manned bomber. In this field we have been

co-operating with the United States for many years and now, with the

setting up of the Joint Air Defence Command in Colorado Springs, we should

be able to develop a joint system of operational control which will be more

effective in an emergency. However this arrangement is not likely to help

us in the production and provision of the necessary improvements in the

weapons systems to meet the continuing bomber threat.

As you are perhaps aware, we have had under development in

Canada a supersonic aircraft known as the CF105, designed to deal with

the manned bomber threat after the early 1960's. We have had the

greatest possible co-operation with the United States Air Force in the

development of a type of aircraft which was considered by both countries

to be a requirement for the air defence of North America during the 1960's.

This aircraft is to be equipped with the U.S. Navy weapon the "Sparrow"

and a large part of the electronic equipment will have U.S. content. It is

expected that the total United States content in the CF105 will be approxi-

mately 20% in the development and pre-production aircraft and 10 to 15%

if this aircraft goes into production. The development of this aircraft to

date has cost $250 million, and its development will be continued for the

next two or three years, to cost about $530 million, making a total of

$780 million. Our requirements for this aircraft will be relatively small,

somewhere around 100, and therefore the individual cost of the aircraft

will be about $5 million, plus the cost of development. If this were the

only requirement for our air defence, we could perhaps make provision

for it in our succeeding defence budgets; but in order that aircraft of this

...4

TOP SECRET

TOP SECRET

- 4 -

type and the type to be used by the United States can operate in Canadian airspace we will be required to introduce a semi-automatic ground environment into Canada. The introduction of SAGE in Canada will cost in the neighbourhood of $107 million. Further improvements are required in the radar and other associated communications which will also bring greater expense within the next few years. NORAD has also recommended the introduction of the Bomarc missile into the Ottawa - North Bay area to supplement the manned interceptor, to round out the U.S. Bomarc chain, and to push the defences 250 miles further north. This development will be a further commitment of some $164 million.

All these commitments coming at this particular time, between 1960 and 1963, will tend to increase our defence budget by as much as 25 to 30%. (All these projects also contain a very large element of U.S. content, which may give rise to other fiscal problems) In approaching these joint problems in the past, we have been able to work out cost-sharing arrangements whereby each country contributed a portion of the capital costs and maintenance in Canada of these projects, which are designed for the defence of both countries but which because of geography had to be constructed in Canada. These projects included the Pinetree System, the DEW Line and the Mid Canada Line. We believe that perhaps a wider application of this principle of cost-sharing is now necessary to enable us to continue our joint defence measures without Canada having to shoulder heavy additional defence burdens because of our geographical position. Some approaches have already been made to a solution of these cost-sharing problems in informal discussions with the USAF. Some initial discussions on the cost-sharing of SAGE and Bomarc projects have been commenced. Suggestions have also been made in other quarters that perhaps the United States could assist in the production of the CF105 by equipping the U.S. squadrons at Harmon Field and Goose B; with this aircraft. These are all very useful approaches which are worthy

...5

TOP SECRET

These pages from the July 1958 top secret briefing of George Pearkes clearly states that provision could have been made for the Arrow but that it plus NORAD requirements would increase the defence budget 25 to 30 percent. (National Archives)

TOP SECRET

CHIEF OF THE GENERAL STAFF

21 Aug 58

Chairman
Chiefs of Staff

1   Reference your "Report on the Development of the CF105 and Associated Weapon System 1952-58" dated 19 Aug 58 and, in particular, paragraph 5 of the paper titled "Development of CF105 Weapon System".

2   Upon reading paragraph 5, one is left with the impression that our air defence plan is designed for the defence of Canada. My understanding is that our air defence plan is not for "the Defence of Canada", but is a part of a Canada-US air defence plan for the defence of North America. This Canada-US plan places first priority on the defence of SAC bases, second priority on certain other installations, and only third priority on certain centres of population in North America, of which four are in Canada, namely, Montreal, Toronto, Hamilton and Vancouver.

3   I think it is wrong to leave the impression with the Minister and the Government that our air defence plan is primarily for the defence of Canadian territory when, in fact, any defence of Canadian territory is but a by-product or extra dividend to the main purpose, which is the defence of SAC bases and Northeastern United States.

(HD Graham)
Lieutenant-General
Chief of the General Staff

TOP SECRET

This letter from Lieutenant-General H.D. Graham states clearly that the Canadian Air Defence plan was for the defence of American territory not that of Canada.

203

1035CT (DA'ng)

Ottawa, Ontario
30 Nov 60

Air Member
Canadian Joint Staff
2450 Massachusetts Ave NW
Washington 8 DC

Iroquois - Engine History & Status

     As requested by W/C AW Armstrong the history and status of the Iroquois engine have been prepared. The status was taken in Feb 59 but was recently checked and has not varied appreciably. Engine X116 has been shipped to the United Kingdom for inspection by Bristol/Siddeley. All other engines and parts have been stored and preserved. Engine X106 was, of course, removed from the B47 before the aircraft was returned to the USAF.

     It is estimated the 50 hour PFRT engine could be prepared in 2 months and the test completed to clear the mechanical configuration in 3 to 4 months. Should a slightly more advanced configuration be required, such as an additional stage to the HP spool as Orenda proposed to the USAF, the timing would be in the order of 8 months.

     The six new test cells, with simulataneous data recording instrumentation, could be employed for Iroquois development. The altitude test tunnel could be completed in approximately 8 months.

     The engine history as tabled is a frank and factual resume and, although many problems and errors are mentioned, it is RCAF technical opinion the engine had overcome the major mechanical difficulties. The aerodynamic configuration, as stated in the historical summary, was cleared by a 50 Hr PFRT before the program terminated.

(WR Cole) W/C
AEng 5

W/C WR Cole/DB
6-6437

Orig
Circ
Local
File

This memo shows Iroquois engine X116 was shipped to Bristol/Siddeley in the United Kingdom, where it remains today.

CABINET PAPER—PRIVILEGED

Property of the White House—For Authorised Persons Only

CURRENT SITUATION

    The present strong interest of Canada in production sharing is the result of the decision made by the Canadian government in September to curtail drastically the CF 105 supersonic interceptor aircraft program, and to introduce into the Canadian air defense system the U.S. produced BOMARC missile and SAGE control equipment. This decision recognized the rapid strides being made in missiles by both the U. S. and Russia and the high cost of the CF 105 in relation to its potential contribution to North American defense.

    The specially developed Astra fire control and Sparrow missile systems for the CF 105 were terminated in September, with the subsequent cancellation of the complete program 20 February. Reaction to this decision from the press and the opposition has been most unfavorable, and will greatly increase the strong pressures which have existed on production sharing.

    With over $300 million already expended in the development of this system and a potential production program of another $1.25 billion for 100 aircraft, this was a heavy blow to Canadian industry and the pride of their people. The implications on the Canadian economy can be measured in terms of their defense budget, which is in the order of $1 billion annually.

    The decision to terminate the CF 105 was predicated in part on the agreements to provide Canada with better chances to share in production of defense items of mutual interest. The Deputy Minister of Defense Production has stated in effect that if production sharing does not work, Canada has no alternative but to use her limited defense budget for whatever items she is able to produce, whether or not it makes a maximum contribution to North American defense.

    Since September negotiations have been underway on the basis of Canada paying one-third of the cost of two 30 missile BOMARC sites, one SAGE super combat center and a radar improvement program. The Canadian share of $125 million would be associated with site construction and unit equipment, with the United States share of about $250 million applied to the procurement of BOMARC and SAGE technical equipment. It has been agreed that this is the only practical way to make the split, however, the Canadians fear it will not give them any assurance of sharing in the production of the electronic and missile hardware. Since construction on Canadian soil is normally done by Canadian contract, Canadians are assured that substantially all of their $125 million will be spent in Canada in any event. However, they do not want to become a "brick and mortar" economy.

    The Air Force has consistently opposed any agreement to assure Canada a given share of the production, based on the conviction that technical competence, cost and delivery considerations must be the deciding criteria. If Canadian competence can be demonstrated and reasonable decisions agreed to on individual items, it is our position that the end result will be a reasonable share for the Canadians.

    From the recent statement by the Prime Minister to Parliament it is assumed that the Canadians have accepted the U. S. position on this matter.

CABINET PAPER   C J-59-59

For Information   3-5-59

This secret American document notes the impact of the production sharing arrangements on the termination of the Arrow. The rest of it explains that the arrangements were not working. (Eisenhower Library)

CF-105 ARROW PROGRAM

I PRE-TERMINATION ACTIVITY

1. GENERAL BACKGROUND

The CF-105 Arrow Program commenced as a research project in 1953. In 1955 contracts were placed with Avro and Orenda for full scale development including the production of airframes and engines for use in an evaluation program. Subsequently, work was commenced on allied programs known as Astra, which was to provide an integrated electronic system, and Sparrow, which was to provide the armament. The two latter programs were cancelled in September, 1958, and were replaced by the MA-1 electronic system and the Falcon Missile.

By February, 1959, the following quantities of airframes and engines had been ordered from Avro and Orenda.

Avro Aircraft Limited -

        5 Mk.1 Aircraft   (J-75 engines)
       32 Mk.2 Aircraft   (Iroquois engines)

Orenda Engines Ltd. -

       20 prototype Iroquois engines
       87 preproduction engines

2. PRE-TERMINATION COSTS

The cost of work completed before termination and the estimated costs to complete 37 aircraft plus 83 aircraft are detailed below. Costs vary slightly from those previously reported as a result of audits.

COST OF 37 AIRCRAFT PROGRAM
(Millions of dollars)

	To 20 Feb/59	To Complete	Total
AIRFRAMES			
Development	67.7	24.9	92.6
Tooling	30.3	13.9	44.2
Production & Support	81.9	126.5	208.4
ENGINES			
Development	55.4	53.0	108.4
Tooling	13.6	3.6	17.2
Production & Support	58.4	10.0	68.4
MA-1	1.7	13.3	15.0
J-75 & MISCELLANEOUS	9.6	12.6	22.2
TOTAL 37 A/C	318.6	257.8	576.4

ADDITIONAL 83 AIRCRAFT

	Total
Production at $3.75 each	311.2
Support (electronics, equipment and spares)	181.0
Combat stock of Falcon missiles	42.6
	1,111.2

NOTE: The additional 83 aircraft would have provided for the revised program of 20 development/evaluation aircraft plus 100 operational aircraft.

3. PHYSICAL PROGRESS & PLANNED DELIVERY

5 Mark 1 aircraft had been completed and flown at the termination date. The next three aircraft were in the final assembly line. Thirteen prototype Iroquois engines had been completed and 7 were in process. No Iroquois engines had been installed in aircraft.

Had the program continued on the basis of 120 aircraft, deliveries would have been:

1959	1960	1961	1962	1963	Total
12	12	30	57	9	120

II POST TERMINATION

1. ADMINISTRATION

An interdepartmental Ad Hoc Committee with representation from National Defence, Audit Services and Treasury Board staff, was established by DDP to co-ordinate all matters relating to termination of the program, to set policies and to monitor the settlement of problems arising from termination. Special contracts were placed with Avro and Orenda to consolidate all terminated contracts and to ensure the orderly channelling of contractual matters.

2. EFFECT ON INDUSTRY

The immediate effect of termination was felt most by employees of the two prime contractors. All employees were released the same day but rehiring began immediately and the re-engaged employees worked extra hours to inaugurate procedures to handle termination. Employment dropped at Avro from 8,800 to 2,000 and at Orenda from 5,000 to 1,100. Subcontractors in the Toronto Area were similarly affected but to a lesser degree. The prime contractors and some of the major subcontractors were faced with heavy overhead costs which had to be absorbed by greatly reduced work loads.

Final costs of the Arrow program that first appeared in *Storms of Controversy's* third edition. Completing the development of thirty-seven aircraft would have cost $257.8 million, yet the program was cancelled. It is now known that separate from the Arrow project, the Department of National Defence actually returned over $220 million in unspent funds from other programs — money that could perhaps have been used to complete those Arrows. (National Archives)

AVRO AIRCRAFT
- LIMITED -

SECRET

MINUTES OF SPECIAL MEETINGS NUMBERED 25 OF
MANAGEMENT COMMITTEE OF AVRO AIRCRAFT LIMITED
HELD IN THE BOARD ROOM, MALTON, REFERENCE
ARROW TERMINATION - AT 2 P.M., THURSDAY, THE
19TH DAY OF FEBRUARY, 1959.

MEETING NO. M25

PRESENT: J. L. PLANT (CHAIRMAN)
                        E. F. ALDERTON
                        J. C. FLOYD
                        G. HAKE
                        J. A. MORLEY
                        W. H. RIGGS
                        D. H. ROGERS

IN ATTENDANCE: A. H. STEWART
                        N. E. KINDELL (SECRETARY)

MEMBER ABSENT: J. TURNER

After noting the regrettable absence of Mr. J. Turner who was confined to bed sick,
the Chairman opened by stating that he had called this Special Meeting of Management
Committee by reason that it was necessary for the Committee to formulate Management
plans in the event that the Government decided to terminate the ARROW Program on or
before March 31st next. While the Chairman recognised that the formulation of such
plans (quite apart from their execution) was part of the costs of carrying out of the
Government's termination instructions, and that the proper task of the Company at this
time was to get on with the important job of developing the ARROW with the highest
priority in the best interests of Canada and its people, nevertheless certain preliminary thinking was needed to be done by Management in the unfortunate event that the
Canadian Government, in its wisdom, resolved to cancel the ARROW Program. The Chairman
then stated that he need not caution the Meeting that the matters to be discussed and
the action necessary as a result of subsequent discussion were of the highest confidential
nature and were not to be discussed or delegated to subordinates except as specifically
permitted in the Minutes appearing hereafter. Discussion then ensued and the decisions
reached appear minuted under the appropriate subject headings listed below.

M25-1   CONTINUING WORK PROGRAMS AFTER ARROW TERMINATION

        That Mr. Morley shall forthwith provide under confidential cover to Members a
        statement of the work that will be under firm contract after termination of the
        ARROW Program, and for which fund support will be forthcoming, listing:

                Nature of Contract;
                Brief description of work required;
                Schedule and timing;
                Dollar content by fiscal years.

        That based on this information, Members (including Special Projects Group) as
        noted below shall compile at the earliest possible date the following inform-
        ation:-

        (a) Facilities Required

This record of this meeting dated 19 February 1959, clearly shows A, V,
Roe was continuing the Avro Arrow but was making preliminary plans
should the government elect to cancel the program on or before 31
March. The very next day, before full preparations could be made, the
Arrow was cancelled. (Document courtesy AHFC.)

Notes

Chapter 1

1   Shaw, E.K. *There Never Was an Arrow*, Ottawa: Steel Rail Publishing, 1979.

2   On January 28, 2002, the World Trade Organization ruled that Canada had violated international trade laws in helping Bombardier in the Air Wisconsin deal. In response the Canadian government indicated the deals were closed and would not be revisited, in light of the WTO ruling. The *Ottawa Citizen*, January 29, 2002.

3   Shaw, E.K. *There Never Was an Arrow*.

4   Ibid.

5   *Jet Age*

6   *Maclean's*, December 1, 1949.

7   By 1955, Floyd had become a Fellow Royal Aeronautical Society and had been chairman of the Toronto section of the Institute of the Aeronautical Sciences. He was a member of the National

Research Council Sub-Committee on Aeronautical Research and had presented a number of papers to engineering societies in both Canada and the United States. The data and information he presented was eventually incorporated into standard textbooks on jet aircraft power systems. In 1951, Floyd became the first non-American to be awarded the Wright Brother's Medal, the Nobel Prize of aviation, for his work on the first commercial jet transport to fly in North America, the C-102 Jetliner.

Chapter 2

8   RG 70 Volume 401 File 14008-8-1949.
9   Ibid.
10   Ibid.
11   *Maclean's*, December 1, 1949.
12   RG 24 Volume 5403 File S-60-3-71
13   Ibid
14   *Engineering Journal*, November 1949.
15   RG 12 Volume 760 File 5010-10-147V2
16   Ibid.
17   Ibid.
18   Ibid

Chapter 3

19   RG 24 Volume 5403 File S-60-3-71
20   Ibid V3
21   RG 24 Volume 5403 File S-60-3-71
22   Ibid.
23   RG 12 Volume 666 File Air Services 22-7-7
24   Ibid.
25   Ibid.
26   RG 24 Volume 5403 File S-60-3-71
27   Ibid.
28   Ibid.
29   Ibid.
30   RG 12 Volume 760 File 5010-10-147V3
31   Ibid.

Chapter 4

32 MG 31 D 224 Volume 7 or House of Commons May 30, 1952

33 MG 31 D 224 Volume 7

34 The *London Free Press*, "Crash Memorial A Personal Project For Area Farmer," April 5, 2001.

35 MG 31 D 224 Volume 7

36 Ibid.

37 Campagna, Palmiro, *The UFO Files: The Canadian Connection Exposed*, Toronto: Stoddart Publishing, 1997.

38 Avrocar Flight Evaluation 270 921 AFSC, Defense Technical Information Center, Virginia

Chapter 5

39 Campagna, Palmiro. *Storms of Controversy: The Secret Avro Arrow Files Revealed* 3rd edition, Toronto: Stoddart Publishing, 1998.

40 Department of Defense Appropriations for 1961, Hearings Before the Subcommittee on Appropriations House of Representatives, Eighty-sixth Congress Second Session Re Appraisal of Air Defense Program Revisions in 1960 and 1961 Air Force Programs.

41 Crosby, Ann Denholm. *Dilemmas in Defence Decision-Making*, New York: St. Martin's Press, Inc, 1998.

42 Ibid.

43 Ibid.

44 Cohen, J. *The Role of the Arrow in the Defense of North America*, 72/Tactics/19, Issue 2, January 19, 1959.

45 Ibid.

46 Ibid.

47 Department of National Defence, Directorate of History Files 73/1223, Ottawa.

48 RG 49 Volume 427 File 159-44-B, part 1

49 Eisenhower Library, File: DDE Trip to Canada, Memcons, July 8–11, 1958, Canada-U.S. Defence Problems.

50 Ibid.

Chapter 6

51   RG 24 Volume 83-84-099 File 1933-103-2 V.3

52   73/1223 series 1 Raymont Collection, Directorate of History, Department of National Defence, Ottawa, Canada.

53   Ibid.

54   RG 24 Volume 83-84/049-1593 File 1933-03-2 (Vol2)

55   McLin, Jon, B. *Canada's Changing Defence Policy, 1957–1963*, Baltimore: Johns Hopkins Press, 1967.

56   RG 24 Volume 83-84-099 File 1933-103-2 V.3

57   Ibid.

58   Ibid.

59   Ibid.

60   RG 49 Interim 135 Volume 67 File 151-9-1 part 3.

61   Department of National Defence, Directorate of History Files 73/1223 Series V File 2500E.

62   Ibid.

63   Department of National Defence, Directorate of History, File 113.014 D1, NADOP 59-63

64   Ibid.

65   Department of Defense Appropriations for 1961, Hearings Before the Subcommittee on Appropriations House of Representatives, Eighty-sixth Congress Second Session Re Appraisal of Air Defense Program Revisions in 1960 and 1961 Air Force Programs.

66   Eisenhower Library, Cabinet Paper, *Cooperation with Canada in Defense*, from CI-59-59, dated 3-5-59.

67   Ibid.

68   Ibid.

Chapter 7

69   MG 26 N2 File: National Defence, General, Volume 110

70   Department of National Defence, Directorate of History, 73/1223 Series 1 File 68, The Development of the Introduction of the Bomarc Ground to Air Missile and the MB-1 Air to Air Guided Missile on Canadian Manned Interceptors for the RCAF for the defence of Canada.

71   Ranelagh, John. *The Agency: The Rise and Decline of the CIA*, New York: Cambridge Publishing Limited, 1986.

72   MG 26 N2 File: National Defence, General, Vol 110

73   Dr. Roy Pearkes interview April 1967, from University of Victoria, British Columbia.

74   Ibid.

75   Lowe, Frank. "Is the RCAF Obsolete", *Weekend Magazine*, Vol. 9. No. 33, 1959.

76   Eisenhower Library, memorandum For Meeting With Prime Minister Diefenbaker

77   Department of National Defence, Directorate of History, File 79/469, Folder 19.

78   Ibid.

79   MG 26 N2 File: National Defence, General, Vol 110

80   Eisenhower Library, Summary Record United States-Canada Political-Military Meeting November 19, 1958.

81   Eisenhower Library, CI-59-59, 3-5-59 Cooperation With Canada in Defense, CABINET PAPER - PRIVILEGED

82   Eisenhower Library, memorandum For Meeting With Prime Minister Diefenbaker

83   RG 24 Accession 83-84/216 Volume 3592 File 964-104-3 vol 3

84   RG 24 Volume 6435 File 1038CN - 183 Vol 10.

85   MG 26 N2 File: National Defence, General, Vol 110

Chapter 8

86   Directorate of History, Department of National defence, 73/1223.

87   RG 24 Volume 24097 File DRBS 9731-11

88   The government eventually paid Orenda for their out of pocket development costs. In this way Orenda's private venture in the PS-13 became property of the crown. This explains why, in 1959, the Iroquois could be terminated and destroyed. Like the Arrow, it was government property. Cancellation of the Iroquois resulted in the closing of the Orenda test establishment at Nobel near Parry Sound.

89   Directorate of History, Department of National defence, 73/1223.

90   Ibid.

91 Personal Correspondence, Footit to Campagna March 8, 1991. (First discussed in *Storms* original edition.)

92 House of Commons, Special Committee on Defence Expenditures, Chairman Halpenny, Minutes of Proceedings and Evidence, No 1, Tuesday May 3, 1960, Wednesday May 11, 1960, Expenditures for Fiscal Year 1958–1958.

93 "An Open Letter To The Prime Minister, Don't Insult me, Mr. Chretien", The *Ottawa Citizen*, December 28, 2001. At the time of the prime minister's comments, spending for the military was down while equipment, especially helicopters, were aging and needed replacement.

Chapter 9

94 RG 24 Volume 6435 File 1038CM - 183-5.

95 The *Globe and Mail*, "U.S. security crackdown could ground Canadian Satellite", June 29, 1999.

96 RG 24 Volume 6435 File 1038CM - 183-5.

97 Ibid.

98 Callwood, June. "The Day The Iroquois Flew," *Maclean's*, February 1, 1958.

Chapter 10

99 Campagna, Palmiro. *Storms of Controversy: The Secret Avro Arrow Files Revealed*, third edition, Toronto: Stoddart Publishing, 1998.

100 Other Avro inductees to the Aviation Hall of Fame are Jan Zurakowski, 1974; Jim Floyd, 1993; Don Rogers, 1998; Bill Baker, 2000; and Paul Dilworth, 2000.

Chapter 11

101 Moore, Christopher, "What Is It about The Avro Arrow," *The Beaver* magazine, August/September 1999.

102 Ibid.

103 Personal Correspondence, Paul Hellyer to Palmiro Campagna, dated April 6, 1995.

104 MG 32 Series B19 Volume 29 File 44-47 CF 105 Arrow Aircraft Vol.1 Part 1 1957–1958.

Bibliography

BOOKS

A Dictionary of Accounting. Oxford University Press, 1999.

Campagna, Palmiro. *The UFO Files: The Canadian Connection Exposed*. Toronto: Stoddart Publishing, 1997.

Campagna, Palmiro. *Storms of Controversy: The Secret Avro Arrow Files Revealed*, third edition. Toronto: Stoddart Publishing, 1998.

Crosby, Ann Denholm. *Dilemmas in Defence Decision-Making*, New York: St. Martin's Press, Inc. 1998.

Dow, James. *The Arrow*. James Lorimar and Co., 1979.

Floyd, Jim. *The Avro Canada C102 Jetliner*. Toronto: The Boston Mills Press, 1986.

Goodspeed, D.J. Lieutenant-Colonel, *The Armed Forces of Canada 1867–1967*, Ottawa: Directorate of History, Department of National Defence, 1967.

McLin, Jon B. *Canada's Changing Defence Policy, 1957–1963*. Baltimore: Johns Hopkins Press, 1967.

Milberry, Larry. *The Avro CF-100*. Toronto: CANAV Books, 1987.

Ranelagh, John, *The Agency: The Rise and Decline of the CIA*. New York: Cambridge Publishing Limited, 1986.

Shaw, E.K. *There Never Was an Arrow*. Ottawa: Steel Rail Publishing, 1979.

Smye, Fred. *Canadian Aviation and the Avro Arrow*. Oakville: Randy Smye, Ontario,1988.

Pigott, Peter. *Flying Canucks II: Pioneers of Canadian Aviation*. Toronto: Hounslow Press, 1997.

Stewart, Greig. *Shutting Down the National Dream*. Scarborough: McGraw-Hill Ryerson Limited, 1988.

Wilkinson, Les et al. *Arrow*. Toronto: Boston Mills Press, 1986.

Zuuring, Peter. *The Arrow Scrapbook*. Dalkeith, Ontario: Arrow Alliance Press, 1999.

ARTICLES

Anglin, Gerald. "Our All-Out Gamble For Jet Supremacy", *Maclean's* magazine, Toronto: Maclean Hunter Publishing Ltd., December 1, 1949.

Aviation Week. "First Jet Transport: Avro XC-102", Nov 1, 1948.

Avrocar Flight Evaluation 270 921 AFSC, Defense Technical Information Center, Virginia.

Baldwin, Derek. "Avro arrow test model found in lake: 40 years after flight: Scaled-down jet survived supersonic impact with water", The *National Post*. June 19, 1999.

Baxter, James. The *Ottawa Citizen*, "Canada won't end cheap loans: Pettigrew", January 29, 2002.

Bliss, Michael. "Shutting Down the Avro Myth", The *Globe and Mail*. *Report on Business* magazine, February 1989, Vol 5 No 8.

Callwood, June. "The Day The Iroquois Flew", *Maclean's* magazine. Toronto: Maclean Hunter Publishing Ltd., February 1, 1958.

Cohen, J. *The Role of the Arrow in the Defense of North America*. 72/Tactics/19, Issue 2, January 19, 1959.

Connant, Melvin. *Foreign Affairs, an American Quarterly Review*. April 1962.

Bibliography

Corcoran, Terence. Editorial, *Financial Post*. January 11, 2001.

Das Satya. "Missiles of another war", The *Edmonton Journal*. April 30, 2000.

Davis, John R. "Can Roe make the big switch?", Executive Decision, March, 1959.

Elliott, James. "ARROW-NAUTICAL History", The *Hamilton Spectator*. October 1, 2001.

The Engineering Journal. "Inferiority Complex", *The Journal of the Engineering Institute of Canada*, Toronto: November 1949.

Gordon, Mary. "Women honoured for pioneer roles in legal profession", The *Ottawa Citizen*. June 15, 2001.

Harbron, John D. "Avro talks up new ideas", Executive, April 1961.

Johnson, Brian D. "Raising the Arrow", *Maclean's* magazine. Toronto: Maclean Hunter Publishing Ltd., January 13, 1997.

Keith, Ronald, "Fact Versus Rumours-An Appraisal of the Avro Projects", *Canadian Aviation*. April, 1952.

The *Leader-Post* (Regina), "NORAD project axed", May 8, 2000.

The *London Free Press*, "London Space Dreams Lift Off, Arrow Shuttle Planners Certain Space Tourism Can Fly", January 15, 2001.

Ibid. "NORAD membership tied to missile defence System", October 5, 1999.

Ibid. "Crash Memorial A Personal Project For Area Farmer", April 5, 2001.

Ibid. "Crash Memorial A Personal Project For Area Farmer", May 5, 2001.

Lowe, Frank. "Is the RCAF Obsolete", *Weekend Magazine*. Vol. 9. No. 33, 1959.

MacKenzie, Maj-Gen. Lewis. "An Open Letter To The Prime Minister, Don't Insult me Mr. Chretien", The *Ottawa Citizen*. December 28, 2001.

Mackinnon, Mark and Bertrand Marotte. "Bombardier ties with Ottawa run deep. May Have helped win loan agreement", The *Globe and Mail*. January 13, 2001.

McArthur, Jack. "Dosco: A story of British disaster abroad", The *Toronto Star*. May 14, 1968.

Mitchinson, Paul, "The enemy within: KGB espionage was more

extensive than even the McCarthyites imagined", The *National Post*. October 14, 1999.

Moore, Christopher. "What Is It about The Avro Arrow", *The Beaver* magazine. August/September 1999.

NORAD, Office of Information Services, various pamphlets concerning SAGE/Bomarc and NORAD workings.

Pre-Flight (various issues), the Aerospace Heritage Foundation.

Pugliese, David. "Canada: missile crash site", The *Ottawa Citizen*. May 2, 2001.

Pugliese, David. "Fighting a losing battle", The *Ottawa Citizen*. January 27, 2001.

Robertson, Fraser, "Looking Into Business", The *Globe and Mail*. August 10, 1957.

Scoffield, Heather. "U.S. security crackdown could ground Canadian satellite", The *Globe and Mail*. June 29, 1999.

Scoffield, Heather. "Hawker-Siddeley shareholders tender to sweetened Glacier bid", The *Globe and Mail*. September 3, 2001.

The History of Air Canada, Air Canada Pamphlet, circa 1967.

Trickey, Mike. "Help pay or lose protection, Canada told", The *Ottawa Citizen*. May 3, 2000.

Turcott, Yvon, vice-president public affairs, Bombardier. "Bombardier is repaying all federal loans", The *Ottawa Citizen*. February 7, 2002.

Walker, David M. "Bring knowledge management to DOD", *Jane's Defence Weekly*. May 30, 2001.

Young, Scott. "The Way Up", *Jet Age* magazine. A.V. Roe Canada Limited, Winter Issue.

Zurakowski, Janusz. "Horizons Unlimited", *Jet Age* magazine. 1952.

CANADIAN ARCHIVAL RECORDS

RG 12 Volume 760 File 5010-10-147V2
RG 12 Volume 760 File 5010-10-147V3
RG 12 Volume 666 File Air Services 22-7-7
RG 24 Accession 83-84/216 Volume 3592 File 964-104-3 volume 3
RG 24 Volume 1556 File 1913-103
RG 24 Volume 5403 File S-60-3-71

RG 24, Volume 6255, File 1035-CT pt 3

RG 24 Volume 6435 File 1038CM - 183-2 and also -5

RG 24 Volume 6435 File 1038CN - 183-4

RG 24 Volume 6435 File 1038CN - 183 Volume 10.

RG 24 Volume 6474 File 1035CT-100 pt 3 and 7

RG 24 Volume 5403 File S-60-3-71 V3

RG 24 Volume 24097, File DRBS 9731-11

RG 24 Volume 83-84-099 File 1933-103-2 V.3

RG 24 Volume 83-84/049-1593 File 1933-03-2 Volume 2

RG 49 Volume 427 File 159-44-B, part 1

RG 49 Interim 135 Volume 67 File 151-9-1, part 3

RG 70 Volume 401 File 14008-8-1949

MG 26 N2 File: National Defence, General, Volume 110

MG 31 D 224 Volume 7

MG 32 Series B19 Volume 29 File 44-47 CF 105 Arrow Aircraft Volume.1 Part 1 1957-1958

73/1223 series 1 Raymont Collection, Directorate of History, Department of National Defence, Ottawa, Canada.

73/1223 Series V File 2500D and E Raymont Collection, Directorate of History, Department of National Defence, Ottawa, Canada.

File: 113.014 D1, NADOP 59-63, Department of National Defence, Directorate of History.

File 79/469, Folder 19 Department of National Defence, Directorate of History.

73/1223 Series 1 File 68, The Development of the Introduction of the Bomarc Ground to Air Missile and the MB-1 Air to Air Guided Missile on Canadian Manned Interceptors for the RCAF for the defence of Canada. Department of National Defence, Directorate of History.

Dr. Roy Pearkes interview April 1967, from University of Victoria, British Columbia.

House of Commons, Special Committee on Defence Expenditures, Chairman Halpenny, Minutes of Proceedings and Evidence, No 1, Tuesday May 3 1960, Wednesday May 11, 1960, Expenditures for Fiscal Year 1958-1958.

AMERICAN ARCHIVAL RECORDS

Department of Defense Appropriations for 1961, Hearings Before the Subcommittee on Appropriations House of Representatives, Eighty-sixth Congress Second Session Re Appraisal of Air Defense Program Revisions in 1960 and 1961 Air Force Programs.

Eisenhower Library, memorandum For Meeting With Prime Minister Diefenbaker

Eisenhower Library, Summary Record United States- Canada Political-Military Meeting November 19, 1958.

Eisenhower Library, CI-59-59, 3-5-59 Cooperation With Canada in Defense, CABINET PAPER - PRIVILEGED

Eisenhower Library, Preparations for President's Visit to Ottawa, May-June papers 1958

Eisenhower Library, File: DDE Trip to Canada, Memcons, July 8-11, 1958, Canada-U.S. defence Problems.

Personal Correspondence, Footit to Campagna March 8, 1991 (First discussed in Storms original edition).

Personal Correspondence, Paul Hellyer to Campagna dated April 6, 1995.

Index

ABM (anti-ballistic missile), 101, 102
Acme Screw and Gear Limited, 62
Adamson, Rodney, 57, 59, 70, 128
ADC (Air Defense Command), 71–74
AHFC (Aerospace Heritage Foundation of Canada), 148, 156, 170
AICBM (anti-intercontinental ballistic missile), 104, 105
Air Defense Planning Group, 89
Air Registration Board, 36
Air Wisconsin Airlines, 13
Aircraft & Armament Experimental Test Establishment, 65
AITA (Air Industries and Transport Association), 124, 126
Alaskan Air Command, 71
Algoma Steel Corporation, 62
American Airlines, 39

American Electric Boat Company, 22
American Joint Chiefs of Staff, 73, 74
Ames, Jack, 158
AN/FSQ-7, computer, 78
Andrew, Christopher, 161
Arrow 2000 project, 162
Associated Aircraft Limited, 14
Astra fire control system, 123, 136, 138, 142, 149-153, 179
Atkin, Edgar H., 19
atomic warhead, 77, 94, 97, 113
Avery, Burt, 154
Avon engine, 23, 26, 28, 51, 54
Avro, 11, 14, 18, 27, 31, 32, 42, 43, 46-56, 58, 59, 61, 63-70, 78, 81, 82, 83, 87, 90, 114, 123, 124, 125, 128-132, 134-137, 139-143, 146-148, 150-155, 157-162, 165, 166, 169-175, 178

Avro Arrow *see also* CF 105, 11, 43, 63, 65, 70, 78, 81, 87, 90, 143, 165, 171, 178
Avrocar, 66, 68-70, 124, 157

B47, 155, 156
Bain, Jim, 23, 26, 27, 32
Baker, James T., 38
Baker, R.J., 48
Battle of Britain, 64, 65
Bell, Ralph, 19
Bennett, Henry, 55
Bickell, John Paris, 16, 17, 19
Bliss, Michael, 42
BMEWS (Ballistic Missile Early Warning System), 74, 101
Boeing, 12, 14, 32, 50, 79, 80, 106, 121
Bomarc, 74-103, 105-110, 115-117, 121, 122, 128, 133, 135, 137, 138, 142, 145, 148, 152, 153, 176, 177
Bombardier, 12, 13, 39, 50, 54, 58, 62, 124, 146, 150, 174, 178,
Boyd, Winnett, 20, 54
Bras D'Or, 126, 130
Bristol Aircraft, 61, 156
Browne, Herbert, 95
Brownridge, Earle K., 156
Bush, George, 101

C-102 jetliner, 32, 43, 44, 47, 52
C-103, 52
CAA (Civil Aeronautics Administration), 38
Cabinet Defence Committee, 90, 97, 100, 130-132, 134, 135, 137
Callwood, June, 160
Campbell, Hugh, 97, 118, 123, 142, 166, 176
Canadair Limited, 12
Canadian Applied Research., 62
Canadian Car & Foundry Company, 14

Canadian Department of Transport, 35
Canadian General Transit, 62
Canadian Government Trans-Atlantic Air Service, 21
Canadian National Railway, 21
Canadian Pacific Railway, 21, 157
Canadian Steel Foundries Limited, 62
Canadian Steel Improvements Limited, 61, 156
Canuck, see also CF-100, 77
CANUS 59, 115, 116, 122
Carravelle, 50
Central Aircraft Limited, 15
Central Intelligence Agency, 66, 115
Certificate of Airworthiness, 35-38, 45, 48
CF-100, 38, 41, 42, 43, 48, 50-59, 63-67, 70, 72, 73, 77, 90, 103, 112-114, 116, 118, 129, 130, 133, 135, 137, 140, 172
CF105, 93, 121, 123, 127, 133
CF-EJD-X *see also Jetliner*, 32
Chamberlin, Jim, 20, 161
Chidlaw, Benjamin, 74
Chief of the Air Staff, 49, 55, 90, 97, 104, 105, 122, 123, 132, 137, 138, 142, 151, 152, 166, 176
Chinook, 20, 54
Chrysler, 68
CINCNORAD, 76, 101, 104, 107, 121, 122
Civil Aeronautics Authority, 36
Civil Aeronautics Board, 49
Claxton, Brooke, 55
Cockshutt Plow Company, 15, 61
Colorado Springs, 73, 119
Comet, 25, 30, 31, 38, 47
commercial jet, 12, 23, 31, 173
Committee on the Postwar Manufacture of Aircraft, 19
Comparative Cost Analysis of the Triangular Route Toronto–New York–Montreal–Toronto When

Using Either The AVRO Jetliner, or The Canadair North Star, 45
Computing Devices of Canada Ltd., 149
CONAD (Continental Air Defence Command), 74
Connant, Melvin, 115
Continental Air Command, 72
Convair, 53
Cooke-Craigie, 131
Cooper-Slipper, Mike, 65
Cope, Peter, 64
Cowley, A.T.N., 36, 45, 52, 53
Crosby, Ann Denholm, 75, 76, 85
Crown Assets Disposal Corporation, 168, 169
Curtis, Wilf, 18, 20, 55
CUSSAT (Canada–US Scientific Advisory Team), 92, 97
Czerwinski, Waclaw, 55

Daciuk, Henry, 168
Davies, Stuart, 56
Davis, R.C., 44
De Havilland Aircraft, 14
death row, 167
Defence Research Board, 66, 90, 132, 137, 138
Deisher, Walter P., 19
Department of Defence Production, 99, 108, 132, 166
destruction of Arrows, 165-168, 176
DEW (Distant Early Warning line), 74, 102, 113
Diefenbaker, John George, 75, 76, 96, 111, 114, 120, 123, 137, 157, 160, 165, 166, 176
Dilworth, Paul B., 20
Distinguished Flying Cross, 65
Dobson, Sir Roy, 11, 17, 18, 19, 28, 53, 157, 158
Dominion Steel and Coal Corporation, 62
Douglas DC-9, 50
Douglas DC-3, 22

Douglas, James H., 87
Dulles, John Foster, 87, 116
Dyment, Jack, 23, 25, 27, 32

Earnest, Les, 81, 84
Easton, Jack, 161
ECM (electronic counter measures), 81, 151, 152
Eggleton, Art, 95
Eisenhower, President Dwight D., 160
Embraer, 13
Erb, Brian, 162

F-101B Voodoo, 77
F-102 Delta Dagger, 77
F-106 Delta Dart, 77, 112
F-108, 84, 102, 103, 105, 107, 177
F-89, 77, 103
Fairchild Aircraft Limited, 14
Falcon missile, 77, 97, 132, 142, 143, 150, 153
Federal Aircraft Limited, 14, 17
Fleet Aircraft Limited, 14
Flight Test Center, 69
Floyd, James C., (Jim), 20, 23, 24, 25, 28-31, 42, 47-50, 52, 53, 55, 56, 66, 68, 140, 170, 174
fly-away cost, 129, 136, 142, 143, 154, 179
flying saucers, 67
Foo Fighters, 67
Footit, Ray, 55, 123
Fort Eustis, 69
Foulkes, General Charles, 71, 75, 85, 101, 105, 115, 116, 121, 122, 128, 134, 176
Frost, John, 20, 56, 67, 69

gap-filler radar, 86, 90, 91, 93, 99, 100, 134
Gartshore, David, 169, 170
Gas Turbine Division, 20, 171
Gates, Thomas S. Jr, 120
GE J-79, 156
General Dynamics, 22

General Motors, 15
Genie missile, 138, 147, 151, 152, 153, 154
Glacier Ventures International Corporation, 158
Gloster Aircraft Company, 65
Gloster Meteor, 65
Goodyear, 38, 68
Gordon E. Cox, 38
Gordon, Crawford, 12, 21, 29, 37, 38, 51-53, 55, 61, 157, 165, 166
Graham, H.D., 71
Gray. I.A, 44
Green, Howard C., 120
Grinyer, Charles A., 154, 171

Hart, R.S., 16
Haswell, Stan, 66
Hawker-Siddeley, 17-19, 26, 28, 62, 124, 158, 179
Hellyer, Paul, 143, 176
Hendricks, Air Vice Marshal, 147, 151, 152
Hiller, 68
Hovercraft, 69
Howe, Clarence Decatur, 16, 17, 19, 21-23, 26, 28, 32, 34, 36, 37, 38, 41-43, 45, 47, 50, 51, 53, 55, 58, 133
Hughes MX-1179, 148, 149
Hughes, Howard, 53

ICBM (Intercontinental Ballistic Missile), 74, 84, 94, 101, 102, 104-107, 114-116, 177
Iltis, 13, 150
inferiority complex, 34
Iroquois engine, 114, 123, 131, 132, 136, 137, 154, 155, 156, 157, 160, 171, 175, 179

J75 engine, 131, 132, 171, 179
Jackson, Alan, 162
Jamming, 81, 82

Jetliner *see also* CF-EJD-X, 21, 22, 24-39, 41-57, 59, 61, 63, 65, 67, 172-174, 178

Keast, Harry, 20, 154
Keith, Ronald A., 57
Korean War, 50, 53, 55, 72, 112
Kuter, Laurence S., 76

La Macaza, 81
Lancaster, 16, 17, 18
Lancaster XPP, 17
Light Alloys Limited, 61, 156
Lowe, Frank, 119
Lucas-Rotax Limited, 156
Lynes, Glen, 66

MacDonald Brothers, 61
MacKenzie, Lewis, 145
MacPhail, Dr. D.C., 44, 48
Magellan Aerospace Corporation, 158
Magor, Robert, 14, 16
Marsh, Colonel Howard, 13
Massey-Harris in Toronto, 15
Matthys, Mark, 63
Mayday Parade, 113
Maynard, Owen, 162, 172
MB-1 Genie nuclear missile, 77
MCC (Military Cooperative Committee), 72, 73, 75
McDonnell, Bill, 160
McGregor, Gordon, 21, 29, 37, 38
McLachlan, John, 154
McLachlan, Walter, 61
McLin, Jon B., 76
MIDAS, 107
Mid-Canada line, 74
Ministry of Munitions and Supply, 16
Minuteman missile, 107
Missile Master, 78
Mitrokhin, Vasili Nikitich, 148, 161
Morley, Joe, 26
MSG (Military Study Group), 73, 75, 76, 89, 92, 97

NADOP (North American Defense
Objective Plan), 102, 103
NASA, 43, 124, 125, 161, 162, 171,
172
National Airlines, 38
National Missile Defense, 95
National Research Council, 19, 20,
43, 67, 90, 133, 167, 176
National Steel Car Corporation, 14,
15, 16
Nene engine, 51
Nesbitt, L.M., 44
Nike Ajax missile, 73
Nike Hercules missile, 73, 74, 78,
97, 101, 106
NMD (National Missile Defence),
95
Noorduyn Aviation Limited, 14
NORAD, 70, 71, 72, 75, 76, 77, 85-
87, 95, 99, 101-105, 107, 115-
117, 119, 123, 129, 130, 150-
153, 160, 176, 177
Nortel, 12
North Bay, 81, 90, 95, 96, 97, 105
North Star, 22, 23, 26, 28, 32, 33,
34, 45, 46, 47, 53
Northeast Air Command, 73
Northwest Airlines, 13
Nott, Herb, 120, 160, 167, 168
nuclear weapons, 76, 94, 96, 102,
113, 114, 128, 153

Office of the Auditor General, 129
Operation Keystone, 148
Orenda Aerospace Corporation, 158
Orenda engines, 51, 54, 55, 61, 124
Orrell, Jimmy, 32, 65
Ostrander, Bob, 55, 63, 64
Ottawa Car, 14

Parkin, J.H., 44
Partridge, Earle E., 74
Pearkes, George R., 75, 85- 87, 100-
102, 105, 106, 108, 111, 115-
123, 128, 142, 143, 152, 160,

165, 166, 176, 177
Pearson, Lester B., 111, 112, 114,
116, 117, 119, 120, 121, 123,
124, 125, 126, 143
Pike, Chris, 66
Plant, John, 48, 123, 140, 171
Potocki, W.O., 66, 69, 171
Pratt & Whitney, 20
Project Silver Bug, 68
Project Y, 67, 68
Project Y2, 67, 68
Putt, General D.C., 67

RCA, 136, 149, 150, 151, 152, 153
RCAF (Royal Canadian Air Force),
14, 15, 18, 19, 21, 43, 44, 47,
51, 53-56, 64, 67, 72, 73, 77,
84, 88-90, 93- 97, 100, 105,
112, 116, 117, 120, 121, 123,
131, 132, 134, 136, 138, 139,
140, 141, 144, 149, 151-157,
165, 166, 171, 177
rebuilding a flying Arrow, 163
Rees, H.S., 35
Regional Jet, 50
Renfrew Aircraft & Engineering
Company Limited, 156
Rentzel, Delos W., 31
Richardson Boat Division, 157
Rogers, Don, 32, 65
Rogerson, Harold, 56
Rolls Royce, 20, 22, 23, 26, 28, 45,
51, 131
Roth, John, 12
Roy, Reginald, 11, 17, 53, 76, 117,
119, 121, 123, 142, 157, 158, 177

Sabre jet, 54, 124, 137
SAC (Strategic Air Command), 71,
83, 85, 90, 91, 92, 93, 94, 97,
103, 122, 128, 155
SAGE (Semi-Automatic Ground
Environment), 78, 79, 81- 91,
93-100, 106-110, 122, 123, 128,
134, 142, 143, 176, 178, 179

SAGE/Bomarc, 81, 83-89, 93-97, 99, 100, 108, 110, 122, 123, 128, 134, 143, 178, 179
Sandys, Duncan, 67
Saunders, Bob, 169, 170
Saunders, Gerald, 169
Scott, Bill, 169, 170
Second World War, 11, 14, 67
Senate Armed Services Committee, 105
Sevigny, Pierre, 165
Shaw, Edith Kay, 160, 178
Skyray, 77
Slemon, Roy, 76
Smye, Fred, 14, 15, 17-20, 28, 29, 38, 41, 47, 51, 52, 53, 56, 61, 62, 140, 157
Solandt, Dr. Omond, 67
Soviets, 102, 103, 112, 113, 115, 148, 161
Sparrow missile, 97, 104, 123, 132, 133, 135-138, 142, 149-153, 177, 179
Speas, Dixon, 38, 41
Spriggs, Frank, 17
Sputnik, 114, 115
St. Laurent, Louis, 96, 111
Stephenson, T.E., 44
Stewart, Greig, 42
Symington, Herb, 21, 26

TCA (Trans Canada Airlines), 17, 21-29, 32, 37, 38, 44-49, 124

Truscott, G.G., 44
Turbo Research Limited, 20
Turcot, Yvon, 13
Turner, William (Bill) L., 147
TWA, 53

unanticipated militarism, 84, 85, 94
USAF (United States Air Force), 42, 43, 48, 49, 50, 56, 67, 68, 72-74, 76, 80, 81, 84, 97-100, 106, 107, 110, 113, 115, 121, 122, 136, 141, 149, 150, 153-157, 180
Vickers, 14, 22
Victory Aircraft Limited, 16
Voodoo, 112, 113, 120, 174
VZ-9A, 68

Warren, Bruce, 55, 63, 64, 66
Waterton, Bill, 54, 63
Weapon System 606A, 68
Weekend Magazine, 119
Willer, Murray, 26
Wright Air Development Center and Training Command, 42

XIM-99 missile, 80
YIM-99 missile, 80

York Gears Limited, 62, 156
Young, Scott, 30

Zuuring, Peter, 163

Printed in the USA
CPSIA information can be obtained
at www.ICGtesting.com
JSHW012024140824
68134JS00033B/2864